# Virtual Japanese

## Enigmas of Role Language

Satoshi Kinsui

Osaka University Press

## Osaka University Press

Osaka University West Front, 2-7
Yamadaoka, Suita-shi, Osaka, Japan
565-0871

Published in Japan
by Osaka University Press
First published 2017

Virtual Japanese:
Enigmas of Role Language
by Satoshi Kinsui

Copyright © Satoshi Kinsui, 2003
Original Japanese edition published by Iwanami Shoten, Publishers, Tokyo
English translation copyright © Osaka University Press

All rights reserved. No part of this publication may be
translated, reproduced or transmitted in any form or by any means,
electronic or mechanical, including photocopy, recording,
or information storage and retrieval systems,
without permission in writing from the publisher.

ISBN 978-4-87259-548-2

# *Acknowledgements*

This book is an English translation of Iwanami Shoten's *Vācharu Nihongo: Yakuwarigo no Nazo* (Virtual Japanese: Enigmas of Role Language), published in January 2003. As of January 2016, the Japanese version has had 14 printruns and has sold approximately 14,000 copies. Role language is a concept that was created by the author and was used for the first time in Kinsui, Satoshi (2000) "Yakuwarigo tankyū no teian" (A proposal of the research of role language) (Satō, Kiyoji (ed.) *Kokugoshi no Shin-shiten* (*A New Perspective on the History of Japanese*), *Kokugo Ronkyū* 8, pp. 331–351, Meiji Shoin). This concept came to be widely known within and outside of academia after the original 2003 publication.

Role language, as also described in detail in this book, is a characteristic way of speaking; it has a special set of spoken language features that include vocabulary, grammar, and pronunciation, which correspond to the speaker's social and cultural stereotypes. As one can find numerous types of role languages in Japanese, it has attracted considerable interest. By 2016, the author was involved in writing and editing that led to one solo publication, two papers, two symposium documents, and one small dictionary, in addition to the original work. In Japan, role language is used as an attractive concept by undergraduate students who are writing their theses on Japanese language studies. Furthermore, it has also attracted the attention of young people outside of Japan who are interested in manga, anime, and the renowned Japanese gaming software industry. Moreover, foreign students from America, Europe, and other Asian countries are studying the role language concept under the author's supervision.

The author was born in Osaka in 1956 and studied Japanese linguistics at the Graduate School of the University of Tokyo. Since then, the author has conducted research on the history of the Japanese language, especially the history of grammar. In 2006, the author's book *Nihongo Sonzai Hyōgen no Rekishi* (History of Existential Expression in Japanese) (Hituzi Syobo) was awarded the Shimmura Izuru Prize, which is granted for research excellence in Japanese language studies. The concept of role language emerged from a description of the use of the verb, *oru* "おる," which is related to existential expressions.

I am indebted to many people who have assisted me in the publication of this book. I would especially like to express my gratitude to Professor Hiroko Yamakido who read through and provided detailed comments on the first translation. I would also like to express my gratitude to Professor Mihoko Teshigawara who gave me permission to reproduce "Modern Japanese 'Role Language' (*Yakuwarigo*): Fictionalised Orality in Japanese Literature and Popular Culture" that is appended at the end of the book for the convenience of English-speaking readers. Finally, I would like to express my profound gratitude to all the members of the Osaka University Press, especially Ms. Shiori Bando, for their continuous support from the planning to the publication of this book.

October 2017
Satoshi Kinsui

# *Contents*

Acknowledgements      iii

CHAPTER 1    Does a Doctor Speak \<Doctor's Language\>?                  
                     The Role Language of an Elderly Male      1

   1. Dr. Ochanomizu      1

   2. Dr. Temma      5

       The doctor character who does not speak \<Doctor's Language\>      5

       Is \<Doctor's Language\> equal \<Elderly Male Language\> ?      6

       The Gap with Reality      8

   3. Seeking the Origin of \<Doctor's Language\>      9

       The Early Works of Osamu Tezuka      9

       The Founder of SF in Japan: Jūza Unno      12

       *Shōnen Kurabu* (Boy's Club)      12

       *Tatsukawa Bunko* and The Entertainment Shorthand Book      14

       The World of *Gesaku* (Popular Novels)      16

       From *Yotsuya Kaidan* (The Yotsuya Ghost Stories)      18

       Formation of Edo Language      19

       The Origin of \<Doctor's Language\> and \<Elderly Male Language\>      19

CHAPTER 2    Stereotypes and Role Language      21

   1. What is stereotype?      21

       The Worries of a Novelist      21

       Research on the Concept of Stereotype      23

   2. Real Life versus Virtual Reality      24

       Role Language and Register and Register Difference      24

       The Dissociation between Reality and Role Language      25

   3. Culture, Media, and Stereotypes      26

       Categorization into Subtypes      26

       Dual Process Model      26

       Dissociation Model      28

   4. The Hero's Journey      28

CHAPTER 3    \<Standard Language\> and \<Non-Standard Language\>      33

   1. What Constitutes \<Rural Language\>?      33

       From *Yūzuru* (Twilight Crane)      33

       The Origin of \<Rural Language\>      36

   2. The Structure of \<Standard Language\> and Role Language      39

       \<Standard Language\> as a Role Language      39

       Spoken and Written Languages      40

       Degree of Role Language      41

       Role Language Degree and Self-Identification      43

   3. The Formation of \<Standard Language\>      44

| | |
|---|---|
| Before <Standard Language> | 44 |
| The *Genbun Icchi* Movement and the Standard Language | 45 |
| Mass Media and <Standard Language> | 47 |
| The Fall of <Kyoto–Osaka Language> | 48 |
| 4. History of the Osaka and Kansai Characters | 49 |
| Pāyan | 49 |
| Stereotypes of the Osaka and Kansai People | 50 |
| The Roots of the Osaka and Kansai People | 51 |
| The Osaka and Kansai People in Modern Mass Media | 56 |
| Lewdness, Violence, and the Osaka and Kansai People | 58 |
| The Transformation of the Stereotypes | 60 |
| | |
| CHAPTER 4   Male Language: Its Root is <Samurai Language> | 63 |
| 1. A Change of <Standard Language> | 63 |
| *Amefuri* (Rainy Day) | 63 |
| Change of a Role Language Degree | 65 |
| 2. The History of <Male Language> | 66 |
| <Student Language> | 66 |
| The History of -*tamae* (please) | 71 |
| *Boku* (I) and *Kimi* (You) | 73 |
| *Boku* (I) and *Ore* (I) | 75 |
| 3. Role language as a Kamen (Persona) | 78 |
| | |
| CHAPTER 5   Where is the Princess?  Female Language | 79 |
| 1. Ochōfujin (Madame Butterfly) | 79 |
| 2. Gender Differences in Language | 81 |
| From Grammatical Features | 81 |
| 3. Women in *Ukiyoburo* (The Bathhouse of the Floating World) | 84 |
| 4. Edo Language and Modern <Female Language> | 86 |
| 5. The Emergence of *teyo dawa* | 89 |
| The Mother and Daughter in *Ukigumo* | 89 |
| The Criticized *teyo dawa* | 90 |
| 6. The Spread of the *teyo dawa* Language | 93 |
| Girls' Schools as Media | 93 |
| The *teyo dawa* Language as Seen in Novels | 94 |
| 7. The Further Spread of the *teyo dawa* Language | 97 |
| Beyond Girls' Schools | 97 |
| Nationwide Spread | 98 |
| 8. The Decline of the *teyo dawa* Language | 101 |
| Changes in <Female Language> after the World War II | 101 |
| The Grammar of -*te yo* | 103 |
| Young Girls and <Young Lady from a Good Family Language> | 105 |
| <Male Language> and <Female Language> as Role Languages | 107 |
| | |
| CHAPTER 6   Perception to Aliens | 109 |
| 1. <*Aruyo* Language> | 109 |
| 2. Categorization of the *Ijin* (Alien) | 113 |

*Contents* vii

| | |
|---|---|
| 3. Language Projection | 113 |
| Various Types of Projections | 113 |
| Black people and <Rural Language> | 114 |
| 4. The Prototype and Development of <*Aruyo* Language> | 116 |
| Use of Pidgin Language | 116 |
| Yokohama Dialect | 117 |
| The *Arimasu* and *Aru* Types | 119 |
| Perception of the Chinese | 120 |
| From *Norakuro* | 121 |
| 5. Beyond Role Language | 123 |

| | |
|---|---|
| Appendix | 125 |
| Modern Japanese "Role Language" (*Yakuwarigo*): | |
| Fictionalised Orality in Japanese Literature and Popular Culture | 125 |
| 1. Introduction | 125 |
| 2. Some Key Concepts of Role Language | 127 |
| 2.1  Formation of Role Language | 127 |
| 2.2  Function of Role Language in Fiction | 127 |
| 2.3  Role Languages versus Sociolects/Actual Speech Styles | 128 |
| 2.4  Types of Role Language | 128 |
| 2.5  Role Language Research | 129 |
| 3. Analyses of Established Role Languages in Japanese Fiction | 130 |
| 3.1  Elderly Male Language | 130 |
| 3.2  Chinese Person Type: *Aruyo* Language | 132 |
| 3.3  Regional Dialect Speaker Types | 133 |
| 3.4  Gendered Types: <Female Language> and <Male Language> | 134 |
| 4. Crosslinguistic Studies of Role Languages | 136 |
| 5. Conclusions | 138 |

| | |
|---|---|
| Sources of Texts | 143 |
| References | 149 |

CHAPTER 1

# Does a Doctor Speak <Doctor's Language>?
## The Role Language of an Elderly Male

## 1. Dr. Ochanomizu

In the world of manga (Japanese comics), the professor/doctor (called "hakase") frequently appears. For example, the book *Manga Hakase Dokuhon* (The Handbook of Manga Hakase (Doctor/Professor) Characters) (Seto and Yamamoto, 1999) describes 157 doctor characters that have appeared in manga since the 1947 release of Osamu Tezuka's work *Kasei Hakase* (Dr. Mars). Among these characters, this chapter focuses on the language used by Dr. Ochanomizu (see Figure 1-1) in *Tetsuwan Atomu* (Astro Boy) (Osamu Tezuka's manga series that began in 1952). One example of Dr. Ochanomizu's use of language is as follows:

"*Oya ja to? Washi wa Atomu no oya-gawari ni nattoru wai!*"
  parent      I                    parent-substitute  become
"A parent? Yeah! I am Atom's (surrogate) parent!"                    (p. 92)

"*Atomu dou ja.*"
        how
"What do you say Atom?"                    (p. 99)

"*Ningen no furi o shite kemuri ni tottsukarete minka?*"
  human      pretend do   smoke    get.caught   try
"Won't you pretend to be a human and try to be caught by the smoke?" (p. 315)
                    (Osamu Tezuka, *Tetsuwan Atomu* 1, ©Tezuka Production)

Figure 1-1 Dr. Ochanomizu
(Osamu Tezuka, *Tetsuwan Atomu 1*, *The Complete Works of Osamu Tezuka*, 221, Kodansha, 1979 ©Tezuka Production)

These are good examples of the role language spoken by Doctor characters in manga. At this point, let us refer to the kind of role language of elderly males as <Doctor's Language>. This type of role language is not only spoken by Dr. Ochanomizu but has been commonly used by many Doctor characters over the years. The following are three more examples:

Dr. Agasa *"Iya, kono ko no oya ga jiko de nyūin shitan de, <u>washi</u> ga sewa o tanomare<u>tottan ja</u> ga, <u>washi</u> mo hitorigurashi de nanika to taihen nan <u>ja</u>..."*
"Well, this kid's parents suffered an accident and they have been hospitalized. So, I have been asked to take care of him. But, since I live alone, it's kind of difficult ..."
(Gōsho Aoyama, *Meitantei Konan* (Detective Conan) 1, p.61)

Dr. Ōkido *"Kono naka kara suki na pokemon o erabidashi ..., yasei no pokemon to tatakawase, katsu to saishu dekirun <u>ja</u> ..."*
"You can select the Pokemon that you like from among these ... pit it against the

Figure 1-2 Professor Agasa
(Gōsho Aoyama, *Meitantei Konan* (Detective Conan) 1, p.61)

*Does a Doctor Speak <Doctor's Language>?*　　　　　　　　　　3

Figure 1-3 Professor Ōkido
(Kōsaku Anakubo, Poketto Monsutā (Pocket Monsters), 1, p. 20)
©Nintendo · Creatures · GAME FREAK · TV Tokyo · Sho Pro · JR Kikaku @Pokémon)

wild Pokemon, and if you win, you can collect them ..."
(Kōsaku Anakubo, Poketto Monsutā (Pocket Monsters), p. 20)

Dr. Tamanegi *"Shinhatsumei no tesuto o shite ottan <u>ja</u>. <u>Washi</u> wa soko no kenkyūjo no Tamanegi <u>ja</u>. Hayaku tasukete kure."*
"I was testing my latest invention. I am Tamanegi from the research institute. Come quickly and help me quickly."
(Shirō Yadama, *Tamanegi-hakase Ichi-gō Tariran*, p. 10),

Table 1-1 shows the linguistic features that appear in <Doctor's Language> contrasted with <Standard Language>;

In most cases, these contrasting features overlap with the contrasting characteristics of Eastern and Western Japanese dialects. It is well known that if the features of the Japanese dialects can be divided into two. Eastern and Western dialects of Japan. The dialect border can vary depending on the respective features, but it is concentrated around the area bordering Toyama and Niigata Prefectures in the north, through the Japanese Alps, and from Aichi Prefecture to Shizuoka Prefecture in the south (Figure 1-4 a map of dialect distribution). These contrasting features of Eastern and Western dialects, particularly grammatical features, are extremely similar to the contrasts shown in the earlier table 1-1.

Some minor differences exist however. For example, while the dialogs of Doctor Ochanomizu end with *ja*, *da* is also used in many instances to conclude the dialog. Rather than using *ja* grammatically all the time, *ja* is sometimes used to add a particular flavor to the character. In addition, the adverbial form *akoo naru* (to become red) are not normally used. Furthermore, the *ame-ya* and *shira-hen* forms in the Western Japanese dialect are generally not used.

4

Table 1-1

|  | <Doctor's Language> | <Standard Japanese> |
|---|---|---|
| Assertion<br>(It is rainy today) | *Kyō wa ame ja*<br>today rain | *Kyō wa ame da*<br>today rain |
| Negation<br>(I don't know) | *Washi wa shira-n*<br>I know-not | *Watashi wa shira-nai*<br>I know-not |
| Existence of Human<br>(There is a man there) | *Asoko ni hito ga oru*<br>there person exist | *Asoko ni hito ga iru*<br>there person exist |
| Progressive, State etc.<br>(It is raining) | *Ame ga fut-teoru/toru*<br>rain fall-PROGRESSIVE | *Ame ga fut-teiru/teru*<br>rain fall-PROGRESSIVE |
|  | Western Japanese | Eastern Japanese |
| Assertion<br>(It is rainy today) | *Kyō wa ame ja/ya*<br>today rain | *Kyō wa ame da*<br>today rain |
| Negation<br>(I don't Know) | *Washi wa shira-n/hen*<br>I know-not | *Watashi wa shira-nai*<br>I know-not |
| Existence of Human<br>(There is a man there) | *Asoko ni hito ga oru*<br>there person exist | *Asoko ni hito ga iru*<br>there person exist |
| Progressive, State etc.<br>(It is raining) | *Ame ga fut-teoru/toru*<br>rain fall-PROGRESSIVE | *Ame ga fut-teiru/teru*<br>rain fall-PROGRESSIVE |
| Adjective (adverbial form)<br>(It turns red) | *akoo naru*<br>red become | *akaku naru*<br>red become |
| Verb (imperative form)<br>(Get up!/Do it!) | *okii* / *see*<br>get.up / do | *okiro* / *siro*<br>get.up / do |

In short, <Doctor's Language> partialy possesses grammatical characteristics of the modern Western Japanese dialect. In this sense, it contrasts with <Standard Language>. On the other hand, <Standard Language> is based on the language of the Tokyo Yamanote area, and it possesses grammatical features of the Eastern Japanese dialect as described later.

In the manga, Dr. Ochanomizu is not portrayed as being from Western Japan. Thus, the following question arises:

#### ENIGMA 1
Why does the doctor character use the Western Japanese dialect?

Before discussing this question, let us observe <Doctor's Language> a little more. In Dr. Ochanomizu's language, besides the grammatical forms, first person pronouns and particles also exhibit unique features. In personal pronouns, *washi, wagahai, watakushi,* and *watashi* (all meaning 'I') are used. In particular, *washi* and *wagahai* are typical of the doctor characters. Conversely, *boku* and *ore* are not generally used to refer to oneself. As for sentence-ending particles, *wai* and *nou* are characteristic of <Doctor's Language>. Finally, interjectory particles, such as *ya,* which is used to address someone as in *Atomu ya*, are also noticeable.

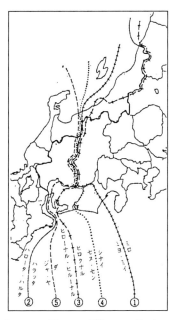

Figure 1-4  Dichotomy between Eastern-Western Dialect in Japan
(adopted from Tokugawa, Munemasa, Nihogo no Sekai (The world of Japanese) 8: Kotoba, Nishi to Higashi (Language, Western and Eastern), Chuo-koron-sha, 1981)

① Verb (*miyo, mii / miro*)    ② Verb (*harōta, haruta / haratta*)
③ Adjective (*hiroo, hiruu / hiroku*)    ④ Negation (*senu, sen / shinai*)
⑤ Assertion (*ja, ya / da*)

## 2. Dr. Temma

### The doctor character who does not speak <Doctor's Language>

After examining the language of doctor characters in manga, there are some doctor characters who do not speak <Doctor's Language>. Moreover, there are obvious differences between the doctor characters that use and do not use <Doctor's Language>. For example, Dr. Temma in *Tetsuwan Atomu* (Astro Boy) (Figure 1-5) represents doctor characters who do not use <Doctor's Language>. One example of his language use is as follows:

*"Urusai yatsu da̲/robotto no kuse ni."*
"What a pestering character! And he is a robot, hah!"
*"Washi̲ ga tsukutte yatta koto o wasurete tondemo nai yatsu da̲/dou da̲ kuchi mo kikenai darō̲."*
"What an ungrateful character. He forgets that it was I who created him/So, how is it?/Can't speak, eh?"

(Osamu Tezuka, *Tetsuwan Atomu* 1, p.59)

Figure 1-5 Professor Tenma
(Osamu Tezuka, *Tetsuwan Atomu* 1, p. 59 ©Tezuka Production)

According to this example, the specific features of <Doctor's Language>, particularly the characteristics of the Western Japanese dialect, do not appear. However, *washi* (or 'I') as well as the negative *n* has been used although rarely.

The most significant difference regarding the external features of doctors Ochanomizu and Temma is that the former is mostly bald with some gray hair, whereas the latter has thick black hair. That is, while Professor Ochanomizu has prominent features of an elderly male, Dr. Temma's appearance is the opposite. In other words, doctor characters who speak <Doctor's Language> are generally elderly professors/doctors. On the other hand, doctor characters who do not look elderly, do not speak <Doctor's Language>, in the comic books. For example, Doctor Shikishima in Tetsujin nijū-hachi-gō (Mitsuteru Yokoyama, 1956–1966) and Sembei Norimaki in *Dr. Surampu* (Dr. Slump) (Akira Toriyama, 1980–1984) belong to this type of doctor character. There are some works in which doctor characters are old men who do not speak <Doctor's Language>, but distinctive <Doctor's Language> expressions (e.g., *ja* 'be' and *wakatteoru* '(I) know') are rarely used by characters who look young.

**Is <Doctor's Language> equal <Elderly Male Language>?**
In manga and anime, some characters who are not professors or doctors but who speak a language that is exactly like <Doctor's Language> appear quite often. These are old men with gray hair or a bald head and sometimes stooping with age.

> Tomozō Jiisan (Grandfather Tomozō): *"Demo Maruko no iu toori ja na/Honto ni minna/okane moraeru kara hataraitoru shi nou."*
> "But, according to what Maruko said must be wright./Really, everyone/works because he can get money."
> (Momoko Sakura, *Chibi Maruko Chan* (Little Maruko) 4, p. 90)

*Does a Doctor Speak <Doctor's Language>?*

Figure 1-6 Tomozō Jiisan
(Momoko Sakura, *Chibi Maruko Chan* 4 p. 90 ©Sakura Production)

*"Sonna otoko ni utsutsu o nukashite <u>oru</u> kara, renshū ni mi ga <u>hairan no ja</u>!"*
"You are so hooked on that man that you can't concentrate on the training!"
(Naoki Urasawa, *YAWARA!* 1, p. 28)

Let us call this language, <Elderly Male Language>. Given that doctor characters who speak <Doctor's Language> are also old men, it will imply that <Doctor's Language> is eventually a type of <Elderly Male Language> (but <Doctor's Language> has also some features of <Student Language>, as I discuss later). Now, the first person pronoun *wagahai* is used by doctor characters but not by ordinary old men. The first person pronoun *washi* is common to both hakase characters and old men. When we closely examine persons who speak <Elderly Male Language> in comic and story books, we see that they are not just aged but are majestic and have a dignified bearing, have powers like a king, are wise as well as guide the main character or protagonist, are characterized as old and feeble persons, harm the main character or are simply senile. Frequently, these characterizations play a meaningful role in the story. The doctor character is the symbol of wisdom (at times, the symbol of evil wisdom); in the story, he is a typical representative of the characteristic old man. We shall discuss this relation between the story and the character the following chapter of this book.

Figure 1-7 Jigorō Inokuma
(©Naoki Urasawa, *YAWARA!* 1, p. 28)

### The Gap with Reality

Now, in what way is <Doctor's Language> or <Elderly Male Language> related to the professor/doctor and the old man in real life? If we consider whether university professors in real life speak <Doctor's Language>, it does not seem at all possible (at least there is no such professor in the university where I work). Most of all, it is not improbable that a person who speaks ordinarily, gradually (or suddenly) begins to speak <Elderly Male Language> when he becomes old.

It is not just that <Doctor's Language> and <Elderly Male Language> do not match language used in real life. The doctor character mostly uses <Doctor's Language> only in children-oriented works, such as manga and science fiction (SF) dramas targeting children; such characters rarely appear in works targeting adults such as novels, real dramas, in other words, works belonging to the "sophisticated" genre. The following example is from a novel targeting adults, but the work may have aimed to benefit from being presented as children oriented by deliberately using childish character settings. This can be understood from the fact that the book adopts the style of a picture book.

> "Sonna koto <u>washi</u> wa <u>shiran</u> yo. Nani se nisen gohyaku nen mo mukashi no koto <u>ja</u> mono, sonna no wakaru wake nai ja nai ka. Shikashi tonikaku sou kimatte <u>orun</u> da yo. Sore ga okite to iu mono da. Shitte <u>orou</u> ga shiranakarou ga, okite o yabureba noroi ga kakaru. Noroi ga kakareba, hitsuji otoko wa mou hitsuji otoko dewa nakunatte shimaun da. Kimi ga hitsuji otoko ongaku o sakkyoku <u>dekin</u> riyū wa soko ni aru no da. Un."

Figure 1-8  Professor Hitsuji
(Haruki Murakami and Maki Sasaki, *Hitsuji-otoko no Kurisumasu* (Christmas of the Sheep Man), p. 30 ©Maki Sasaki 1989)

"Well, I don't know about that. Because, well, that was 2500 years ago, so you can see why it's not possible to know that, right? But anyway, it is decided, it is the law. And whether you know the law or not, if you break it, you will be cursed, and if you are cursed then the sheep man will no more remain the sheep man. This is the reason why you can't compose sheep man music. Yeah."

(Haruki Murakami and Maki Sasaki, *Hitsuji-otoko no Kurisumasu*
(Christmasn of the Sheep Man), p. 30)

Here, there arises the following question.

ENIGMA 2
Though <Doctor's Language> and <Elderly Male Language> role languages do not in all probability exist in real life, why does it seem so true to the associated character archetype?

## 3. Seeking the Origin of <Doctor's Language>

### The Early Works of Osamu Tezuka
We consider the character of Dr. Ochanomizu as an example of <Doctor's Language>, but the character of doctor had been appearing in the early works of Osamu Tezuka, and <Doctor's Language> had been used for these characters from quite early on. In the 1947 (Showa 22) publication *Kasei Hakase* (Doctor Mars), the two doctor characters, namely, the good doctor Būton and the bad doctor Poppo use typical <Doctor's Language> .

Doctor Poppo:
"*Kou shite wagahai wa namaiki na chikyū no yatsura o mechakucha ni kakima-washite yaru no sa./subarashii kangae jaro ga.*"
"And so in this way we shall mess up these impertinent earthlings./That's an amazing idea, eh?"
Doctor Būton:
"*U...n, oshoroshii mokuromi ja.*"
"Hmm ... this is a scary scheme."

(Osamu Tezuka, *Kasei Hakase* (Doctor Mars), p. 33)

Moreover, in the work *Shin Takarazima* (The New Treasure Island) which was released in the same year, and became a best seller with 40,000 copies printed, the captain of the ship speaks <Elderly Male Language>. This captain has the same appearance as Professor Būton mentioned earlier.

Figure 1-9 Doctor Poppo and Professor Būton
(Osamu Tezuka, *Kasei Hakase* (Doctor Mars), p. 33 ©Tezuka Production)

Pete:
*"Boāru? Sore wa boku ga tsukutta kaizoku desu yo!"*
"Boaru? Hey, that's the pirate I made!"
Captain:
*"Nani o iu/Boāru wa kata te kata ashi no reikoku na akunin ja yo."*
"What the hell are you saying/Boaru is a one-handed, one-legged, ruthless villain."

(Osamu Tezuka, *Shin Takarasima*, p. 31)

In fact, we can observe <Doctor's Language> in Tezuka's work *Yūrei Otoko* (the Ghost man), which was created as early as in the study year immediately after he graduated from junior high school (around the year 1945).

*"Sekaijū no hakushi ga atsumatta you da."*
"It looks like doctors gathered Professors from all over the world."
*"Kono naka ni ya taitei nise ga nannin ka oru yo."*
"In here, there are usually several pseudo (people)."
*"Iya washi wa nanto itsudemo sore ga seitō dakara seitō to iun da."*

Figure 1-10 Captain
(Osamu Tezuka, *Shin Takarazima*, p. 31 ©Tezuka Production)

*Does a Doctor Speak <Doctor's Language>?*

"Well no, if it is fair I always say it is fair."
*"Dare ka <u>washi</u> ni bentō o <u>kuren</u> ka naa soo surya <u>washi</u> wa shokuji no kōkateki sesshuhō ni tsuite jisshū shite miseru ga."*
"Will someone give me their lunch box; if they do I shall show them an effective food intake method put into practice."
*"<u>Wakaran</u> ka? <u>Wakaran</u> nara oshie te shinzeyou ichi tasu ichi wa ni <u>ja</u> yo."*
"Do you understand? If you don't, then I will teach. One plus one is two."
*"Shokun! <u>Wagahai</u> no setsu ni sansei shite kure tamae."*
"Gentlemen! Please agree with my theory."
*"Urusai! kikou no tsuba de kono heya no shitsudo ga agatta <u>wai</u>."*
"Be quiet, Your spit is raising the humidity of this room."
*"Naruhodo! Sansai no hakushi-tte no wa kimi ka ne?"*
"I see! The three year old hakase is you, eh?"
*"Shinri o toita yatsu wa hitori mo <u>oran</u>! Aa nagekahashi shidai <u>ja</u>."*
"There is not a single person who said this is the truth! Ah, what a wretched turn of events!"

(Ban, Tezuka Production, Yūrei Otoko, p.139)

Figure 1-11 Proffessors
(*Yūrei Otoko*, p.139 ©Tezuka Production)

**The Founder of SF in Japan: Jūza Unno**

The direct source and the dominant influence of Tezuka's <Doctor's Language> has been for example from Jūza Unno's (1897–1949) novels. Jūza Unno is referred to as the founder of SF in Japan; it is said that in his boyhood days, Tezuka was addicted to Unno's novels. (Cf. Takanaka Shimotsuki (ed.) *Tanjō! Tezuka Osamu* (The Birth of Osamu Tezuka) and other sources). Examples of <Doctor's Language> from Jūza Unno's novels include the following.

> *Jinzō-ningen Efu shi o mukaete, Iwami Hakase wa, ningen to onaji ni atsukatta.*
> *"Nani ka goyou desu ka." to, Efu shi wa itta.*
> *"Umu. Washi ga tsukutta jinzō ningen ja ga, ware nagara umaku dekita mono ja. Kocchi no itta kotoba ni oujite, chanto henji o surun dakara, taishita mon da yo."*

Dr. Iwami received the android Mr. F and treated him in the same way as any human.
"How may I help you?", said Mr. F.
"Hmm. You are an android human created by me, but I have made you well. You reply to what I say, which is a great thing. "

> (Jūza Unno, *Robotto Hakase* (Doctor Robot), (the title is changed
> from *Robotto Efu-shi*), p. 192, First Published in 1939)

> *"Maa, sou kuchibiru o furuwasen demo ii. Iya kimi no human nano wa you wakatteiru. Shikashi ja, kagaku to iu mono wa kimi ga kangaete iru yori, motto Jūdai na monoda. —Sou, Washi o kowai me de niramu na. Yoku wakatte iru yo, kimi wa washi no setsu ni hantai da to iundarou. Tokoroga sore wa washi no me kara miru to kimi ga wakai to iu ka, kimi ga mada ooku o siranai to iu ka, sorekara hasshita koto da."*

"You should not quiver you lips. Well I understand your discontent. But, science is a much more serious endeavor than you can imagine. Sometimes, it is more important than marriage and family life. Don't look at me with those scary eyes. I know very well, you will say that you are against my theory, but seen from my perspective you say this as you are young, or shall I say you don't know that much."

> (Jūza Unno, *Uchū Joshū Dai ichi-go* (The First Female Prisoner in Space), p. 5)

*Shōnen Kurabu* (Boy's Club)

Furthermore, Tezuka was also absorbed in reading *Shōnen Kurabu* (Boy's Club, 1914 (Taisho 3) to 1962 (Showa 37)), which was extremely popular magazine among boys where various role languages, including <Doctor's Language> and <Elderly Male Language> were found (Note: Jūza Unno also contributed to *Shōnen Kurabu*). Next, we show *Shōnen Kurabu*'s popular section, "Kokkei Daigaku (The Humorous University)." Here Dr. Mecharakuchara solved one witty riddle after onother contributed by a reader, and 10,000 entries were received every month.

*Does a Doctor Speak <Doctor's Language>?* 13

Figure 1-12 The Android Human Mr.F
(First published: Jūza Unno (text) / Shigeo Seto (illustration) "Jinzō Ningen Efu-shi" in *Rajio Kodomo no Tekisuto*, 1939, March. From: Masami Akiyama "Zasshi to Manga ni Miru Showa Shoki no Jidō Bungaku" in Shimotsuki (1998), p.34. ©Shigeo Seto.)

Me hakase (Dr. Mecharakuchara) :
*"Kyūhei kun, samui nou. Douja, shitsumon ga aru ka? Gumon wa doshidoshi botsu ni shite kure tamae!"*
"Isn't it cold, Kyuhei! Come on now, haven't any of you got any clever questions? Do me a favor and screen your foolish ideas first! "
[snip]
Kyūhei:
*"Tsugi ni Tōkyō no Hiraoka Masaaki kun ni ippon kenmon o negaimasu."*
"Next, I'd like a "clever question" from Masaaki Hiraoka of Tokyo. "
Hiraoka kun (Hiraoka):
*"Me hakase ichi mon. Boku ga aru hi Yokosuka e itta tokoro ga, sono toki shikan ga futari zure de nani ka motte aruite ita. Sate nani o motte itaka. Saa maitta rou."*
"A question for Dr. Me. So one day, I went to Yokosuka, and I saw two officers (shikan) carrying something. What were they carrying? Stumped, huh? "
Me hakase (Dr. Me) :
*"Nanjira gotoki ni maitte tamaru mono kai. Shikan (4-kan) ga hutari de motte ita mono wa yakan (8-kan) ja. Soshite sore wa yakan jatta noda. Douja, osore ittaka."*
"You think I'd get stumped by the likes of you? What the two officers (shikan, 'four kan') were holding was a kettle (yakan, 'eight kan'). And it was nighttime (yakan) too. How do you like that? Amazed, aren't you? "
[snip]
Me hakase (Dr. Me) :
*"Oshiete kuren demo yoi. Nakanai (naka nai) uguisu ja kara, sore wa usu ja.*

Figure 1-13 Kokkei Daigaku

*Usubon'yari shite ite wa wakaran kamo shiren ga, kenmei naru wagahai niwa yoku wakaru ja.*"
"No need to tell me. A warbler (u-gui-su) that does not sing (nakanai, 'no middle') is a millstone ('u-su'). All you dopes might not get it, but it's easy for someone like me!"

(Kokkei Daigaku, p. 159)

In this way, the language of Dr. Mecharakuchara is the typical <Doctor's Language>. Furthermore, the doctor's appearance in the artwork is also the stereotypical image of manga old doctor characters, and the look is also similar to that of Dr. Ochanomizu.

### *Tatsukawa Bunko* and The Entertainment Shorthand Book

*Tatsukawa Bunko* was a popular publication, a little before *Shōnen Club*. From around 1911 (Meiji 44), a professional storyteller of Osaka prepared storytelling material, including adventure and action of popular historical figures like Sarutobi Sasuke, Taikō (Toyotomi Hideyoshi), and Mito Kōmon, and this was very popular. This began in Osaka, but similar publications were also composed in Tokyo. *Tatsukawa Bunko* is primarily a historical drama, and we must consider the relation between the language of the character and <Samurai Language>. For example, one can say that the language of Tozawa Hakuunsai in *Sarutobi Sasuke* is related to <Doctor's Language> and <Elderly Male Language>. Hakuunsai was a mysterious old man who imparted the art of *ninpō* to Sasuke; in terms of the role he played, he is very close to the character of doctor (the *Rou* (old) used in examples refers to Hakuunsai).

Rou: "*Korya Sasuke Sasuke, nanji wa naze shōtai naku nekonde iru, ore ga koko e kita noga wakaranu ka*" to, shikari tsukerare, Sasuke wa me o kosuri kosuri okinaori, Sa: "*Yaa, kore wa oshishō sama* .......[snip]"
Rou: "*Damare, bujutsu o kokorogakete oru mono ga, zengo o shiranu hodo neru to iu koto ga aru ka, An'ya no tsubute to iu dewa nai ka, itsu nandoki tekini dekuwasu*

Figure 1-14 Tozawa Hakuunsai and Sarutobi Sasuke
(Tatsukawa Bunko, part 40, p. 5)

*yamo wakara<u>n</u>, banji ni yudan wa taiteki j<u>a</u>, kon'ya wa yurusu ga, kono ato itsu kuru yamo wakara<u>nu</u> kara, ore ga kita toki nete iru to, naguritsukeru zo!" to, ii sutete izuko tomo naku tachisatta.*
The master scolded Sasuke, saying, "Wake up!! Sasuke, Sasuke, why are you lying here like dead? Didn't you hear me come in?" Sasuke sat up rubbing his eyes. "Yo ... Master ... (...)" "Shut up! You think people who are in a habit of training in art of fighting can sleep so soundly? How naive can you get! You never know when you'll be faced with an enemy; carelessness is your biggest foe! I'll let you off this time, but I might show up again, and if you're asleep, you're gonna get hit!" As soon as the words had left his lips, he left for somewhere.
(*Sarutobi Sasuke*, p. 9. First written in 1914)

In the background of the creation of *Tatsukawa Bunko* was the popularity of "The Entertainment Shorthand Book." Besides the art of storytelling(*kō-dan*), these books were compilation of the traditional art of narration, such as *naniwa-bushi* (a type of narrative ballad chanted by a reciter with a shamisen (a kind of plucked string instruments) accompaniment) and *rakugo* (traditional comic storytelling), recorded in a modern stenography. The first of its kind was *Kaidan Botan-dōrō* (The Tale of the Peony Lantern) narrated by San'yuutei Enchō, which was published in 1884. However, similarly structured publications subsequently appeared in Tokyo and Osaka, which eventually led to the publication of magazines. In other words, *Tatsukawa Bunko* began with the idea of the speaker writing directly, thus eliminating the need for stenography.

One can find <Elderly Male Language> even in the shorthand book mentioned

16

above. These are the dialogues of the character of Ryōseki Oshō from *Kaidan Botan-dōrō*. Ryōseki Oshō has supernatural power that is described as "unlimited ability to perceive causes and effects of things and foresee what will happen 100 years in the future." This character guides/advises the main character (Kōsuke) and describes a mysterious prophecy.

Ryō:
*"Kōsuke dono wa doumo nogare gatai kennan ja, nani karukute usude, sorede sumeba yoroshii ga, doumo fukade jarou, ma ga warui to kirikorosareru toiu wake ja, doumo kore wa nogareraren innen ja."*
"Verily are you in gravest danger, Mr. Kosuke; if you escape only lightly wounded, it would be a blessing, but I fear you will be severely hurt or dishonorably killed. It looks to be an inescapable fate."
(Sanyūtei Enchō, *Kaidan Botan-dōrō*, p.235, first published in 1884)

**The World of *Gesaku* (Popular Novels)**
Tracing further back before shorthand books, the earlier works with dialogues in <Elderly Male Language> are *kabuki* and *gesaku*. We will discuss kabuki later. Let us now examine "Yabuisei no Buyōjō" from Kanagaki Robun's (1829–1894) *Ushiya Zōtan Aguranabe* (1871 (Meiji 4)–1872 (Meiji 5)), a representative work of the *gesaku* genre that survived in the beginning of the Meiji era.

*"Aa kyō wa samukatta samukatta. Tamani byōka kara hito ga kita to omottara gurou nado ni wa nakanaka temo tsukerarenu nanshō no yousu jakara kirinukeyou towa omottaga, mamayo, ayaui hashi mo wataran kereba magureatari to iu koto mo nai to kankō shite shinsatsu shiteoru tokoro e shinrui domo kara tachiawaseru to iu seiyōka no zangiri isha me ga dekakete useotta de sonoba o yuzutte suguni dassō mo kimeraren kara dangō site mita tokoroga kyatsu nakanaka no kōsha to miete gurō nazo ga ashimoto emo ottsuku koto dewa nai kara iikagen na gomakashi o itte dasshite kita ga tōsetsu no you ni idō ga sakan ni hirakete wa ichimon-futsū no gurō nazo ga isha no mane o site iru tokoro dewa nai te."*
"Oh, it was cold today. As a person came from a house where someone was sick with a difficult disease, which doesn't occur too often, I went to see the patient, and I found that it was a disease that someone like me couldn't possibly cure. So I just thought "to hell with it"! But I felt I should just stick with it because if I don't try to cross a dangerous bridge, I don't have a hope of even getting it right by accident. But after finishing the examination, the relatives crowded around because a Western-style doctor whom the relatives decided to call had shown up, and because I could not pass over the patient to him and escape immediately I tried talking to him, then I saw that he was quite capable and I had no chance of catching up to him and that I've just gotten away with deceiving people—for medicine nowadays is so advanced that an uneducated guy like me should just give up pretending to be a doctor."
("Yabuisei no Buyōjō," *Ushiya Zōtan Aguranabe*, 3-pen jō, 18 chō, omote)

*Does a Doctor Speak <Doctor's Language>?*　　　　17

Figure 1-15 Yabuisei no Buyōjō
(*Ushiya Zōtan Aguranabe*, 3-pen jō, 18 chō, omote)

Here, note that this character is not just old, but he has the distinction of being a medical doctor—a position that can be considered to be the precursor to the doctor character that appeared later.

Going further back in time, let us take the example of *Ukiyoburo* (The Bathhouse of the Floating World) (1809–1812) by Shikitei Samba (1776–1822). It is mostly the ordinary people of Edo who appear in this comic novel, and they speak the Edo dialect—a type of Eastern Japanese. There are however, a few exceptions, which include those residing in the Kyoto–Osaka area and the elderly. In Part 1, Volume 1, a rather old man appears who is described as *shichijū bakari no inkyo, okizukin kamiko no sodenashi baori, ju ni san no decchi ni, yukata o motasete tsue ni sugari, kuchi o mugumugu shinagara* (A retired person aged approximately 70, wearing a sleeveless *haori* made of paper and a hood, makes an apprentice of 12 or 13 years old carrying his *yukata* and holding on to his cane, mumbling),

Bantō (Clerk):
"*Go-inkyo san, kyou wa ohayou gozarimasu.*"
"Good morning, sir!"
Inkyo (Retiree):
"*Dou ja bantou dono. Daibu samuku natta no.* [snip] *Ya yuube wa nesobirete komarikitta te. Soreni inu mega ya naita naita. Kono toshi ni naruga, yuube hodo inu no hoeta ban wa oboenu.*"
"What do you think? It's gotten awfully cold (...) You know, it was so rough, I couldn't sleep a wink. And you know what else? That dog! Barking and barking! Not in all my years have I heard a dog bark as much as last night!"
(*Ukiyo-buro*, zen-pen maki jō, pp. 18–19.)

This old man is supposed to be from Edo, but he uses much grammatical forms of Western Japanese. This raises the following question: Why would an old men from Edo speak Western Japanese?

## From *Yotsuya Kaidan* (The Yotsuya Ghost Stories)

It is known from the series of studies by Tōsaku Furuta (see references) that by the late early-modern period, <Elderly Male Language> expression patterns had already been established in *kabuki*. Furuta classified the language usage of the characters that appeared in the kabuki work, *Tōkaidō Yotsuya Kaidan* (The Tōkaidō Yotsuya Ghost Stories) by Nanboku Tsuruya, from the perspective of whether it was the Kyoto–Osaka or Eastern Japanese style. Here, the Kyoto–Osaka style refers to speech that uses the Western Japanese type of grammar, which includes the following: *ja* affirmative endings, negative expressions *nu* and *n*, the *u-onbin*, or the euphonic changes of *u* of the *a/wa godan dōshi* (Type 1 verbs or one of the conjugation classes of verbs in Japanese ending in *-u*) such as *kou-ta* (bought) and *shimou-ta* (completed), and the euphonic changes of *u* of adjective continuative forms such as *you wakaru* (understand well) and *akou natta* (became red),On the other hand, the Eastern Japanese style refers to sentence endings that include *da*, the negative expression *nai*, the *soku-onbin*, or the euphonic changes to a double consonant of the *a/wa godan doshi* (Type 1 verbs or one of the conjugation classes of verbs in Japanese ending in *-u*) such as *kat-ta* (bought) and *shimat-ta* (completed), the *hi-onbin* or the non-euphonic change of adjective continuative forms such as *yoku wakaru* (understand well) and *akaku natta* (become red).

As a result of the examination, characters in "*Tōkaidō Yotsuya Kaidan*" can be classified as follows:

a. Those who speak in the Kyoto–Osaka style are samurais, wives of samurais, old people, and people from the Kyoto–Osaka area.
b. Those who speak in the Eastern Japanese style are common people of Edo.
c. Those who use both speech styles are the samurais who are deeply involved in the world of common people and others.

It is natural for the people of the Kyoto–Osaka area to speak the Kyoto–Osaka variety. In addition, as discussed later, the samurai-warriors and their wives speak the Kyoto–Osaka style because <Samurai Language> (the language of the samurai-warriors) is based on the Kyoto–Osaka variety. Here,we will focus on the character of the old man is portrayed as a person who speaks the Kyoto–Osaka style of language, as seen in the following example:

Magobee:
*"Aa, nanja kono shu wa. monomorai ni shite wa, sate hitogara no yoi onna hinin. Kore, konatashu wa kono kawabata ni iyaru kara wa, hyotto kokoe, ano, sugito ni nuutaru otoko to onna no, ukishigai ga nagarete ki wa senu ka. douja, douja."*
"Well, what do you know! For a beggar, you're not so bad! Say, from where you are by the river, did you by any chance see a cedar sliding door come floating by

with bottoms of a man and a woman sewn onto it? How about it? "

(*Tōkaidō Yotsuya Kaidan*, pp. 148–149, First played in 1825)

## Formation of Edo Language

Thus the formation of Edo language seems to be deeply related to the adoption of the Kyoto–Osaka style as <Elderly Male Language>. Hisao Komatsu divided the formation process of Edo language into three overall processes: 1) the primary formation process (Kan'ei period; Keicho (1596) to Meireki (1657); 2) the secondary formation process (Meiwa period: 1764–1771); and 3) the tertiary formation process (Kasei period: Bunka (1804) to Bunsei (1829) (*Edo-jidai no kokugo: Edo-go* (Language in Edo era: Edo Language)). In the primary formation process, the samurai language was formed, but the city as a whole still had a mixture of dialects. In the secondary formation process, a language that should be termed "the common language of the townspeople" was formed. Komatsu noted that subsequently, "the conflict between Kyoto–Osaka and Eastern Japanese dialectal expressions would become a conflict that degenerates into a hierarchical conflict internal to the Edo language rather than a conflict between the dialects" (p. 90). In the tertiary formation process, the underlying Eastern type of expressions gradually infiltrated the higher strata.

<Elderly Male Language> expressions seen in the *Tōkaidō Yotsuya Kaidan* can be considered to represent the hierarchical conflict between generations, as seen in the secondary and tertiary formation processes. In other words, when young and middle-aged persons were quickly using the new common language of Edo or Eastern Japanese expressions as their own language, the elderly did not abandon normative Kyoto–Osaka expressions. Moreover, *kabuki* expressions were being exaggerated it even more and were eventually assigned to certain characters in a graphic and symbolic manner.

## The Origin of <Doctor's Language> and <Elderly Male Language>

Apparently, the origin of <Elderly Male Language> dates back to the linguistic conditions in Edo between the late 18th century and the early 19th century. At that time, even among the people of Edo, the majority of the elderly might speak the Kyoto–Osaka language. In addition, professionals, such as doctors and scholars, were conservative in their language usage, and their antiquated manner of speaking was prominent. This actual situation was further exaggerated and depicted in both *kabuki* and *gesaku*.

After that time, the number of Edo people who spoke the Edo language increased. In the subsequent Meiji era the grammar of Edo language was even adopted as a new <Standard Language>. However, in literary and theatrical works, the elderly continued to be equated with the Kyoto–Osaka style of speech.

In the process of the preservation and development of <Elderly Male Language>, the development of modern media and new genres of works gave great impetus to having <Elderly Male Language> preserved and developed. The traditional *rakugo* and other storytelling forms rode on the popularity of modern publications, such as *Tatsukawa Bunko*, and eventually led to the world of juvenile magazines such as

*Shōnen Kurabu* (Boy's Club). Here, <Elderly Male Language> met the new doctor character, which further proliferated in the world of manga.

This chapter has comprehensively discussed the development of the modern <Doctor's Language> from <Elderly Male Language> and traced back to the Edo period. In fact, the examples covered in this chapter are only a fraction of <Doctor's Language> and <Elderly Male Language> since their oral traditions must have been more widespread. However, even among these, in terms of the extent of diffusion, the *Shōnen Kurabu* and Osamu Tezuka's work must have played especially important roles in terms of the extent of diffusion,.

Particularly significant is the fact that <Elderly Male Language> and <Doctor's Language> were accepted by child-oriented media, such as novels and manga for young boys. This is because the knowledge of cultural stereotypes, such as role language, is formulated in childhood and does not fade even into adulthood. These young boys became creators of new works and continued to use the same type of role language. Through this ongoing cycle, role language, which is practically unrelated to how actual society works, had become inherited by successive generations. Chapter 2 will examine this process in more detail.

CHAPTER 2
# Stereotypes and Role Language

## 1. What is stereotype?

### The Worries of a Novelist

Yoshinori Shimizu, a writer who is extremely conscious about language, writing style, and wording, has published several inspiring works in which he has skill-fully applied various linguistic devices. The following is an excerpt from one of his essays "Shōsetsu no Naka no Kotoba" (Language in Novels):

> In reality, when a boss asks his subordinate to do some work in a company, he wouldn't say *Kyōjū ni yattoite kure tamae* (Make sure you do it by the end of the day). You'll see this is true when you look into the actual dialogue. It can be *Sore, kyōjū ni ne, Kyōjū ni yatte moraeru kana,* or sometimes it can be even *Kyōjū ni yatte chōdai ne* (Could you do it by the end of today?).
>
> However, the dialogues spoken by a boss in a novel cannot merely be ver-batim transcriptions of tape recordings of real-life conversations such as *Yatte chōdai ne?* (Make sure you do it, okay?). One can adopt this style of writing, but in this case, the boss will have to be the main character, and his personality must be portrayed in great detail.
>
> If the boss who only appears in part of the novel (or as a minor character) says *Yatte chōdai ne?* (Make sure you do it, okay?), then it will sound out of place. Hence, it is desirable that the boss who plays a secondary role says conventional, symbolic lines such as *Yatte kure tamae* (Please do it), after which he immedi-ately disappears.
>
> This is the mystery of language in dialogue in a novel.
>
> For example, let us suppose that there is a scene in the novel in which an

old man, who knows about "the olden days," appears and narrates a forgotten legend. In a B-grade novel, the old man would say something like *Washi wa mitanja yo, shitteorunja* (I saw it you know, I know about it). Nowadays, we rarely come across an old man who says *washi*, and very few people other than Mr. Tomiichi Murayama[1] say *ja*. However, adopting this writing style is in accordance with the pattern of a novel since it is conventional and easy to understand.

A novel following a pattern that is stereotypical and easy to understand is considered to be B-grade work. When writing a novel that has depth, such stereotypical dialogues are avoided as much as possible. However, it is impossible to write dialogues verbatim from transcriptions of tape recordings of real-life conversations. The reason being that in real-life situations, there are 80-year-old men who say *Boku chan shitteru mon nē. Mukashi mitan da mooon* (I know. I saw it a long time agooo). Yet, if an old man in a secondary role says such lines, the novel would be torn asunder.

Conversations in a novel are fictionalized language reconstructed for use in the novel itself. I would attempt to use real language and not reconstructed styles but it is nearly impossible to completely write in real language.

(Yoshinori Shimizu, *Nihongo Hisshō Kōza* (Japanese Laughing Course) , pp. 34–36)

What is being discussed in this excerpt is none other than role language. Several examples, such as the *tamae* spoken by the boss and the *-ja* spoken by the old man have been cited, the latter is an example of <Elderly Male Language>, as discussed in Chapter 1. For the time being, let us consider the former to be <Boss's Language>.

In the above excerpt, Shimizu is talking about the gap between role language and the language use in. Furthermore, he notes that despite the gap, role language is useful since it is stereotypical and easy to understand, so one is compelled to use such language. This is exactly our earlier Enigma 2 from Chapter 1.

### ENIGMA 2
Though <Doctor's Language> and <Elderly Male Language> role languages do not in all probability exist in real life, why does it seem so true to the associated character archetype?

Shimizu indicates another important aspect. It is sufficient for the minor character of the boss to use the stereotypical <Boss's Language>. More specifically, if this character is made to make more realistic statements, then it is essential to portray this character in great detail. In addition, he notes that novels that frequently use role language are easy to understand, and thus they are considered to be B-grade works. Recall (from Chapter 1) that in recent years, the use of <Elderly Male Language> and <Doctor's Language> have become conspicuous in novels for children, works for children such as manga, and works that intentionally imitate the style of picture books for children. This raises the following (new) questions:

## Enigma 3

Why are the characters that use role language, such as <Boss's Language> and <Elderly Male Language>, minor characters?

## Enigma 4

Why the majority of the works that extensively use role language are children's literature?

Before solving these enigmas, it is important to first introduce the concept of stereotype.

## Research on the Concept of Stereotype

The concept of stereotype can be found in social psychology and sociolinguistics. In everyday life, we tend to classify people based on their attributes, including gender, occupation, age and race. Individuals who belong to a particular category are believed to possess certain common characteristics that are referred to as stereotypes. Some examples include "The Japanese are hard-working people" or "Women are emotional."

The concept of stereotype was first used in the 1922 work titled *Public Opinion* by journalist Walter Lippmann. In his book, Lippmann positively embraces the use of stereotype as an essential mechanism to continue living efficiently in daily life, which is inundated with information.

In our daily lives, we come across many new aspects and events every day, and it would be impossible to observe closely each and every event. Thus, it becomes important to match the categories to the target based on instinct and culture and assume that this target also possesses the characteristics (i.e., stereotypes) that constitute the given category.

The process of categorizing the target, assuming the characteristics it possesses, and behaving accordingly is a cognitive characteristic that is common to all animals. In fact, the absence of such a process may result in the extinction of the species. For example, if an animal always checked whether the object is bait, then it would never be able to eat.

However, when human beings classify and categorize humans, it creates various problems. In other words, classifying human beings into certain stereotypes according to superficial characteristics, such as appearance, gender, and nationality, without acknowledging their diverse individuality can result in prejudice and discrimination. For example, women's employment opportunities can be hindered due to the bias associated with the following stereotype: "Women are inferior to men in intellectual ability, they are emotional, and they are not accustomed to organizational behavior."

In other words, one can state that stereotyping is a phenomenon connected to the cognitive characteristics of humans. Cognition refers to the processing of knowledge related to the external world while stereotyping involves the organization of the chaotic external world to gain an understanding of the same. In addition, when knowledge related to stereotypes is associated with emotions (mainly

negative ones), this combination of knowledge and emotion constitutes "prejudice". Furthermore, when "prejudice" becomes associated with specific actions
that create unfair outcomes for stigmatized individuals, these actions constitute
"discrimination".

In social psychology, many studies have been conducted on nationality, race,
and gender stereotypes from the perspective of overcoming the prejudice associated with such stereotypes. Furthermore, there have also been studies on blood-
group stereotypes, a phenomenon characteristic of the Japanese culture.

Based on the aforementioned findings, we can see that role language is a linguistic stereotype. With respect to research that focuses on the linguistic aspect of
stereotypes, the differences between male and female language have been relatively
well researched in the field of sociolinguistics. Such an interest is in accordance
with the recent rise in gender research. However, till date, few studies have explored
aspects such as the types of stereotypical languages (namely role languages) and the
type of functions and histories associated with each role language.

## 2. Real Life versus Virtual Reality

### Role Language and Register and Register Difference

In traditional national language linguistics (i.e., Japanese linguistics), research on
phase and phase difference focuses on variations of Japanese language other than
dialectal variation. Register and Register difference is described in the following
excerpt from *Nihongo no Isō to Isō-sa* (Registers and Differences between Registers)
by Akio Tanaka.

> Language exhibits various differences and correspondences depending on
> gender and generational differences or social class and occupational differences.
> In addition, in closed groups such as the army, licensed quarters, and mafia
> groups, a unique group-specific language tend to emerge easily.
>
> On the other hand, language differences and variations also arise due to dif-
> ferences in styles and forms of expression, such as written and spoken styles as
> well as prose and poetry styles. Just as speech has speech-specific styles and let-
> ters have styles specific to letter writing, variations also arise depending on situ-
> ational differences.
>
> Thus, the specific linguistic aspects seen in different social groups, social
> classes, or in forms of expression, styles, and situations are termed "register" and
> the language differences based on these aspects are called "register differences."
>
> (p. 1)

Register and register difference and role language are similar in some ways, and
simultaneously, they are extremely different in others. Let us first consider the differences. While Register differences are obtained when the researchersstudy the
aspects and variations in real life, role language refers to the ideas regarding reality
that we have, so-called 'virtual reality'.

In this regard, one may think that 'reality' is something obvious to everyone, but this is not necessarily the case. Register and register difference are eventually identified after researchers complete fieldwork and literature reviews, and hence it is often not easy to grasp for ordinary Japanese language speakers. Instead, the knowledge that ordinary language speakers possess is the knowledge of role language.

Researchers sometimes use recordings of real-life conversationsas linguistic data in the study of register and register difference; but, they more frequently use fictional works, such as novels and scenarios. In particular, when tape recorders were not available, there was nothing besides written works that could be used as sources of linguistic data. Fictional works, such as novels and scenarios, are worlds of virtual reality created by the authors, in which role language is employed. As Shimizu says, "It is impossible to write dialogues like verbatim transcriptions of tape recording:" the real-life register and register differences indicated by researchers are aspects that have been reductively extracted from role language used in virtual reality after completing certain processes.

## The Dissociation between Reality and Role Language

As seen in the case of <Doctor's Language> and <Elderly Male Language> in Chapter 1, speech style that clearly does not exist in real life is role language, but not register difference. Thus, there are cases in which role language is cleanly different from register and register different.

However, some language usage can be considered both as a role language and real-life phase difference. What would be the nature of the relation between role language and phase and phase difference in such cases? Let us examine the case of female language. It is considered that in modern Japanese, there are word forms and grammatical usages specific to females "female specific," which are only used by females in principle. For example, there are expressions such as *Ashita wa ame da wa* (Tomorrow it will rain) with the rising intonation at the end of the sentence and *Kirei da koto!* (how beautiful it is!) that expresses exitement. Any native speaker of Japanese would know that these expressions are female specific. In fact, they are also used in the dialogues of novels and dramas. However, ordinary speakers do not know how frequent these female-specific expressions are used in real-life conversations. Although it depends on the age and dialect of the speakers, the frequency of these female-specific expressions used in real life is surprisingly low (also see Chapter 5 in this book). This indicates that, our knowledge of a role language is, by no means, a true reflection of the real life. The distance between reality and role language is close, and other role language has no relation to real life varies and ranges from no relation at all to a close relation to real life. In either case, a bias is definitely involved in some form or another, which is a general characteristic of stereotyping.

Considering this, adding the perspective of role language is extremely important to capture the totality of variations in the Japanese language since it would be one sided to observe it only from the perspective of real life, that is register and register difference.

At this point, if role language is not a reconstruction of real life, then the following question is raised:

Enigma 5
How do we obtain the knowledge of role language?

## 3. Culture, Media, and Stereotypes

### Categorization into Subtypes

The problem that real-life conditions are not necessarily truly reflected in stereotypes has been studied in the social psychology domain. To explain this phenomenon, researchers have proposed several models regarding information processing conducted in the human mind. Let me introduce as an example the information processing model from Yumiko Kamise's *Sutereotaipu no Shakai-shinri-gaku: Henken no Kaishō ni Mukete* (Social Psychology of Stereotypes: towards the Solve of Prejudice).

For example, when a particularly strong stereotype is attached to a specific category, even if one comes across a target in the real world that does not match this stereotype, we tend to exclude the target as an "exception" rather than discard the stereotype. This is termed categorization into subtypes. For example, when a person who holds the stereotype "Women are not good at working" comes across a woman working hard and performing on the job well, the individual considers that "She is a career woman and so it is an exception" and treats her as a special subtype. Conversely, when a person comes across a woman who matches the stereotype, the stereotype is activated in the form of "Women obviously ..." Hence, in either way, the stereotype itself is ultimately maintained and remains absolutely unharmed. (Kamise, abovementioned book, p. 60)

Such sub-typing is possibly in operation in the case of the female-specific expressions mentioned above. In other words, there are stereotypes of "Women speak in this way", including female-specific expressions. When one comes across an individual who does not matches this stereotype, the person is excluded from the category in the form of "She talks like a man," and the stereotype is retained. Conversely, if one comes across a person who speaks like a woman, then the stereotype is naturally reinforced. Even given an ordinary speech that does not deviate from the feminine style of speaking, the stereotype is not weakened. Ultimately, it becomes difficult for a stereotype to be uprooted once it has been formed.

### Dual Process Model

Kamise also introduces Brewer's (1988) dual process model, which is an interpersonal cognition process model. The following is a summary by Kamise:

Upon encountering a target individual, we first automatically categorize the person based on aspects such as race, gender, and age, and judge the person. When there is not much need to know the person well (the target is irrelevant to oneself), the information processing stops at this stage of automatic processing. However, if there is a need to know the target more, then the perceiver progresses to the stage of integrated processing. Brewer considers this stage to comprise the "category-based processing mode" and the "individual-based processing mode."

In the category-based processing mode, one stereotypes and judges the target individual based on the information that has already been formulated in one's mind. This processing mode is selected when there is no need to know the target individual very well (no relevance of the target to oneself). If the target fits the category, then information processing is assumed to stop at this point; if not, then the target is considered to be a special case, and individuation is conducted to understand the target; the target individual belongs to a social category but is judged to be an exception and a special individual. Categorizing into subtypes, mentioned earlier, is also one of the processes of individuation. Even though the judgment is based on individuation, it is considered to be a category-based processing judgment since a particular social category is activated.

On the other hand, in the individual-based processing mode, an impression is formulated by focusing on the specific characteristics of the target individual. This is a type of information processing conducted for persons having high relevance to the perceiver and here, category-related information is not considered to be important. In this processing mode, information processing is not based on stereotypes but on the process of personalization. In this processing mode, the social category to which the target individual belongs is one of his/her attributes.                                                                                         (pp. 79–80)

At this point, the difference arises whether the perceiver stops at category-based processing or advances to the person-based processing mode, depending on whether the target individual is one with whom the perceiver would want a high level of involvement. Interestingly, this hypothesis explains Enigma 3, which has been raisedfrom the essay by Yoshinori Shimizu early in this chapter.

### Enigma 3
Why are the characters that use role language, such as <Boss's Language> and <Elderly Male Language>, minor characters?

The reader does not need to get highly involved with a minor character, in which, the category-based processing mode is adequate. To employ this processing mode, it is sufficient for a writer to portray a character in accordance with the stereotype. However, in regard to main characters, the reader is required to have a high level of cognitive processing of individuation. For this, it is essential to break the stereotype and attract the reader's attention. Conversely, works that require the reader to conduct only the category-based processing mode ultimately cannot go beyond the level of commonsensical stereotypes. In this sense, they are inevitably categorized under B-grade works.

Both the categorization into subtypes and the dual process model operate under the assumption that stereotypes themselves are not so far from reality. However, considering <Doctor's Language> and <Elderly Male Language>, a target individual true to the stereotype does not exist in real life. Moreover, we possess stereotypical knowledge about a target individual that we are not likely to meet in real life. As far as language is concerned, we can imagine the languages spoken by kings, princesses, robots, aliens, and Native Americans (all speaking Japanese!), even though there is little or no possibility that we will ever encounter such individuals. Furthermore, even if we did, in all probability, they would not speak Japanese. Therefore, we have to explain how a stereotype that does not reflect reality is formulated in a situation like this and how we accept it, however, it is difficult to explain this based on subtype categorization and the dual process model.

**Dissociation Model**
Kamise, in the book cited earlier, introduces the hypothesis of the process model, which clearly explains the abovementioned problem, Devine's (1989) dissociation model.

According to Devine, the knowledge related to stereotypes generally prevailing in the society is called "stereotypical knowledge" or "cultural stereotypes." Such knowledge is acquired from caregivers and the surrounding environment during our childhood, a period in which we cannot critically examine the validity of stereotypical knowledge. Since cultural stereotypes are repeatedly activated from an early age, the combination of knowledge becomes strong. Therefore, it is inevitable that stereotypical knowledge automatically arises without any conscious awareness. In contrast, in the course of growing up and receiving education, we also acquire "personal beliefs" that negate cultural stereotypes and the prejudices based on them, thus making it possible for us to avoid these cultural stereotypes.

In accordance with Devine's model, role language is basically a type of cultural stereotype primarily formulated during childhood. After growing up, the cultural stereotype is revised on the basis of individual experiences, but the previously formed cultural stereotype continues to exist as part of the acquired knowledge.

Here, the surrounding environment would, for example, include old tales and children's stories that parents read to their children, and picture books, comics that children read on their own, and animated programs for children, and television/video dramas. These works mainly contain depictions which can be understood under the category-base processing mode since the individual-specific processing mode cannot be expected from children who are the recipients of the contents in these works. Consequently, the works are full of stereotypical knowledge that the author or authors possess; that is, they are filled with role language. Accepting these works repeatedly results in cultural stereotypes becoming firmly imprinted in children's minds. This could offer one tentative explanation for Enigmas 4 and 5.

# 4. The Hero's Journey

Speakers of <Elderly Male Language> do not only have the attribute of being older, but they generally have a specific role associated with their age in the story.

*Stereotypes and Role Language*

The professor/doctor (*hakase*) is typical of such a specific role. Broadly classified, the character of doctor can be divided into the good doctor and the bad doctor. Examples of both types from Tezuka Osamu's works are Doctor Ochanomizu (good) and Doctor Tenma (bad) from *Tetsuwan Atom* (Astro Boy), and Doctor Poppo (bad) and Professor Būton (good) from *Kasei Hakase* (Dr. Mars). In both cases, the doctors possess wisdom and scientific knowledge that seems somewhat similar to magical powers. However, the good doctor empowers the main character with this power of science and guides him, whereas the bad doctor uses scientific powers to confront, torment, and hurt the main character. (The latter belongs to the genealogy of the "mad scientist.") Furthermore, speakers of <Elderly Male Language> are not limited to the character of doctor, but they can be roughly classified into the following three types:

(a) An advisor who guides, teaches, provides training and wisdom to the main character.
(b) An incarnation of evil who terrorizes and tortures the main character using cunning and mysterious powers (for example, the witch in *Sleeping Beauty* and the Queen in *Snow White*).
(c) A person who repeats misunderstanding and mistakes due to senility, and confuses the main character and people around him. This individual sometimes assumes the role of a relationship mediator (for example, Tomozō Jiisan from *Chibi Maruko Chan* (Little Maruko))

In short, speakers of <Elderly Male Language> (including <Doctor's Language>) do not directly point to individuals that we meet in real life, but those who have been given a specific role within the structure of the story.

There is a profoundly interesting work regarding this aspect of the structure of a story; namely, Christopher Vogler's *The Writer's Journey*. Vogler analyzes Hollywood movie scenarios, and he was deeply impressed by *The Hero with a Thousand Faces* written by the American scholar and mythologist Joseph Campbell. And noted that the contents of this work are extremely useful for writing movie and theater scenarios. Vogler has written a guidebook for scenario writers based on the essence of Campbell's work. According to Vogler, Campbell pointed out that there is a common structure in the myths from countries around the world and referred to it as the "hero's journey." This journey comprises a person or persons playing certain roles (archetypes) whom the hero meets and the temporal alignment of the events and situations that occur during such meetings. The hero's journey is something along the lines of the following (here, the term "hero" is used without any distinction between a male and a female):

One day, a hero living an "Ordinary World" receives a "Call to Adventure" from a "Herald" from another world. The hero "Refuses the Call" once, but he is eventually guided by an old "Mentor," encouraged and empowered, and. subsequently, embarks on a journey. The hero approaches the "First Threshold" and is given "Tests" by the "Threshold Guardian." Through these processes, the

"Allies" and the "Enemies" are gradually identified. The "Enemy" works under the "Shadow" that curses and torments the hero. Sometimes, the "Shadow" itself torments the hero. "Tricksters" cause confusion and laughter for the hero through mischief and failures and make him aware of the necessity for change. The "Shapeshifters" are tempters of the opposite sex, and the hero is beset by doubts as he cannot read their minds. Finally, the hero attempts an "Approach to Inmost Cave," overcomes the hardships, and earns the cherished "sword" (reward). the hero follows the "Road Back," but he dies on the way. After being restored to life, he carries a mysterious miracle cure and returns home.    (ibid.)

This type of "hero's journey" can easily be seen (partially or entirely) in other myths, folk tales, and fairy tales. For example, in the Japanese folk tale of *Momotaro* (The Peach Boy), one can see a fairly simple version of this journey. Vogler further breaks down this structure and notes that by superposition, repetition, expansion, and the addition of modern character portrayals, a story that is worthy of appreciation can be created in modern times; He shows that irrespective of the genres of popular movies, dramas, and novels, what ever its genre is (adventure and action films, SF, mysteries, and love stories), have the structure of the hero's journey in some way or another. Works that Vogler use as direct examples of this structure include *The Wizard of Oz*, *The Lion King*, *Star Wars*, *Titanic*, and *Close Encounters of the Third Kind*. It is apparent that the hero's journey captivates the emotions of audiences even today.

Then, why does the hero's journey create such a deep impression on people? According to the claims of Campbell and Vogler, it is based on the personal experiences of those before us and it is, so to speak, a stereotype of human life. We, who are the receivers, identify ourselves with the hero and gain knowledge about our own life goals and processes from the story. In addition, since children have been exposed to variations of the "hero's journey" since childhood, the framework of the stereotypical life becomes imprinted on their minds well before they encounter real life themselves.

If we consider the "hero's journey' from the perspective of role language, an interesting finding is revealed. It was noted earlier that the speakers of <Elderly Male Language> can be categorized into three types; they assume the role(s) of "Mentor(s)," "Shadow(s)," and "Trickster(s)," respectively. Using well-known movies and novels as examples, Yoda in *Star Wars Episode V: The Empire Strikes Back* appears as a "Trickster" but actually becomes an "Mentor"), Merlin the Wizard in *The Sword of the Stone*, ("Mentor") and Albus Dumbledore in *Harry Potter and the Philosopher's Stone* is a typical "Mentor". Furthermore, the speech of these charactersistranslated into typical <Elderly Male Language> role language, asseen in the following excerpts:

Yoda:
*"Attamaruzo, umaijaro?"*
"This will keep you warm. Isn't it delicious?"
(Original: "Good food. Good.")

Luke:
*"Yoda no tokoro made wa tooi no kai? Koko kara dono kurai kakaru?"*
"Is it a long way to Yoda's place? How long will it take from here?"
(Original: "How far away is Yoda? Will it take us long to get there?")
Yoda:
*"Chikaku<u>ja</u>yo, sugu chikaku ni <u>oru</u>"*
"It is nearby, quite close from here."
(Original: "Not far. Yoda not far.")

(*Star Wars Episode V: The Empire Strikes Back*)

*"Kimi no hahaue wa, kimi o mamoru tame ni shinda. Vorudemōto ni rikai dekinai koto ga aru to sureba, sore wa ai <u>ja</u>. Kimi no hahaue no aijō ga, sono ai no shirusi o kimi ni nokoshite iku hodo tsuyoi mono datta koto ni, kare wa kizukanakatta. Kizuato no koto dewa nai. Me ni mieru shirusi dewa nai ...... Sorehodo made ni fukaku ai o sosoida to iu koto ga, tatoe aishita sono hito ga inakunattemo, eikyū ni aisareta mono o mamoru chikara ni naru no<u>ja</u>. Sore ga kimi no hada ni nokotte <u>oru</u>. Kuireru no you ni nikushimi, yokubō, yabō ni michita mono, Vorudemōto to tamashii o wakeau you na mono wa, sore ga tame ni kimi ni fureru koto ga deki<u>n</u> no <u>ja</u>. Kakumo subarashii mono ni yotte kokuin sareta kimi no you na mono ni fureru nowa, kutsū de shika nakatta no<u>ja</u>."*

(Matsuoka, Yūko (translation) *Harī Pottā to Kenja no Ishi*, p. 440)

"Your mother died to save you. If there is one thing Voldemort cannot understand, it is love. He didn't realize that love as powerful as your mother's for you leaves its own mark. Not a scar, no visible sign ... to have been loved so deeply, even though the person who loved us is gone, will give us some protection for ever. It is in your very skin. Quirrell, full of hatred, greed and ambition, sharing his soul with Voldemort, could not touch you for this reason. It was agony to touch a person marked by something so good."

(J. K. Rowling, *Harry Potter and the Philosopher's Stone*, Kindle version, No. 3647)

In this way, speakers of this distinctive role language are assigned a specific role within the story. If they are not assigned roles in this manner, then they will become background figures who appear and quickly disappear. Native Japanese speakers who have grown up in Japan generally learn the structure of the mythological stories together with the role language.

Then, what type of language does the hero, with whom the reader and the listener identify himself/themselves, speak? This is typically <Standard Language>. Indeed, one can find several exceptions, but these exceptions are possible since there are adequate explanations of the background along with the characterizations. If this is not the case, then we are unable to easily identify ourselves with such <Non-Standard Language> speakers. Conversely, we are already prepared to unconditionally identify ourselves with speakers who use <Standard Language>. This raises the following question:

32

Enigma 6
Why does a hero speak in <Standard Language> and what type of language
is it?


NOTES
[1] Tomiichi Murayama was the 81st Prime Minister of Japan from 30 June 1994 to 11
January 1996. He was born in Ōita prefecture and He often used *ja* instead of *da* as an
Ōita dialect in his private talks.

CHAPTER 3

# \<Standard Language\> and \<Non-Standard Language\>

## 1. What Constitutes \<Rural Language\>?

### From *Yūzuru* (Twilight Crane)

Among the representative works of playwright Junji Kinoshita (1914–) is *Yūzuru* (Twilight Crane), which was published in 1949 in *Fujin Kōron*. It was derived from the ancient folktale titled *Tsuru no Ongaeshi* (The Grateful Crane), and it was also composed as an opera by Ikuma Dan in 1952. In the story, an injured crane that is helped by Yohyō (a farmer) transforms into a beautiful woman named Tsū, who subsequently marries him. With the intention of helping Yohyō, she gives him cloth woven from her feathers under the condition that he "shall not come and peep in." Eventually, Unzu and Sōdo, two evil friends of Yohyō, urge him to get Tsū to weave more cloth for money. Although Tsū is saddened by the fact that Yohyō's once-pure heart had become polluted, she continues to weave cloth for him. However, because Yohyō forgets about the promise that he made and quietly watches his wife weave the cloth from her feathers, Tsu transforms back into a crane and flies away forever.

Here, Yohyō, Unzu, and Sōdo speak \<Rural language\> and this language exhibits extremely interesting characteristics, as seen in the following excerpt:

Yohyō:
*"Mou are de oshimai da̱to Tsū ga iu da̱ mon."*
"Well, Tsū keeps said that that's the last one."

Figure 3-1 Tsū and Yohyō, in *Yūzuru*

Unzu:
*"Soge na omē. Mata moukesasite yaru ni."*
"What? But I'll make you earn a sum again!"
Yohyō:
*"Uun ...... Ora Tsū ga <u>itoshūte</u> nara<u>n</u>."*
"Well ... I love Tsū so deeply, I can't help it..."
Sōdo:
*"Itoshi karoga? <u>da</u>de dondon to nuno o orasete kane o tameru <u>da</u>."*
"Don't you? So you've got to make her keep weaving and accumulate money."
(Junji Kinoshita, *Yūzuru*, pp. 246–247)

Here, the underlined *da* is a feature that belongs to the Eastern Japanese dialect, but *itoshūte* and negative form *n* underscored with a wavy line are features that belong to the Western Japanese dialect (refer to the table on p. 4). Furthermore, the form *sogena* is often heard in Kyūshū, the southern part of Japan and conjectural forms such as *itoshikaro* are also generally considered to belong to the Western Japanese style. In this regard, the conversations of these three characters are not in any particular dialect and are a fabricated dialect composed of mixed expressions that sound particularly rural.

On the other hand, Tsū's dialogues are in perfect <Standard (female) Language>.

*<Standard Language> and <Non-Standard Language>*     35

Tsū:

*"Yohyō, atashi no daiji na Yohyō, anta wa doushita no? Anta wa dandan ni kawatte iku. Nandaka wakaranai kedo, atashi ni wa kotoba mo wakaranai hitotachi, itsuka atashi o ya de ita you na, ano osoroshii hitotachi to onaji ni natte itte shimau. Doushita no? Anta wa. Dousureba ii no? Atashi wa. Atashi wa ittai dou sureba ii no?"*

"Yohyō, my precious Yohyō, what has happened to you? You are gradually changing. I don't understand what has been happening, but you are becoming someone living in a world different from mine, and you are becoming similar to those terrible people who once shot me with arrows, whose language I do not understand. What is the matter with you? What should I do? I, what in the world should I do?"

(ibid., pp. 247–248)

This manner of using different speaking styles for different dialogues reflects the intention of the author Junji Kinoshita. Let us cite the following comments by Kinoshita regarding *Yūzuru* :

In short, the result is that, interesting and effective language expressions were picked from various regional dialects and these were combined and mixed based on my own sensibilities. At first, I did this spontaneously and naturally, but gradually with a conscious effort, and then in *Yūzuru* (1949) the dialogues are written using a slightly three-dimensional style. Through the kind of language used by the three men and the language used by the female character Tsū (I call it pure Japanese), I have attempted to bring out the commonalities and differences in the world of the three men and Tsū's world, and eventually express the rupture between the two worlds.

(Junji Kinoshita, *Gikyoku no Nihongo* (Japanese Language in Drama), p. 273)

Here, Kinoshita concisely describes the effect of <Rural Language> and <Standard Language> by superimposing it on the structure of the work. Who would the readers or the viewers of the play empathize with? It is bound to be the character of Tsū. In short, Kinoshita called <Standard Language> "pure Japanese" because the Japanese readers/viewers would without a doubt be able to psychologically associate with the language. By the virtue of this, Tsū is qualified as the heroine. In contrast, the three men's language prevents the readers/viewers from empathizing, and therefore they cannot assume anything beyond peripheral or background roles. In addition, the reason that the men's language inhibits empathy is not simply because the Eastern and Western dialects are mixed (although that may be also a part of the effect). Even if their language comprised a pure Eastern Kantō dialect or the Kyūshū dialect, there would not have been much change in the resulting effect. Furthermore, the effect has no relation to the dialect spoken by the readers/viewers in daily life. In fact, if the readers/viewers are native speakers of the Japanese language who have grown up in Japan, then they will first empathize with the speakers of <Standard Language> regardless of the dialect they use, and then <Non-Standard Language> speakers will be treated as peripheral or background characters. Conversely, by making the characters use <Rural Language>, the author definitely positions the speakers as peripheral and background characters. For this to occur, the differences regarding whether it is the Eastern Japanese or Western Japanese types of language do not become much of an issue.

The following is another example of the dialogues with mixed Eastern and Western dialects:

*"Aa ...... Iya, washi wa ...... Na, joyaku san ...... Anta, washi wa hazukashii de ...... Nani mo konnani chikaku de yaran demo, yokattaro ni, ...... Washi ni taisuru, Tsuraate dattan dabe ka ...... Mou anna yatsu, musuko da towa omowan wa ...... Demo, anta, mura no shū niwa, damatte oite kureru bē na?"*

"Oh no, I ... hey, Mayor Deputy ... I'm so embarrassed ... He didn't have to do it this close (in this neighborhood) ... It was a terrible retort made toward me, wasn't it? ... that guy I could never see him as my son! But you, you can keep this a secret from the townspeople, can't you? Take it with you to the grave?"

*"Shikashi, issho ni itta futari ga, mō shitte oru de ......"*

"But the two who went together, they must already know ..."

*"Sō ...... Sō dabe nā ...... Izure, washi jishin mo, sekinin toran to ikan benā ......"*

"Yes ... yes that's right ... sooner or later, I too will have no choice but to take responsibility ..."

(Kōbō Abe, *Yume no Heishi*, p. 208)

### The Origin of <Rural Language>

As discussed in Chapter 1, during the Edo period up until the mid-18th century, the Edo language was still in a mixed dialect state. Among these dialects, the Kyoto–Osaka dialect was considered to possess relatively high prestige. However, in the latter half of the 18th century, the people of Edo started having the consciousness of being *Edokko* (natives of Edo), an Edo language with the features of Eastern Japanese style emerged from the townspeople, who constitute a lower stratum of social hierarchy.

While Edo Language gained citizenship status in the city of Edo, <Rural Language> emerged in the *gesaku* (a popular novels) genre of Edo. The following is an excerpt from Ota Nanpo's (1749–1823) *sharebon* book (a late-Edo period novelette about life in the red-light district) titled *Sesetsu Shingoza* (published around 1776–1777 (An'ei 5–6)). This excerpt, shows an exchange between Dengouemon, who appears in the red-light district of Yamashita (in the vicinity of the present-day Ueno), and a prostitute. According to his attire and language, it is understood that he is a rural samurai from a rural area.

Den:
*"Kono hashigo o noboru bē ka no* [snip] *"*
"I wonder if I should climb this ladder (...)"

*<Standard Language> and <Non-Standard Language>* 37

I:
*"Nani ohakimono kae. Sōshite ōki nansenshi. Nakunaru kocchaa gozaisen."*
"What is it? Shoes? Leave them right there, please. Don't worry, you won't lose them."
Den:
*"Īya souja ozannē. Ura ga kuni sā jā gara torichigaetemo karyō nō tsundasu mono o." to teinei ni shimai nikai e.*
"Well, that's not the case ... Where I'm from, if you take the wrong shoes, you must pay a fine," he said, while cared ally putting his shoes away and going upstairs.
I:
*"Oenē henchiki da no* [snip] *Anna zouri sē shimatte sa."*
"What a strange person! (...) Going through all that trouble for a pair of sandals!"
(Ōta Nanpo, *Sesetsu Shingoza*, pp. 238–239)

Here, the patron, Dengoemon, cannot behave in accordance with the rules of the red-light district of Edo, and therefore he is despised as a "henchiki" (strange fellow) by the prostitute Ito. As seen in this early example, speakers of <Rural Language> in the Edo *gesaku* genre are depicted as rustics who speak and act in a manner that is removed from the code of metropolitan Edo, and hence they are laughed at and despised by the Edo people. Thus, they are treated as foreigners in the Edo community, which is clearly depicted in the contrast between <Edo language> and <Rural language> (See Chapter 6 in this book).

In Part 1, Volume 1 of *Ukiyoburo* (The Bathhouse of the Floating World) (published around 1809 (Bunka 6)), Sansuke, the male bathhouse attendant who is the "manservant from the countryside," talks about a "strange incident" of *washii kuni sa ita toki* (when I was in the country). In this excerpt, he is ridiculed by everyone as he talks about the tale of the yam that turns into an eel.

Sansuke:
*"Iyahaya harasuzī yoru kondate. Mono hanbun unagi da to omotta yamanoyomo me ga, fushinjū no hikazu sa heta uchi ni, yomo no katachi ga gara nakunatte, minna hā unagi ni natte shimattā. Hanbun yamanoyomo da mon ga, garagara unagii natta mondukuru, acchii nutakuri, kocchii notakuri, tsukamu bei to shite mo, yobi no mata sa, nurunuru nurunuru kandēte, nyorōri nyorōri unagii nobori suruda. Sā tamagemē monka. Gashōgi ni kattsukandara occhinu bē. Tsuchii umetara unagii ochite yomo ni demo narubei ga. Yamanoyomoni bei nacchā motokko ni naranē."*
"Oh man, it's too funny! This yam, which I was sure was half an eel, totally lost its yam shape after a few days under construction and became all eel. This thing that was once half a yam became an eel completely, slithering here, wriggling there, escaping between my fingers when I tried to get a hold of it. Isn't that a surprise? If I grabbed it, this "eel" would probably die; if I buried it, the eel would die, and it'd turn back into a yam. It comes nothing if it turns back into a yam."

*Minamina* (Everyone):
*"Ahhahahahahahahaha." to hikkurikaette warau.*
(falling over in hysterics) "Ahahahahahaha!"

(*Ukiyoburo*, Vol. 1, Part 1, pp. 31–32)

Furthermore, Shikitei Sanba, the author of *Ukiyoburo*, makes Naozane Kumagai speak the Bandō (Kantō) dialect and Taira no Atsumori speak the Kyoto dialect in the comic novel *Daisensekai Gakuya Saguri*. In other words, by making the heroes of *Heike Monogatari* (the Tale of Heike) use <Rural language> and the Kansai dialect, he strips away their hero status and thoroughly defamiliarizes and mocks them.

Kumagai:
*"Anda. Ashiko e mumā bottatte igu nowa, Ura ga kata no mon jā anmē. Tekigata no mon danbei. <ōkina koe shite> Yai, yai, teki dara unu machiyagare, <to suko-shi tachi yodomi> Hatena, to kangae, ō sore sa, mikata daraba motokko yo. Maa yobatte mibei. <to ōgoe hariage> Ōi ōi, soko sa igu no wa dare dāe. Teki ka mikata ka. Teki dara nanore sa. Koreyai. Ōi ōi, heike no teeshō dono dappei. Fukkee sasshai. Teki ni serakaa miseru chū ga arumonda. Konjō gitanē kechina yarō da. Aze, umi no hou ē bei, mumā norikomu da. Hā, fukkeesaneegana."* [snip]
"What's this? Who is that driving those horses over there? They're not on my side. They may be the enemy. (in a loud voice) Hey, hey, if you're an enemy, stop where you are! (pausing a moment) Wait, now that I think about it, if they're allies, it'd be a windfall. Well, I'll call and see what happens. (with voice raised) Heyy! Heeeey! Who is that over there? Friend or foe? If you're an enemy, name yourself! Hey! Hey! You're a general of the Taira clan, right? Turn back! What kind of man shows his back to the enemy? What a sorry, yellow-bellied lot! Why are you only going toward the sea on horses? Won't you turn back already?" (...)
Atsumori:
*"Ya nanjai. Kyōtoi dosugoe de washi o maneku ga. ○ hahā Genji gata to mieru wai. Nani yara iute jaga, namino oto to tokino koe de tonto kikoen."*
"Oh, what's this? Calling for me in such a gloomy, hoarse voice ... ah! He looks like a samurai of the Minamoto clan! He's saying something, but I can't hear him over the sound of waves and all the shouts of fighting!"

(*Daisen Sekai Gakuya Saguri*, pp. 384–385)

In the plays of the Edo *gesaku* genre considered up to this point, <Rural Language> mainly referred to the language of the Kantō regions situated near the Edo area. In contrast, in the *gesaku* plays of Kyoto–Osaka, <Rural Language> referred to the language of the various regions surrounding the Kyoto–Osaka area. The following is an excerpt from the comic novel *Katō Hōgen Hakomakura* (published around 1822 (Bunsei 5)), with its setting of red-light district around the Kyoto-Gion area. Although we cannot specify which region the patron is from, he is presented as a rustic from around the peripheral Kyoto–Osaka area. One can especially understand the rustic feel in the expression *tsuite oru*.

*Dan* (Patron):

*"Iya iya hometa tote nani mo kudasareru niwa oyobanu ga. Orera ga kunimoto ni ima komachi to iute. shikona no tsuite oru geisha ga. ichiban jō kiryō ja to omouta ga. otemae yori wa ototta mono ja."*

"Well, I know it won't get me anywhere flattering you, but where I'm from, there was a geisha nicknamed 'The Modern Beauty,' who I thought was the most beautiful woman in the world, but she's nothing compared to you."

(*Katō Hōgen Hako-makura*, p. 120)

Thus, in the early modern times, a large and linguistically homogenous layer of Edo and Kyoto–Osaka readers/viewers was growing. The urban dwellers took language to be the base of their identity; while they identified with the characters speaking the same dialect as themselves, they ridiculed and despised the characters who spoke <Rural Language> from the nearby regions. This structure is a precursor of the function of <Rural Language> in the early modern times. However, the basis of self-identification depended on regional characteristics such as Edo or Kyoto–Osaka regional features, which was not so far removed from day-to-day experiences. Native speakers of the Japanese language had not yet acquired a language that strengthened their self-identification, regardless of the dialect that they used in everyday life, like in the case of <Standard Language> of the modern period.

## 2. The Structure of <Standard Language> and Role Language

### <Standard Language> as a Role Language

The concept of <Standard Language> is extremely relevant in this book. However, here, the term "standard language" is used with a slightly different meaning than the concept of "standard language" used in daily life or in the fields of traditional Japanese linguistics. More specifically,

- <Standard Language> used here is understood not only as a language associated with issues, such as vocabulary, phonology, grammar, and usage, but also as a speech style and literary style in which these aspects are integrated.

In other words, we should consider <Standard Language>, not as an individual phenomena (as in examples such as the fact that the verb *suteru* 'throw' in standard language is *hōru* in the Kansai dialect, or that the accent pattern in the word *ringo* 'apple' is low–high–high in the standard language), but as a comprehensive system that includes these aspects.

Furthermore,

- <Standard Language> is considered to be a type of role language. However, it is a special type of role language that forms a standard for other role languages.

Considering <Standard Language> as a special type of role language does not infer that it is a phenomenon in real-life society, but it should simply be regarded as a concept and knowledge we have. Avoiding the prescriptive and regulatory images of standard language before the World War II, the term "common language" was employed after the war. However, in Japan, common language is the language that is widely used in Japan, and hence it is a phenomenal as well as a practical concept. For the concept that is being considered here, <Standard Language> is a suitable term. However, there is absolutely no intention of prescribing <Standard Language> as an idealized, pure Japanese, but it is viewed as a concept or knowledge that has been ingrained since childhood by mass media and education just as in the case of other role languages, regardless of whether one likes it. This raises the following question: What is the special characteristic of <Standard Language> that is different from other role languages?

**Spoken and Written Languages**
In this book, <Standard Language> is considered to be having a rather broad scope. <Standard Language> can be subdivided as follows:

1. Written Language

   (a) Plain style (*da*, *dearu* style)
   (b) Polite style (*desu*, *masu* style)

2. Spoken Language

   (a) Public or formal speech style
   (b) Private or informal speech style
      i  Women's Language
      ii Men's Language

Written language is presumed to be used in newspaper articles, essays, theses, novels (especially the so-called third-person novels), etc. as its name suggests. In spoken language, public/formal speech style is used to address an audience (e.g., style used by television and radio announcers, teachers, and politicians). In both written language and public/formal speech style, the gender of the speaker is not actively reflected. In contrast, in private/informal speech style used in everyday interactions, the language of women and men can be differentiated from the absolute and relative scales of first person pronouns, sentence-final particles, and interjections (refer to the Chapter 4 and 5).

These categories are not assumed to be aspects that can be perfectly distinguished from one another. For example, it can be considered that public/formal speech style is based on the polite style (*desu*, *masu* style), but this is practically indistinguishable from the polite style in written language. Furthermore, in television news programs, the announcers use the public/formal speech style when reading the news on air. However, the announcers use elements of private/informal speech in the program, such as the sentence-ending particles *yo* and *ne* in talking to their assistants next to them. In this regard, there is no clear distinction between them; rather, it is smooth and continuous. Furthermore, private/informal language is a speech style that ranges from the punctilious and decorous announcers' interviews to fairly rough speech styles, such as "Ore wa shiranē yo" 'I don't know' which is usually considered to be the "Tokyo dialect, the speech style that is ???" perceived as deviating from the scope of <Standard Language>. In short, I would like to understand <Standard Language> as a system that shows continuity as a whole with gradual gradations from written language to private/informal speech styles.

Some may feel a sense of incongruity to the fact that written language is included in the set of role languages. As stated in "The Definition and Indicators of Role Language" in the Appendix, role language is defined as a language that "enables the visualization of a particular character image" of the speaker. In other words, role language is assumed to be a speech style spoken by specific individuals. If this is the case, then written language does not fit the definition of role language. However, the reason that written language is considered to be a part of role language is because written language (especially the plain style (*da, dearu* style) is "a language that no one speaks"; that is, it is a language that "no one can imagine someone to be speaking." Conversely, by slightly changing the vocabulary and usage of the written <Standard Language> as well as the intonation and sentence-ending particles, a specific character image emerges. In this sense, the written <Standard Language> has the characteristic of being the origin or the reference point of role language. Hence, it must be included in role language.

### Degree of Role Language

Let us introduce the concept of the "degree of role language," which is a measure of the "extent to which a speech style (literary style) conjures up the image of a speaker with distinctive characteristics." In the near future, it may be possible to linguistically and psychologically quantify the exact degree, but at the present moment, this shall be treated as a tentative and intuitive scale.

From the above discussion, in the sense that the plain style of written <Standard Language> cannot conjure up the image of a speaker with any specific characteristics, it has zero degree in the role language scale. For example, the following is an example of such language.

*Sono hi wa taihen yoi otenki de atta. Shikashi tenki yohō ni yoreba, yokujitsu wa ame ga furu kanousei ga arurashikatta.*
On that day, the weather was really fine. However, according to the weather forecast, there seemed to have been a possibility of rain the next day.

In contrast, let us temporarily assume a private/informal style that distinguishes between male and female speeches?, although it lacks any personality, to be degree 1 in the role language scale. The following is an example of such language:

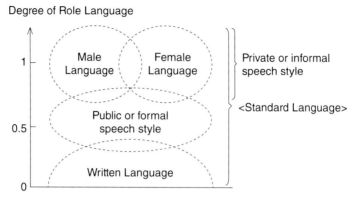

Figure 3-2  Degree of Role Language

A.
*Kyo wa taihen ii otenki da ne?*
The weather is really fine today, isn't it?

B.
*Ē, honto. Demo tenki yohō wa, ashita wa ame darou to itte ita wa.*
Yes, truly. But the weather forecast said that it might rain tomorrow.

In this conversation, one can guess from the usage that A is a male and B is a female. The speakers are probably not small children, however, besides this, there is no feature that actively indicates the age, occupation, or circumstances of the speakers. This type of speech style is given degree 1. Then, <Standard Language> is a language (speech style and literary style) distributed between and in the periphery of written language with a role language degree of 0 and private/informal speech style (male and female language) with a role language degree of 1. Moreover, public/formal speech style falls between written language and private/informal speech style with a role language degree of 0.5. These relationships are illustrated in Figure 3-2.

Conversely, a speech style that emphasizes a strong personality will have a fairly high degree of role language, as seen in the following.

*"Mattaku ja. Shikashi tenki yohō wa, ashita wa ame ka mo shiren to itte otta zo"*
"Yeah, totally. But the weather forecast was saying that it might rain tomorrow, you know."
*"Nda nda. Dakendo, tenki yohō wa, ashita a ame sa furu ka mo shinnētte itteta be*
"Yep. Hey, but the weather forecast said it might rain tomorrow, I say."

Since there is little significance in discussing whether this should be given a role language degree of 5 or 10, let us just say that the degree would be relatively high.

In contrast, the earlier interaction (with the role language degree of 1) is relatively low on the scale of the role language.

### Role Language Degree and Self-Identification

Here, let us consider Enigma 6: Why does a hero speak in the <Standard Language> and what type of language is it?

As stated earlier, the hero refers to the term used in Campbell/Vogler's "Hero's Journey." In the mythological structure of the story, the listener and reader/viewer conducts self-identification with the hero, and as he fakes a journey of the story, which is a veritable epitome of life, and grow up together with the hero. This term, used as a cover term, is not gender specific. Thus, it can also include a female (heroine). According to this definition, for a character to be a hero, it is essential that he/she possesses characteristics that make it easy for the listener and reader/viewer to identify with him/her. Among these characteristics, if one focuses on linguistic aspects, then <Standard Language> must be the language that the hero is using.

Indeed, there are many exceptions. For example, in historical dramas, the "hero" is forced to speak <Samurai Language>. Thus, the measure of the role language degree increases, and the ordinary reader finds it a little difficult to identify with the character. However, if the workings of the mind of the main character are clearly depicted, then such a difficulty can be overcome. So is not a necessary condition that the hero must speak <Standard Language>, but if there are no special circumstances, then speaking <Standard Language> can result in a quick characterization of the hero.

More specifically, written language with a role language degree of 0 is not a language of any particular character type. Thus, it cannot be the language of the hero. The typical hero's language would be a role language degree of $1 + \alpha$. The "$+ \alpha$" part is bound to constitute the hero's individual characteristics. Meanwhile, written <Standard Language> with a role language degree of 0 is not a language of any particular character type, So, it is suitable for freely depicting the workings of any character's mind, that is, an internal language. Consider the following.

*Tarō wa hidoku kanashikatta.*
Tarō was extremely sad.

Here, this is not an observation of a specific person. Instead, you can feel that it is a genuine, objective portrayal of the internal workings of Taro's mind. Now consider the following:

*Tarō wa monogottsu kanashū omashita.*
Tarō was extremely sad.

In this case, it becomes a portrayal from the perspective of someone who speaks <Osaka Dialect>. In this case, it is difficult to feel that it is genuinely depicting the inner workings of the character. Why has <Standard Language> been given this type of privileged position? This question is, in a sense, a reversal. We call a language (speech style) that has been given such privileged position <Standard Language>. However, this type of standard language did not exist in Japan before the Edo period. <Standard Language> was established as one of the requirements for Japan to develop as a modern state in the modern era. What type of language would facilitate identification and be suitable as a hero's language was examined by the Literary Arts Improvement Movement(, of which the *Genbun Icchi* <unification of the spoken and written language> Movement was a part. See below.) of the Meiji period. Before the time the *Genbun Icchi* movement had ended, the citizens were starting to be trained through school education and mass media, such as newspapers and magazines. In other words, this training encouraged self-identification with the speaker of <Standard Language> through the speaking of <Standard Language>. Consequently, the native Japanese speakers in Japan were able to easily identify with the speakers of <Standard Language> in the story, regardless of the linguistic community to which they belonged. Conversely, even if the language was the dialect that the readers/viewers used, the speakers in the story were automatically categorized as minor or background characters. This is the background behind the development in which <Standard Language> is equated with <Hero's Language>.

As clarified in Chapter 1, <Standard Language> is a kind of eastern Japanese dialect. However, up until the beginning of the Edo Period, the center of Japanese culture was the Kansai region in western Japan. The following sections discuss how the standard dialect was formed and what kind of fate <Kansai Dialect> and other western Japanese dialects had?

## 3. The Formation of <Standard Language>

### Before <Standard Language>

As discussed in Section 3 of Chapter 1, the linguistic situation in Edo before the Meiwa period (1754–1771) was a mixture of dialects. The Kyoto–Osaka language, a western Japanese dialect, held high prestige. Originally, <Samurai Language> was specifically based on the grammar of the western Japanese dialect due to the high prestige held by the Kyoto–Osaka language. Furthermore, at that time, as the economy was prospering in Kyoto–Osaka and the culture of the townspeople was flourishing, and high artistic works based on the Kyoto–Osaka language, such as the *jōruri* (a form of traditional Japanese puppet theater) by Chikamatsu Monzaemon (1653–1724), were created. However, around the Meiwa period, the distinctive Edo language, which included eastern Japanese dialectal features, began to be used first among the lower strata of the townspeople, and it spread to the members of the middle and upper classes from the Kasei period (1804–1829). The use of Edo language flourished in the works of the *gesaku* genre, such as *sharebon* (late-Edo period novelettes about life in the red-light districts), *kibyōshi* (illustrated story books with yellow covers), *kokkeibon* (comic books in the Edo period), and Edo-*kabuki*. On the other hand, as in the case of the performances of *Ningyō-jōruri* or jōruri-themed *Maruhon-kabuki*, the Kyoto–Osaka language was used when the performances were held in Edo. At that time, many people from the

Kyoto–Osaka area lived in Edo, and the Kyoto–Osaka language would have been relatively familiar to these Edo residents.

Although, in the later Edo period, there were some Edo people who spoke Edo-go in the Kyoto–Osaka region, there was little influence of Edo language on the majority of the residents. *Sharebon* that were set in the Kyoto–Osaka districts were naturally written in the Kyoto–Osaka language, and plays that were popular in the Kyoto–Osaka region such as *jōruri* and *Kamigata-kabuki* were all performed in this language.

Now, works in Edo language or the Kyoto–Osaka language were solely treated for the entertainment of the people. The intellectuals of those times, who mainly belonged to the samurai class, were exclusively engaged in reading and writing texts in ancient Japanese, *kanbun* (classical Chinese) and transcribing Chinese classics into Japanese. Even in the *gesaku* works written in Edo language and the Kyoto–Osaka language, descriptive portions were written in *kanbun* and transcribed into Japanese. Furthermore, letters in those times were written in *sōro-bun* (epistolary style of Japanese literature), a writing style somewhat between classical Chinese and spoken language. Eventually, seen in Japan as a whole, the major literary style was written language based on the transcriptions of classical Chinese into Japanese and *sōro-bun*. Even in spoken language, Edo language and the Kyoto–Osaka language could have had an impact not only in their respective cities but also in various parts of Japan. However, they remained limited to genres such as *gesaku, kabuki*, and *jōruri*.

The Edo period did not have <Standard Language> nor a unified <Hero's Language> that could inspire self-identification in the various Japanese speakers. However, Edo language might have been <Hero's Language> for the people of Edo, and the Kyoto–Osaka language might have been <Hero's Language> for the people of the Kyoto–Osaka region. Moreover, for intellectuals who could read Classical Chinese and Japanese, the written language of these texts was <Hero's Language>. Therefore, even if role languages had existed during that time, There shouldn't be role language that could familiar with anyone anywhere.

## The *Genbun Icchi* Movement and the Standard Language

In the beginning of the Meiji era, Japan made a "fresh start" as a modern state. As a nation-state, this meant advancing modernization in various aspects such as political, economic, military, and cultural. The issue of language was deeply connected to all of these issues and in this regard, it is termed as the "national language problem." This language problem can be broadly divided into the following two points:

1. The development of an efficient language system that can accurately convey necessary and sufficient information as well as reduce the burdens in education and communication

2. The establishment of a language that has high prestige and that is suitable as a national language

Among the conflicting principles of efficiency and high prestige, the discussion was to become complicated. However, the national language problem can be generally summarized as follows:

1. Improvement in the script and writing system
(problems associated with Japanese characters or script)

2. Establishment of a written-language grammar

3. Genbun Icchi (unification of the spoken and written language)

4. The establishment and spread of the standard language

Among these items, the latter two are directly related to the establishment of <Standard Language>. *Genbun Icchi* was a discussion that was inspired by the minimal difference in the spoken and written languages of Western languages. In short, it referred to the goal of unifying the spoken language (*gen* = speech) and the written language (*bun* = writing). However, since a unified and standard spoken language had not been originally determined, the *Genbun Icchi* movement became linked to the establishment of <Standard Language>.

Initially, among the languages pictured to unite with of the written as the spoken language were informal literary styles such as the *sōrō-bun* (epistolary style of Japanese literature), the *-de gozaru* type of <Samurai Language> that adhered to formalities, and the Kyoto–Osaka type of speech with *-ja*. However, these gradually converged into the Tokyo speech style. In 1895 (Meiji 28), Professor Mannen (or Kazutoshi) Ueda from Tokyo Imperial University noted the following in his paper titled "Hyōjungo ni tsukite (On the Standard Language)" published in the inaugural issue of the magazine *Teikoku Bungaku* (Imperial Literature).

> If I may, I'd like to say a word about a standardized Japanese language which must be newly established. On this point, it is my belief that the current Tokyo dialect possesses the characteristics that could lead it to eventually receive this honor. Certainly, when the Tokyo dialect is mentioned, some people immediately think of it as slang as in "*beranmē*," or rough language of working-class men, but it's not like that at all. When I talk about the Tokyo dialect, I mean the language spoken by educated Tokyoites. In addition, all I'm saying is that the Tokyo dialect has the characteristics that make it deserving of the honor someday in the future; not that it has it now. In order for the dialect to be fit for the standard language of the whole nation, it still needs a little more refinement.
> (Mannen Ueda, "Hyōjungo ni tsukite (On Standard Language)," p. 92)

This was not only Ueda's perspective, but it was also shared by other intellectuals of that time. The following are three possible reasons why the language of Tokyo was considered to be a suitable candidate for the standard language.

*<Standard Language>* and *<Non-Standard Language>*        47

1. Since the Edo period, Edo/Tokyo had been the political and economic center, and with a large population (including many migrants from the countryside), the language of Tokyo was, to a certain extent, functioning as the de facto lingua franca.

2. In the late Edo period, Edo language had even penetrated the *samurai* class and had become quite refined as the language of the intellectual class.

3. Since Edo language had been often used in the *gesaku* genre and the performing arts, it had acquired a written style and to some degree, it developed the linguistic techniques that could be used as a language to communicate with the general public.

Regarding 3, Shimei Futabatei states *"Yo ga Genbun Icchi no Yurai"* (How I Came to Use *Genbun Icchi*) (1906) (Meiji 39) in order to to create the *Genbun Icchi* style of *Ukigumo* (Drifting Clouds), a reference was made to *Kaidan Botan Dōrō* (The Tale of the Peony Lantern), a shorthand book by San'yūtei Encho (for *The Tale of the Peony Lantern*, refer to Chapter 1, Section 3).

Furthermore, Akito Mizuhara points out the following:

From the end of the Edo period to the Meiji era, various novels and *ninjō bon* (a love story in which the characters are ordinary townsfolk) abroad the daily lifestyles of Edo were circulated nationwide. Due to such types of novels, it can be considered that the understanding of the Edo (Tokyo) language had progressed considerably, at least among the intellectual class who could read the written language.

In Meiji 18 (1885), the following was posted in the June publication of the newspaper *Jiyū-tō* (*Light of the Freedom*):

In the past, Tokyo speech used to be learned from the *ninjō bon* of the Tamenaga style. Since reading *furigana*-laden (phonetically annotated) newspapers are a sufficiently effective (and convenient) method nowadays, brazen students have managed to learn the Tokyo dialect without ever setting foot in Tokyo...

In other words, they learned the words used in Tokyo from Tamenaga Shunsui's books and the like, and, by reading newspapers with *furigana*, they learned the Tokyo dialect without ever having visited Tokyo.

(Akihito Mizuhara, *Edo-go/Tōkyō-go/Hyōjungo*
(Edo language/Tokyo language/Standard Japanese), p. 65)

## Mass Media and <Standard Language>

Along with the development of new mass media during the latter half of the 19th century, new genres in literary and performing arts also emerged. First, there were publications following the introduction of the printing press (1870s), which included books, newspapers, magazines, textbooks (textbooks and schools are discussed in chapter 5) and others. Along with these various publications, modern novels developed with there new media, and novels poetries, modern *tanka*, and *haiku* had emarged.

Theater media had existed since the Edo period, but in addition to the classic and traditional genres, the modern genre also emerged. The former included *kabuki, jōruri, rakugo*, and *kōdan* (storytelling) while the latter included *shin-geki* (new dramas), translations of plays , *naniwa-bushi* recitations, and *manzai* (stand-up comedies). Apart from actual theater performances, the genre of motion pictures was newly added in 1897 (Meiji 30) showed documentaries, news reports, foreign dramas, historical dramas, and even modern plays.

Motion pictures were already a visual reproduction medium, but SP records emerged as a form of audio reproduction media from the early 1900s. Apart from classical and traditional theater and music, new genres of entertainment emerged, such as speeches, *naniwa-bushi* recitations, new dramas, operas, fairy tales, and fantasy operas. In addition, from 1925 (Taisho 14) on, radio was added to broadcast media and apart from regular news broadcasts, music and theater plays were also aired.

Through these approaches, new mass media emerged in the Meiji and Taisho eras, and it became possible to transmit the information to the general public through print, video, and audio (with further additions of new media after World War II). This gave a huge impetus to the spread of <Standard Language>. Rather, one can say that in the absence of mass media, <Standard Language> would have been meaningless. In addition, most of the contents of mass media were created in Tokyo (a discussion regarding contents created in Kyoto–Osaka area will be provided later). For example, almost all the literary figures and writers were from Tokyo or they had come to Tokyo from the countryside. In most cases, they wrote novels with Tokyo as the milieu and had characters who spoke the language of Tokyo. For example, *Tōsei Shosei Katagi* (The Character of Modern Students), *Ukigumo* (Drifting Clouds), *Takekurabe* (Comparing Heights), *Konjiki Yasha* (The Golden Demon), *Hototogisu* (The Cuckoo), and *Onna Keizu* (A Woman's Pedigree) are all in this category.

In short, novels written in Tokyo and about Tokyo were read by readers all over the country, and the self-identification with characters who spoke the language of Tokyo was occurring at a national scale. A similar process was occurring through all types of mass media. Thus, the following association was established: <Tokyo Language> = <Standard Language> = <Hero's Language>. Simultaneously, mass media played an important role in the emergence of <Non-Standard Languages> and various role languages, which were subsequently nurtured and spread. Through mass media, role languages in the form of cultural stereotypes were imprinted in the minds of children who would eventually grow up to become content creators and would continue to spread role languages to the society through mass media. Mass media itself generated and spread various role languages, including <Standard Language>, and it became their life-support system.

### The Fall of <Kyoto–Osaka Language>

In the Edo era, before the emergence of <Standard Language>, <Kyoto–Osaka

*<Standard Language> and <Non-Standard Language>*

Language> was considered to be the language of the "Imperial Palace", and it enjoyed much higher prestige compared with Edo-go. It can be assumed that the Kyoto–Osaka language could also have become <Hero's Language>, at least among the people of Kyoto and Osaka. However, during and after the Meiji era, once <Tokyo Language> became <Standard Language>, <Osaka Language> or <Kansai Language>, descendants of <Kyoto–Osaka language>, were reduced to the status of a dialect. Rather, it was became something different from other dialects; that is, an intense, vivid role language. This raises two questions: 1) In what way are the people who speak <Osaka Language> and <Kansai Language> portrayed? 2) What stereotypes are the Osaka and Kansai people associated with?

## 4. History of the Osaka and Kansai Characters

### Pāyan

Mitsuo Suwa, the main character in Fujiko Fujio's manga *Pāman* (serialized in *Shōgaku Sannen Sei* (and of theirs) in 1966–1968, the television anime version started in 1967), is a lazy and wimpy boy who is given a mask and a cloak by a superman from outer space. The boy then transforms himself into Pāman and begins rescuing people. Due to the superman's whims, the number of Pāmen increases to Pāman 2 (a chimpanzee in a zoo), Pāman 3 (a girl), and Pāman 4 (a boy from Osaka named Pāyan). Pāyan, from his very first appearance, is shown to be a stingy person who leaves his peers dumbfounded.

Pāman:
*"Kimi wa Pāman no chikara o kanemōke ni tsukatteru no ka?"*
"Are you using the power of Pāman to make money?"
Pāyan:
*"Sou ya, sore ga donai shita?"*
"Yea, that's right. Is there anything wrong with that?
Pāko:
*"Mā, akireta"*
"Wow, scandalous!"
Pāman:
*"Pāman no tsutome o nan to omotteru no da. Sono chikara wa seigi o mamoru tame no mono dazo!"*
"What the hell do you think is the duty of a Pāman? That power is for protecting justice, you know!"
Pāyan:
*"Seigi wa chanto mamotteru gana. Sono aima ni chotto arubaito shitoru dake ya."*
"I am protecting justice alright. Just making some extra money in the meantime."
Pāyan:
*"Seigi dake dewa moukaran yotte na, ahahaha."*
"Protecting justice alone doesn't yield money, ahahaha."

Pāko:
*"Iyā nē!"*
"Disgusting! "

(Fujiko F. Fujio, *Pāman* 1, p.176)

### ENIGMA 7
Why is it often the case that speakers of <Osaka Language> and <Kansai Language> is portrayed as being stingy and miserly?

## Stereotypes of the Osaka and Kansai People
Pāyan is portrayed as a person for whom money comes first, and this is one of the stereotypes of the Osaka and Kansai people or characters who speak Osaka-ben and Kansai-ben, respectively. In addition to this, the characteristics that are generally expected from the Osaka and Kansai people are given below:

1. Jovial, Cheerful, Talkative

2. Stingy, Miserly, Greedy

3. Gourmet, Glutton

4. Gaudy

5. Lustful, Vulgar

6. Gritty (energetic, especially when overcoming adversity)

7. Yakuza or mafia, Gangsters, Scary

If there is a character in the story who speaks <Osaka Language> or <Kansai Language>, then he/she will quite certainly have one or two or more of the above features.

These characteristics can be further divided into three groups: 1, 2–6, and 7. Among these, the 2–6 group can be summarized by focusing on the characteristics of affirmation as well as the pursuit of pleasures and desires. However, the pleasures and desires mentioned here do not refer to the pursuit of political, religious, and social ideals or abstract and lofty aspects such as acquisition of social prestige. Instead, they refer to the intuitively easy-to-understand desire for money, appetite for food, and sexual desire. Since social prestige is not in this pursuit, they are considered to be stingy, gluttonous, indecent, and lustful and are ridiculed and despised by those around them. When they dress gaudily, it arises from the behavioral principle that if one is spending money, then it has no meaning if the result is not visible. The goal of their extraordinary efforts is referred to as not idealistic but an extremely easy-to-understand acquisition of real wealth.

These characteristics are frowned upon and viewed with disgust by idealistic

*<Standard Language> and <Non-Standard Language>*     51

people or by people who are moderate, but with the quality described in characteristic 1 above, they also become a lovable clown. That is, there is another "self" in them, who coolly observe their own behavior based on their pursuit for they desires, and turns their failure that comes from his actions going too far into laughter, which amuses and relax people around them.

Furthermore, their actions and language, while laughing off the arrogant hypocrites and authoritarians who hide their true desires, also convey the message to look more directly at their desires to those who are stuck or tied to certain ideals and norms. In other words, the role given to the Osaka and Kansai characters is none other than that of a "trickster." Let us examine the following excerpt from "The Writer's Journey," which discusses the psychological function of tricksters in a story:

> Tricksters serve several important psychological functions. They cut big egos down to size, and bring heroes and audiences down to earth. By provoking healthy laughter they help us realize our common bonds, and they point out folly and hypocrisy. Above all, they bring about healthy change and transformation, often by drawing attention to the imbalance or absurdity of a stagnant psychological situation. They are the natural enemies of the status quo. Trickster energy can expresses itself through impish accidents or slips of the tongue that alert us to the need for change. When we are taking ourselves too seriously, the Trickster part of our personalities may pop up to bring back needed perspective.
> (Vogler, *The Writer's Journey*, Second Edition, p. 77)

Here, if such "impish accidents or slips of the tongue" are replaced by "extreme realism, excessive verbiage, and incessant jokes," then it would become the stereotype of the Osaka and Kansai people.

Finally, regarding Characteristic 7, its origin seems to differ from those of Characteristics 1–6. When the pursuit of realistic pleasures becomes linked with aggression, it leads to *yakuza* (mafia and gangsters) and although one cannot call it an irrelevant nature, the original stereotype of the Osaka and Kansai people seems to comprise a non-violent and weak nature. I'll discuss this aspect later.

**The Roots of the Osaka and Kansai People**
Now, this stereotype of the Osaka and Kansai people seems to have been more or less completely formed by the latter part of the Edo period. First, let us examine Jippensha Ikku's *Tōkaidōchū Hizakurige* (Shank's Mare) (1802–1809). Two individuals, Yaji and Kita, after entering Kyoto and Osaka, are saying the word "Atajike nē" (*kechi*/miserly) repeatedly. From their observations, they emphasize the fact that the people of Kyoto and Osaka are greedy and have no mercy toward people from other regions.

Kitahachi:

*"Iya kiranakutemo gōsē ni itē kamisori da."*

"Jeez, that razor hurts; and it doesn't cut a thing!"

Kamiyui (barber):

*"Itai hazu ja waina. Kono kamisori wa, itsuyara toida mama ja sakai"*

"It should hurt. Because it hasn't been sharpened once since it sharpened before at one time ore another."

Kitahachi:

*"Ē, messō na. Naze, soru tabini toganē no."*

"Are you kidding me? Why don't you sharpen it every time you use it?"

Kami-yui:

*"Iya sonai ni togu to, kamisori ga heru sakai. Hate hito san no tsumuri no itai nowa, kocha san-nen mo koraeru gana."*

"Well, if I sharpened it that much, the blade would wear away. You know, I can even endure the head pain of other people for 3 years. "

(*Tōkaidōchū Hizakurige,* 5-hen Tsuika, p. 298)

Kitahachi:

*" [snip] Mochi nara tatta mittsu yottsu irete, negi no chitto bakari sarae-konda mono o, ichi-momme zutsu towa, naruhodo Kyō no mono wa atajikenē. Ki no shireta konjō-bone da."*

"(...) Only putting 3 or 4 rice cakes in with just a little bit of sliced green onion, only a few grams; it's true Kyoto people are stingy, they are bona fide misers."

(6-hen ge, p. 363)

Kitahachi:

*"Kou, Sahei-san, takoku no mono da to omotte, ammari hito o baka ni shita. Yūbe kutta mono ga, nani konnani kakaru mono ka. Sotai kamigata mono wa atajik-enee. Kino shireta berabō domo da."*

"Hey Sahei, Because you think I'm from out of town, you go out of your way to make a fool out of me, huh? Why was what we ate last night so expensive? Every last one of these Kyotoites is stingy; they're all a bunch of tremendous assholes."

Sahee:

*"Iya omai gata ga ata ja wai na. Nan-ja aro to, kūta mono harōte kudansenya, Washi ga suman waina."*

"No, you're the greedy ones. If anything, if I don't get paid for what you eat, I'm out of business."

(8-hen ge, p. 472)

In general, the author of *Tōkaidōchū Hizakurige* has portrayed the people of Kyoto and Osaka as cunning and impudent. At the inn in Kyoto (7th part), there is a scene depicted, in which Yaji and Kita used their quick wits to avoid paying a high price but were instead outwitted by the owner of the inn.

Next, in Shikitei Sanba's *Ukiyoburo* (The Bathhouse of the Floating World) (published 1809–1813) and *Ukiyodoko* (The Barber Shop of the Floating World)

*<Standard Language> and <Non-Standard Language>*     53

(published 1813–1814), three characters from Kyoto and Osaka appear, and they clearly exhibit the characteristics listed in 1–4 above. First, in Volume 2, Part 1 of *Ukiyoburo*, there is the conversation between *Kamigatasuji no Onna* (a woman from Kyoto–Osaka area; hereafter referred to as Kami) and Oyama san (a woman from Edo). Here, Kami's appearance is described as "a squab woman, with fair complexion and thick lips, with eye rims shaded in deep red, black lustrous lipstick applied thickly, and her thick hair ornament is rolled up with white paper to prevent tortoiseshell from being bent by steam from hot water." (In Volume 3 (final part), this type of make-up worn by the Kyoto–Osaka women is criticized by the Edo women as "excessive.")

Now, when Kami hears Oyama san lament her fatness, she states the following to make Oyama san laugh,

Kami:
*"Kai na. Kocha mata, kaza-make sei de ee ka to omōta. Washi nado hashiri-kokura shō nara, yoko ni nete kokeru hō ga, yatto hayai ja."*
"Is that so? I thought it'd be enough just to not lose to the wind again. If someone like me was in a race, I'd go faster if I lay on the ground and rolled."
(*Ukiyoburo*, 2-hen maki jo, pp. 102–103)

Next, the talk shifts to the topic of lunch, and Kami brags about the splendid Kyoto–Osaka style soft-shelled turtle and eel dishes. Oyama-san replies by criticizing the Kyoto–Osaka style of eel dishes as "stingy" and emphasizes that "if the dish cools down as one is eating it, an Edo person would leave the dish as it is and eat another eel that is freshly roasted." Kami criticizes the manners of the Edo people who present wasteful habits as something to be proud of. Oyama-san retorts by saying that the people of Kyoto–Osaka are able to live because even they are appreciated in Edo.

Kami then criticizes the Edo accent and language, after which Oyama-san presents counterarguments by picking examples from classics and emphasizing that the Edo language also has historical roots. Against Kami, who believes and does not doubt the superiority of the Kyoto–Osaka language, Oyama-san is not defenceless and fights back by citing old poems. Here, one can already see the emergence of <Tokyo Language> and the gradual ouster of the western dialects of Japan.

In Volume 4 (middle part) of *Ukiyoburo*, we have the character of a Kyoto–Osaka merchant named Kechi Bē (literally, "stingy guy"), (in the latter half, it is incorrectly written as Kechi Suke, (literally, "stingy assistant") ), who lives alone. First, Kechi makes the *ukiyoburo* clerk laugh by talking in an amusing way about his lonely in a single household.

Kechi:
*"..... Ja ni yotte o-shiru no kawari ni, meshi wa miso-zai ja. Hate miso o nebutte sayu o nomiya, hara no naka de ē kagen no oshiru ni narozoi."*
"So I'm saying, instead of soup, the meal is '*miso-zai.*' If you lick some *miso* and

drink hot water, it'll become a tasty soup in your stomach."
Banto: "Hahahaha."

(4-hen maki chū, p. 255)

Then, he fiercely haggles with a travelling vegetable vendor and manages to buy groceries at the price that he wanted. Moreover, he is also able to wangle some dried *shiitake* mushroom for free.

Banto:
*"Kechi-suke san. Ōkina koe da nē. Watakushi ra ga kadoguchi de donaru koe ga ni-san chō wa hibike-yashō. Yaoya darōga, senzai-uri darōga, omē ni tsukamatte wa ikanē. Dōshite mo kamigata mono wa josai nē ze. Hito oba korori to saseru ne."*
(Clerk) "Kechisuke, you have such a loud voice! As loud as when shouting at the door, it must still be reverberating 2 or 3 blocks away! Whether it is a green grocer or a flower vendor—once you get hold of them, they can't beat you! No matter what—people from Kansai are smart and can control people freely."

Kechi:
*"Yō korori shō-zoi. Shita ga nanigoto mo kī-nagō senya yukanu-wai."*
(Kechisuke) "You're a fine one to talk! If things are not done patiently—nothing works well."

(4-hen maki chu, p. 268)

In *Ukiyodoko* (Volume 1, middle part), we have the character of a Kyoto–Osaka merchant called Sakubē, who is an extremely talkative and an excessively frugal person. However, he is not simply a miserly individual, but he is always jovial and narrates his failures in an amusing way. He is portrayed as a character who is loved by all for this reason.

Saku:
*"Yaya mō ino ino. Tonikaku hanashi ga nago-natte naran wa. Shikaraba. Iya minasan kore ni."*
"Ahh, let's go home, time to go home. The story is intolerably getting long. So with that, I'll be heading out, everyone."
Bin:
*"Mo chitto o-hanashi nasē."*
"Talk a little while longer."
Saku:
*"Iya iya ita tete akan wai no."* <to dete-iku>
"There's no point staying the whole time." (said while leaving)
Chō:
*"Karuwaza no kōjō to iu otoko dano."*
"He's like a master of ceremony for acrobats."
Tan:
*"Momo iro no kataginu o haotte charumera o fukō to iu hito da."*

"He's the kind of person who would put on a pink jacket and play the cha-rumera (an oboe-like instrument)."
Bin:
*"Ki no karui okata sa."*
"A very cheerful person."

(*Ukiyodoko*, Sho-hen, Kan chū, pp. 127–128)

Thus, Ikku and Sanba portrayd exaggeratedly the relentless obsession with money and infinite verbosity as the Kyoto–Osaka characters. However, in regard to violence, the patient and flexible nature of the Kyoto–Osaka people is high-lighted, whereas the short-temperedness of the Edo people and their indiscretion of immediately resorting to violence are admonished, and merits of settlement through negotiation are expounded.

*Sa sa iwansu na soko jate. Sorya tate-ire ja nai totto no yoko-ire ja. Honma ni otoko o tateru to iu mono wa rippa ni kuchi kite kotobaron no rizume ni shite tokushin sasu wa. Hate sore de tokushin nai naraba iu-temo sen ga nai sakai totto hottoku ga ei wai no. Sorya baka-mono ja to omōte hate make-ta ga eiwa.* [snip] *Jiman ja nai ga kamigata niwa sonai na bakamono wa dekenu ja. Osaka no jinki ga arai to iute mo sonna ja nai. Kyōto wa besshite ō-jō no chi ja sakai otoko mo onago no yō de banji ga yasakata ni yū ja wai no.*
"Alright, don't say it anymore. That isn't a "vertical entry" (i.e., a fight. It also means putting something in vertically), it's a "horizontal entry" (i.e., putting something in sideways. It also refers to committing some act of oppression). A truly chivalrous person can speak elegantly, pursue a discussion, and persuade with logic. Then, if you still can't persuade someone, it's best to just let it be. Just realize the whole thing is stupid and let them have the win. (...) It's nothing to be proud of, but Kyoto people aren't capable of that. Even if Osaka people are said to have short tempers, it's not like that. Kyoto is particularly special as it is the location of the royal palace, so men have the feminine charms of grace and kindness."

(*Ukiyodoko*, Sho-hen, Kan chū, p. 121)

The aforementioned features are the portrayals of the people of Kyoto–Osaka through the eyes of Jippensha Ikku and Shikitei Sanba, two Edo natives. Although it is essential to examine the depictions in the works of other writers, considering the vividness of the portrayal and the continuity of the stereotype of the Kyoto–Osaka people seen later, one can consider that these stereotypes of their were, to a considerable degree, established during the late Edo period.

These characterizations can be considered, to a certain extent, as reflecting the true culture of the Kyoto–Osaka region. Along with the *ukiyozōshi* (Edo-period variety of realistic novels by Saikaku Ihara), one can conjurn the Kyoto–Osaka culture with Osaka as the center, there was an ethos that placed importance on the realistic and economic aspects of life. Moreover, there is the presence of business practices that help seize certain opportunities through repeated conversations that may be considered to be a waste of time in everyday life, against the backdrop of insular market tendencies. Such practices do not exclude but wholeheartedly welcome various interactions.

Sanba brilliantly demonstrates how, by placing these characteristics in the Edo environment, it can make them more conspicuous. Edo is the city of samurais and it was ruled by Confucian asceticism, idealism, and behaviorism. On the other hand, the Kyoto–Osaka people came to Edo to make money, and they appeared to the native Edo people as particularly miserly. It can also be considered that the repetitive and strong modulations in the *gidayū* ballad drama and *ningyō-jōruri* (puppet theater) performance styles, which were popular in Edo at that time, influenced the modeling of the Kyoto–Osaka people. Finally, in an ethos of Edo, in which an idealistic and heroic nature was respected, the Kyoto–Osaka people were naturally assigned the role of tricksters.

### The Osaka and Kansai People in Modern Mass Media

In the beginning of the modern period, Japan selected the new policies of *Fukoku Kyōhei* (measures for the wealth and military power of the country) and the *Datsu-a Nyū-ō* (Leave Asia, Join Europe). In addition, the descendants of the former samurai continued to lead the modern empire after which a more austere, reticent, active, and heroic nature came to be valued. Therefore, in stories originating from Tokyo, the people from Osaka and Kansai were inevitably portrayed as tricksters.

Furthermore, the dissimilation effect of the movement for the standardization of language in the modern period must be considered. In *Ukiyoburo*, although *kamigatasuji no onna* (a woman from Kyoto–Osaka area) receives tough resistance from Oyama san, she harbors no doubts about the prestige of her own language. However, in the modern period (from the end of the Meiji era through to the Taisho period), the *Genbun Icchi* movement had concluded. In addition, amidst the movement promoting the development of <Standard Language>, the recognition that <Standard Language> is "a language spoken in Tokyo by educated people" became difficult to remove. In this regard, the equation has become the following: <Hero's Language> = <Standard Language>.

Radio, which became the means that propelled the spread of <Standard Language>, was also the tool that transmitted <Osaka Language> and <Kansai Language> nationwide. However, <Kansai Language> that was heard was in short, *manzai* (comic dialogue) representative of the duo Entatsu and Achako. Entatsu and Achako also appeared in films and were successful. In the process, which occurred in the 1930s, one can say that the association of Kansai Language = *Owarai* (comedy) had become fixed in mass media. Let us examine an excerpt of the famous *manzai* "Sō-Kei Sen" (Waseda versus Keio Baseball game) by Entatsu and Achako.

Entatsu:
*"Shikashi, boku ne, ima koso konna hosoi yaseta karada o shite imasu ga, koredemo gakkō ni iru jibun wa, rippa na mono dattan desu yo."*
"Now I have such a thin, skinny body, but when I was in school, I had a great

physique."
[snip]
Achako:
*"Atarimae ya, kimi wa doko no gakkō ya?"*
"Of course. Which school did you go to?"
Entatsu:
*"San-kō desu."*
"3-Kō (usually, this refers to Dai-San Kōtō Gakkō, the third national senior high school that previously existed in Kyoto)."
Achako:
*"San-kō? Hahan, Kyōto de benkyō shitan desu ka?"*
"3-Kō? Ah ha, you studied in Kyoto, eh?"
Entatsu:
*"Boku wa ne, doumo fushigi to, Ōsaka ni sunde ite, imadani Kyōto o shiranain desu."*
"Actually, I live in Osaka but know nothing about Kyoto yet."
Achako:
*"Sonna aho-rashii koto, San-kō yattara Kyōto ya naika."*
"That's so absurd. If it's 3-Kō, it's Kyoto, isn't it?"
Entatsu:
*"Īya Nishinomiya desu."*
"No, it's in Nishinomiya."
Achako:
*"Nishinomiya? Sonna tokoro ni San-kō-tte arimasen yo."*
"Nishinomiya? There's no 3-Kō in such a place."

Figure 3-3 Entatsu and Achako

Entatsu:
*"Nishinomiya Dai-San Jinjō-Kōtō-Shōgakkō."*
"Nishinimiya the third Normal Elementary School."
Achako:
*"Nan-ya, boku no yūteru no wa, ue no gakkō no koto ya."*
"What the…I'm talking about high (high level) school."
Entatsu:
*"Boku no gakkō wa oka no ue ni atta."*
"My school was also on top of a hill."

(Entatsu and Achako "Sō-Kei Sen," pp. 92–93)

After World War II, even after the addition of television, programs originating from Kansai were almost entirely comedy shows. Typical representatives of such programs were the 1959 (Showa 34) *Bantō Han to Decchi Don, Tonma Tengu*, and the 1962 (Showa 37) *Tenamon'ya Sandogasa*.

Conversely, dramas originating from Kansai that were not *owarai* (comedies) included Kazuo Kikuta's *Gametsui Yatsu* and Kobako Hanato's *Konjō Mono* ("guts" drama). The former was performed in 1959 (Showa 34) at Geijutsuza theater in Hibiya, Tokyo, and it had a successful long run. It was also made into a film in the following year. The character of *Oshika bā-san* (Granny Oshika. played by Aiko Mimasu, both in the theater play and in the film) manages a cheap hotel in Kamagasaki, Osaka and was portrayed as an extremely stingy person. The play became very popular, making Kazuo Kikuta's coinage of *gametsui* famous as well.

Kobako Hanato's works *konjō mono*, include the 1967 (Showa 42) *Semba, Hosoude Hanjōki* (with a successful long run from 1970) (Showa 45), *Doterai Otoko* from 1973 (Showa 48), and the 1979 *Ayu no Uta*, he was from Shiga Prefecture, and the heroes and heroines in his dramas were not the reflection of Kansai people, but merchants from the Oumi region. However, due to the success of these dramas, the image of <Kansai character = miser and gritty character> had became fixed in society. Pāyan is an extension of this particular image.

### Lewdness, Violence, and the Osaka and Kansai People
In the analysis thus far, the link between the Kansai people and the image of a lewd and violent nature is rather unclear. Indeed, there is Saikaku Ihara's *Kōshoku Ichidai Otoko* and *Kōshoku Gonin Onna* in the erotic category, but for this stereotype in the modern period, we need to seek the origin elsewhere. In this regard, Tōkō Kon's (1898–1977) *Kawachi* (the south east area of Osaka Prefecture) *Mono* (such as *Shundeini-Shō* (1957)) may well be the point of departure. *Kawachi Mono* was written around the latter half of the 1950s. Most of his works were made into films, such as *Shundei-ni* (1958), *Mimizuku Seppō* (1959), *Kotsuma Nankin* (1960), and *Kawachi Fudoki Oiroke Seppō* (1961). Let us examine an energetic and wild Kawachi dialogue from *Tōkei*.

*"Yō. Miteru bakari ga nō ya nai de. Mōkeru zeni nai-non ka. Nakattara Enryo nō yūte mii. Kiyō ni kashitaru de. Seya kendo na. Kashite morote kaesu kaishō nai no*

*<Standard Language> and <Non-Standard Language>*

*wa, yametatte. Oi. Sokora ni iru wakai no. Wai ra wa shamo no kenbutsu ni use sarashitan ka. Soretomo Keai ni kitan ka. Doccha ya. Hakkiri shitatte. Soko no ossan. Doya. [snip] Kawachi-mon wa hyaku ya ni-hyaku no zeni de shian sarasun ka. Warawareru de. Sonai shibuchin no tokoro o, ano ko ni mise tomo nai wa. Sā. Hatta. Hatta. Hatte waruiwa oyaji no dotama dake ya. Mē muku hodo mōke sasitaru de. Koredemo you haranno ka. Hotara, wai ga itaru. Wai ga aite ja. Sā, hatte mii. Gashintare me ga ......"*

"Hey, just looking at it does not mean you are competent. Don't you have the funds to create it? If you don't, say so without hesitation, and I'll duly lend you some. But please make sure that you have the capacity to return what has been lent. Hey, you young people there. Have we come to see "Shamo" (roosters for chicken fight) or have we come to hold "Shamo no" (rooster fights)? Which is it? Be clear. You there, old man, what do you say? (...) People of Kawachi think twice about spending 100 or 200 gold pieces, eh? That makes me laugh. I don't want to be such a cheapskate in front of that girl. Come on, lay a bet, lay a bet. If you hit (meaning, bet money), the only bad thing will be a father's head. I'll make you earn an eye-popping amount. Is this still not enough for you to bet? In that case, I will go. I am the bet opponent. Well then, try and bet, you miser."

(Tōkō Kon, *Tōkei*, p. 9)

In 1961 (Showa 36) , Tōkō Kon's original film *Akumyō* (Notoriety) premiered. This story was about the yakuza (mafia) of Kawachi. In this case, the Kansai dialect and violence were clearly linked. *Akumyō* became a hit after which it was made into a series. Furthermore, the so-called "mafia films" were made from the 1960s, but the milieu selected ranged from <Standard Language> speaking areas such as Tokyo, Yokohama, and Kawasaki along with Osaka, Kobe, Kita-Kyūshū, and Hiroshima. For example, Kōsaku Yamashita's *Gokudō* (*Hoodlumism*)(1968) (Showa 43, later made into a series) is a typical example. After 1975 (Showa 50), works set in Kansai dramatically increased.

Now, in regard to lewdness, it is important to mention Akiyuki Nosaka's maiden work *Erogoto-shi tachi* (*The Pornographers*). With its extremely vulgar content that matched the full vitality of the Osaka dialect, it left an intensely vivid impression on the readers.

*"Kangaete mitara Tōkyō-ben ga akan nen wa. Aitsura no kuchi kiite tara, honma no koto kate uso yūteru mitai ya, kanjō komottē-hen chūno kana, ame no yoru no tēpu (tape) kate, hito niwa sadame ga omanne, nā, koremo anta no sadame ya oma-hen ka, sadame ni sakarawan to, sa, sono tē doke-toku-nahare, to kō yūtottara, ano gaki kate manzoku shiyottan ya."*

"Come to think of it, it is the Tokyo dialect that is bad. When you listen to them, even if they are speaking the truth, it seems as if they are lying. Maybe it's because there's not much emotion. Even if it was a tape recording of a rainy night, if one would have said '(In the Kansai dialect) a person has a destiny, and isn't this your destiny, don't defy fate, please move your hand,' that man would have been satisfied."

(Akiyuki Nosaka, *Ero-goto-shi tachi*, p. 7)

As far as manga works are concerned, we have the 1975 (Showa 50) *Aa! Hana no Ōendan* (*Oh Glorious Cheer Team!*) by Dōkuman and the 1979 (Showa 54) *Jarinko Chie* (*Little Girl Chie*) by Etsumi Haruki in which violent characters such as Akamichi Aota and Tetsu appear respectively.

In addition, in 1985 (Showa 60), a mafia war between Yamaguchi-gumi and Ichiwa-kai erupted, with Kansai as its battleground. Referred to as "Osaka War," the story made the top headlines in the country's daily newspapers, which further fanned the negative image that the "Kansai is scary."

As seen above, Tōkō Kon's works and the films made based on these works (including the mafia films set in Kansai) created the image of Kansai people = vulgar, violent, *yakuza* in the 1960s. From the 1970s, these stereotypes were amplified, and by the 1980s, when some incidents took peace in real life, it become an unshakable stereotype.

## The Transformation of the Stereotypes

The stereotypes associated with the people of Kansai and Osaka was based on the characteristics formulated in the late Edo period. Multiple layers of characteristics were further added in the modern period. In other words, in the Edo period, the Kyoto–Osaka people were given characteristics such as stingy, verbose, and jovial, and they were rather perceived as non-violent compared with the Edo people. In the modern period, at least since the 1930s, due to the live *manzai* or *owarai* (comedy) dramas broadcast on radio and television, the image Kansai dialect = *owarai* had become clear. In addition, from around 1960, especially with Kobako Hanato's dramas, the characteristic of "gritty" was added. Since the 1950s, from Tōkō Kon's works and others, the image of lewdness and violence was added to these characterizations. Furthermore, *yakuza* and gangster movies set in Kansai further strengthened the various shades to the characterizations.

Recently, there seems to have been another characteristic added to the list: the *manzai* boom, which began in the 1980s. Several young *manzai* pairs from Kansai led an explosive boom in television programs after which it expanded to concerts, thus leading to packed Budōkan (an indoor arena in Tokyo). Following suit, from 1981, a program titled *Oretachi Hyōkin Zoku* (We are Tribe of Fun) began, and several entertainers had become popular through this program. Until then, *owarai geinin* (comedians) were looked down on by the general public, and there is no doubt that feelings of despise were also included in their laughs. However, this boom demonstrated that *owarai* artists could also become heroes. Among the young people, the image of Kansai dialect = *kakko ii* (cool) was being formed.

"Kinki Kids," an idol duo of two men formed in 1993, gave an impetus to this trend. The pair was not only handsome, but they could sing and dance well. Apart from these characteristics that were similar to regular idols, they openly shared the fact that they were from Kansai, and their comedian-like performance, including making a gag, *tsukkomi* or retorting, etc., is a great fascination of them. In fact, they were the first idols to have incorporated the elements of Kansai *owarai*.

<Standard Language> and <Non-Standard Language>    61

Additional evidence that tells the transformation of the Osaka and Kansai character is the high school student detective Heiji Hattori in the highly popular manga *Meitantei Konan* (*Detective Konan*), Volume 10 (Shogakukan, 1996). He is the rival of the high school detective Shin'ichi Kudō, who is forced to drink a potion by bad men after which his body shrinks to the size of the an elementary school student. He was born and raised in Osaka and indeed, he speaks <Osaka dialect/Kansai dialect> However, he has no other specific (Kansai) characteristic. In short, he does not run after money, he is not gluttonous nor is he lustful. In his appearance, he is portrayed as a handsome boy comparable with Shin'ichi Kudō, who is the protagonist. According to traditional stereotypes, he would have been depicted as a much more idiosyncratic character like Pāyan, but he is depicted in a new way as one who is not only "cool" but also a powerful rival to the main character.

However, even if this type of new stereotype has begun to be associated with the Osaka and Kansai people, it does not mean that the association of <Language of Tokyo> = <Standard Language> = <Hero's Language>, which represents the modern Japanese language, will undergo any major transformation. Even though Heiji Hattori is depicted as "cool," he is still the rival of the main character Shin'ichi Kudō, and it cannot be denied that he is simply number two.

Figure 3-4 Hattori Heiji
(Mei-tantei Konan 10, ©Gōshō Aoyama)

CHAPTER 4

# Male Language
## Its Root is <Samurai Language>

## 1. A Change of <Standard Language>

*Amefuri* (Rainy Day)

*Amefuri* (Rainy Day), a nursery rhyme composed by Hakushū Kitahara (1885–1942), was published in the anthology titled *Taiyō to Mokujū* (*The Sun and a Wooden Gun*) (1943) (Showa 18). Although it is a well-known nursery rhyme, surprisingly very few people may be able to sing Stanzas 1 to 5 accurately.

*Ame-furi*

*Ame ame, fure fure, kā-san ga*
*Janome de omukai ureshii na.*
*Picchi picchi chappu chappu*
*Ran ran ran*

*Kake-masho, kaban o kā-san no*
*Ato kara yuko yuko kane ga naru*
*Picchi picchi chappu chappu*
*Ran ran ran.*

*Ara ara, ano ko wa zubu-nure da.*
*Yanagi no nekata de naite iru.*
*Picchi picchi chappu chappu*
*Ran ran ran.*

*Kā-san, boku no o kasha masho ka.*
*Kimi kimi kono kasa sashi tamae.*
*Picchi picchi chappu chappu*
*Ran ran ran.*

*Boku nara iinda, kā-san no*
*Ōkina janome ni haitte ku.*
*Picchi picchi chappu chappu*
*Ran ran ran.*

(Kitahara, Hakushū, *Taiyō to Mokujū* (The Sun and Wooden Rifle),
pp. 186–187.)

(synopsis) When coming home from school (or kindergarten), it started to rain.
My mother came out with a big umbrella for me, so I was very happy. On the
way home, we found a child crying by the trunk of a willow tree. This is what
I said to my mother: "Mother, shall I lend that child my umbrella?" I did so
and spoke to the child: "Hey you, take this umbrella, I'm going home with my
mother under her big one."

The subject of focus here is *kimi kimi kono kasa sashi tamae* 'Hey, you, please use
this umbrella' in Stanza 4. The *boku* ( = I) in this lyrics is a type of character who
sings *Picchi picchi chappu chappu, ran, ran, ran* 'Splishy splishy, splashy splashy,
how happy I am!' since he is happy that his mother is coming to pick him up on
a rainy day. Hence, he is most likely a Grade 1–3 student or even if he is in Grade
4–6, he would surely be on the younger side. For this *boku* ( = I) to say *kimi kimi
kono kasa sashi tamae* seems similar to a middle-aged man's style of speech, from the
perspective of modern sensibilities. Nowadays, even company bosses do not speak
in this manner, as shown in Chapter 2 of Yoshinori Shimizu's essay. Apparently, in
1943 (Showa 18), it was not considered unnatural for elementary school children
to use this type of role language that, in this modern period, should be referred to
as <Boss's Language>. Certainly, from the early Showa period, we can find various examples that show the use of *-tamae* by young boys, which can also be easily
found in the post-war period.

For example, in the following excerpt from *Kaijin Nijū Mensō* (The Fiend with
Twenty Faces), serialized in *Shōnen Kurabu* (Boy's Club) in 1936 (Showa 11), there
is a scene where the boy detective Kobayashi-kun meets face-to-face with *Kaijin
Nijū Mensō*.

"*Namae nanka dou datte ii ga, osasshi no tōri, boku wa kodomo ni chigai nai yo.*
"It doesn't matter what the name is. As (you) must have guessed, there is no
doubt I am a child.
*Daga, Nijū Mensō to mo arou mono ga, boku mitai na kodomo ni yattsukerareta to
atte wa, sukoshi naore da nē. Ha ha ha ha ha ha ha.*"
but if someone who has twenty faces gets defeated by a kid like me, it would be
a little disgraceful, wouldn't it? Ha ha ha ha ha ha ha."

*Kobayashi shōnen wa makenai de ōshū shimashita.*
Undeterred, Kobayashi responded,
*"Bōya Kawaii ne .... Kisama sore de, kono Nijū Mensō ni katta tsumori de iru no ka."*
"How cute, little boy ...., you think you have won against me, the one with the twenty faces, have you?"
*"Makeoshimi wa yoshi tamae. Sekkaku nusumidashita butsuzō wa ikite ugokidasu shi, daiyamondo wa torikaesareru shi, sore de mo mada makenaitte iu no kai."*
"Don't be a bad loser. The statue of Buddha stolen so painstakingly will come alive and start moving, the diamond will be got back, and still you say that you will not be defeated, eh?"

(*Kaijin Nijū Menso* (The Fiend with Twenty Faces), p. 520)

The next example comes from *Tetsuwan Atomu: Kitai Ningen no Maki* (Astro Boy: the Volume of the Gas Human) in the 1952 (Showa 27), where Ken'ichi uses *-tamae*.

Professor Ocahnomizu:
*"Atomu dō ja/Ningen no furi o shite kemuri ni tottsukarete minka?"*
"What do you say Atom?/Won't you pretend to be a human and get caught by the gas?"
Kenichi:
*"Ne dakara/Kono sai hitotsu te o kashite kure tamae."*
"So/this once, (will) you lend me a hand."
Atom:
*"Ōkē."*
"Okay."

(*Tetsuwan Atomu* 1, p. 99)

Thus the *-tamae* of <Boss's Language> was, until a certain period, a part of what should be called <Boy's Language> role language. This raises the following questions:

**ENIGMA 8**
From where did the expression *-tamae* originate?

**ENIGMA 9**
Why is it that *-tamae* was once recognized as <Boy's Language> and it has now become <Boss's Language>?

**Change of a Role Language Degree**
As discussed in Chapter 3, <Standard Language> comprises a sequential gradient, including written language, public (formal) speech style, and private (informal) speech style. Private speech style is further divided into <Male Language> and <Female Language>. These speech styles were considered to have a role language

Figure 4-1 *Tetsuwan Atomu* 1
(p. 99 ©Tezuka Production)

degree of 1 (or 1 + α).

The *-tamae* in question here is no doubt <Standard Language>, but in the modern period, it is perceived as a word used by "males who are elderly" and have a "certain social standing" over their subordinates. In other words, it is <Boss's Language>. Moreover, it is hardly ever used in real life. However, examining pre-war documents, the usage of *-tamae* had a wider range that included young boys, in fact, it seems to have been common usage. That is, its role language degree has imperceptibly risen in ordinary language.

In regard to <Female Language>, the transition was a bit more complicated. Expressions such as *iya da wa* (I don't like it), *yokutte yo* (It's good), and *suteki da koto* (That's lovely) are recognized as typical female language. Above all, there was a strong impression that *-te yo* and *-koto* were used by upper-class females. In short, this is <Young Lady from a Good Family Language>. Until around the year 1897 (Meiji 30), however these usages were rejected by experts as vulgar and rough. Then, they came into vogue in girls' schools, and from the end of the Meiji era to World War II, they had become quite common. Gradually, these usages have become outdated in real life, and they are currently nothing more than the notional <Young Lady from a Good Family Language> used in mass media.

In this chapter and the next chapter, from the perspective of male and female language, we shall explore the process of what was included as well as excluded in <Standard Language>.

## 2. The History of <Male Language>

### <Student Language>
Among the words that symbolize the Meiji era, there is the word *shosei* (student). In today's society, this is roughly equivalent to the word *daigakusei* (university

student). However, this word also refers to young people who attended private schools, those who lived with their caretakers without going to school, going to school performing chores, and went to search for job opportunities. Furthermore, there is also the word *onna-shosei* (female student), but basically *shosei* referred to male students.

Shōyō Tsubouchi's (1859 (Ansei 6)–1935 (Showa 10)) novel *Ichidoku Santan Tōsei Shosei Katagi* (literally, the character of modern students that makes you sigh three times every time you read it) (published 1885 (Meiji 18)–1886 (Meiji 19)), portrays the daily life of *shosei* in the early Meiji period, vividly and with some exaggeration. The following is a lengthy excerpt from the novel.

*Konata ni nao mo tattaru mama. Bon'yari shian no shosei no senaka. Pon to utarete. Oboezu bikkuri.*

Here we have someone about to strike the back of a *shosei* (student) who is standing lost in thought. The attacked *shosei* jumps in spite of himself.

Sho:
*"Oya dare ka to omottara Sugawa ka. Mada kimi wa nokotte ita no ka."*
"Oh, Sugawa. I was wondering who it'd be. You are still here, huh?"

Su:
*"Oi komachida. Ayashii zo. Ano geigi o kimi wa shicchoru no ka. To iwarete oboezu makka ni seshi kao o warai ni magirasi tsutsu."*
"Hey, Komachida. You look suspicious. Do you know that geisha? Upon hearing this, Komachida's face turned bright red, but he tried to laugh it off."

Ko:
*"Nāni boku ga shitteru monka."*
"What! You think I know? No way."

Su:
*"Sore demo. Erai hisashii aida. Kimi to hanashi o shi-chotta dewa nai ka."*
"And yet you two were talking an awfully long time."

Ko:
*"E. Are wa nani sa. O-kyaku to onigokko ka nanika o shite ite ayamatte boku ni tsukiatatta node. Sorede boku ni wabite ita nosa."*
"Yeah, that was, what do you call it; she was playing tag with a customer and hit me by mistake and was apologizing for it."

Su:
*"Sō kā. Sore ni shite wa taisō teinei danaa."*
"Ohhh, I see, but I have to say, it extremely polite."

Ko:
*"Nani ga."*
"What (is polite)?"

Su:
*"Kare ga shibashiba kimi no hō o. furikaette michotta kara sa. Yoppodo kimi o rabu (love) shite iru zō."*
"She kept looking back at you for a while, it seems like she really loves you."

Ko:

*"Ahahahahaha. Bakaa ii-tamae. Sore wa sō to. Shokun wa mō. Minna kaeshite shimatta noka."*

"Ahahahahaha, please, don't make me laugh. By the way, has everyone already been sent home?"

Su:

*"Un. Ima yōyaku kaeshite yatta. Dorankaado* (drunkard) *ga shichi hachi nin deki-otta kara. Kurase to futari de karōjite kaihō shite minna kuruma ni nosete yatta. Mō kanji wa negaisage da. Ā kitsuka kitsuka."*

"Yes, I finally sent them back. We had 7 or 8 drunk ones, but Kurase and I managed to look after them and load them into rikishas. I won't organize a party ever again. Ahh, that was rough."

Ko:

*"Boku wa mata asoko no matsu no ki no shita e yoi taorete ita mondakara. Zengo no koto wa marude shirazu sa. Soryā shikkei datta nē. Chitto herupu* (help) *sureba yokatta."*

"I was so drunk that I collapsed by that pine tree over there, I don't remember what happened before or after. I'm sorry about that. I should have helped a bit."

Su:

*"Ya hi ga mō shizumu to mieru wai. Inō inō."*

"Ah, looks like the sun is setting. Let's go home."

Ko:

*"Kurase wa dō shita ka."*

"What happened to Kurase?"

Su:

*"Shita no chaya ni machi-yoru jarō. Miyaga ga ankonshasu* (unconscious) *ni nari-otta kara. Sore o kaihō shichoru hazu ja. Ā boku mo yōta. Ā Yōte hā. Makura sū. Bijin nō. Hizā. Samete hā. Nigirū. Tenka nō. Ken."*

"He's waiting in the teahouse downstairs. He's been looking after Miyaga since he passed out. Ahh, I got drunk too. (poetry recitation omitted below)"

Upon reading the conversation of the two *shosei* student characters Komachida and Sugawa, you immediately realize that the conversation is full of insignificant English words. In fact, the majority of the words, such as 'love', 'drunkard', 'help', and 'unconscious', have not been established as loanwords even today. Rather than being practical usages, they were expressions that indicate the simple unpretentiousness of the intellectual elite of that time.

There is also the conspicuous use of Sino-Japanese expressions such as *shokun* (gentlemen) and *shikkei* (rude). The Meiji period is generally known as a period in which the use of Sino-Japanese expressions dramatically increased, but expressions such as *shokun* and *shikkei* were specifically used by *shosei*.

Yet, the language used by Komachida and Sugawa seems to have dialectical differences. First, Komachida's language has absolutely no dialectal features. Komachida was born in Hakusan, Tokyo (Edo), and since his father had been

## Male Language

appointed as a government official (after his distinguished service during the Meiji restoration period), he is surmised to be from the samurai class. "The language of Tokyo's educated class of men," which was the basis of the standard language, was indeed the language of people in the samurai class such as Komachida.

On the other hand, Sugawa's language includes many dialectal elements, as seen in the following example:

- *shicchoru, shichotta, dekiotta, macchoru, nariotta, kaihō shichoru*
- *kitsuka* (= *kitsui*, tough)
- *mieru-wai* (I can see + sentence-final particle)
- *inou* (= *kaerou*, let's go back home)

According to the knowledge of dialects in the modern period, the usage of *-choru* and *-oru* is a characteristic present in Chūgoku to Kyūshū regions. In addition, the predicative form of the adjective *kitsuka* can be considered to be a characteristic of northern Kyūshū. In short, characteristics of the western Japanese dialects are obviously used, with no systematic use of a dialect from a particular area. The author specifically notes the following about such language usage:

> *Sakusha iwaku sugawa no kotoba wa ikanaru chihō no kotoba naruka to fushin o idaku hito mo aru beshi. Ko wa izuko no hōgen to sadamaritaru mono nimo arazu, shosei shakai ni okonawaruru hakuzatsu naru namari kotoba to omou beshi. Kedashi shosei chū niwa kamigata no umare ni arinagara wazawaza Tosa kotoba nado o maneru mono arite ichigai ni izuko no kotoba tomo sadamegatakereba nari.*
> An explanation by the author follows: Without a doubt, there are people who are uncertain where Sugawa's speech comes from. Instead of thinking of it as a particular dialect, think of it as the mixed speech that was present in *shosei* circles. For example, a student may be a Kyoto or Osaka native, but he might deliberately try to imitate the Kōchi dialect, so it becomes difficult to assign a specific dialect to his speaking patterns.
>
> (ibid.)

In other words, there must have naturally been many individuals from western Japan among the *shosei*. Thus, their language was also reflected in <Student Language>, and some of the terms seem to have come into vogue.

In this way, <Student Language> is viewed as a combination of the language of Tokyo (similar to that of Komachida) and the western Japanese dialect (seen in the language of Sugawa). Since *shosei* would eventually become leaders in the political, business, and academic arenas, <Student Language> is the origin of the language of such leaders in Japan. If the language of Komachida is purified, it becomes <Standard Language>. Some part of <Student Language> that goes out of <Standard Language> also often appears as the language of "great people" such as ministers, deputies, company presidents, and scholars.

If the lectures and texts written by the intellectuals of the Meiji era (those written in the *genbun icchi* style) are examined, the characteristics of western Japanese dialects, such as the substantive verb and aspect *-oru* and *-te oru* or the negative *-n*, can be seen more frequently. One reason could possibly be the inherited traditions of <Samurai Language> and <Elderly Male Language> of the Edo period. Another reason could be the impact of the *kanbun kundoku bun* (the Japanese reading of Chinese classics) in the form of academic terminology. An additional possibility could be the impact of the western Japanese dialects used by the *shosei* of the Meiji period, as seen in the language of Sugawa. Consider the following excerpt for example:

• *Yomiuri ni bakotsujingen to iu no o kaite iru tokumei sensei ga aruga, shikirini Niichie (Nietzsche) no kōgeki o yatte iru. Nanpito nimo kaishi eraruru koto dake wa kaite iru ga, chōjin ya, tensei nado no koto ni naruto, sasuga ni zokugakusha no chikai ni iri-gatai to miete, hitokoto mo nobete <u>oranu</u>. Konna tegiwa de Niichie o hihyō shi eraru mono naraba, yoni hihyō hodo yōi na mono wa aru mai yo.*

There is an anonymous article published in the Yomiuri Newspaper called "Bakotsujingen" (literally, words spoken by a horse's bones), which vigorously attacks Nietzsche. It talks about things that anyone can understand, but when it comes to the "ubermensch" (superman) and the eternal recurrence etc., not a single word is written about them as an amateur scholar cannot probably hope to understand such matters. If it's possible to critique Nietzsche like this, nothing is easier on the Earth than criticism.

(Takayama, Chogyū, *Bungei Hihyō* (Literary Criticism), p. 50)

The following is an excerpt from Soseki Natsume's (1867–1916) work *Wagahai wa Neko de Aru* (I am a Cat) (published in 1905 (Meiji 38)–1907 (Meiji 40)). First, the main character Kushami Sensei is a junior high school English teacher, thus a former *shosei*, and his language can be considered to be an extension of <Student Language>.

Meitei: "*Mata kyojin inryoku kane*" to tatta mama shujin ni kiku.
Shujin: "*Sō, itsudemo kyojin inryoku bakari kaite wa <u>oran</u> sa. Tennen koji no bomei o senshite iru tokoro nanda.*" to ōgesa na koto o iu.
"Giant Gravitation again? " asks Waverhouse still standing.
"How could I be always writing only about Giant Gravitation? I'm trying to compose an epitaph for the tombstone of Mr. the-late-and-sainted Natural Man, " replied my master with considerable exaggeration.

(Soseki Natsume, Aiko Ito and Graeme Wilson (translation),
*I Am a Cat*, Charles E. Tuttle Company, Inc. Rutland,
Vermont, & Tokyo, Japan, 1972. p. 143.)

The primary narrative of this novel is a monologue of the cat. However, the cat is impersonating its master; that is, it uses the same language <Student Language> as its master.

*Ganrai koko no shujin wa hakushi toka daigaku kyōju toka iu to hijō ni kyōshuku*

*Male Language* 71

*suru otoko dearu ga, myō na koto niwa jitsugyōka ni taisuru sonkei no do wa kiwamete hikui. Jitsugyōka yori Chūgakkō no sensei no hō ga erai to shinjite iru. Yoshi shinjite <u>oran</u> demo, yūzū no kikanu seishitsu to shite, tōtei jitsugyōka, kin-manka no onko o kōmuru koto wa obotsukanai to akiramete iru.*

The master here is a very humble man who calls himself to be a doctor/professor. Strangely, he has very low respect for businessmen, and believes that a junior high school teacher is superior to them. Even though he truly believes this, given his non-accommodating nature, he ultimately resigns himself to the fact that he is unlikely to receive favors from businessmen and billionaires.

(ibid., p. 108)

Apart from the characteristics of the western Japanese dialects noted earlier, their language has additional similarities

in <Student Language> of *Tōsei Shosei Katagi* (The Character of Modern Students), the language has additional similarities. Let us examine the characteristics of <Student Language>, as observed in Hisao Komatsu's "*Ichidoku Santan Tōsei Shosei Katagi* no edo-go-teki tokushoku" (Edo-language-like features of *Ichidoku Santan Tōsei Shosei Katagi*).

1. *Boku* and *wagahai* ( = I) are extensively used, and the first person of *shosei* ( = student) language comprises these two pronouns.

2. *Kimi* ( = you) is extensively used and this is the only second person pronoun in *shosei* language. Other second person pronoun equivalents used extensively include the name of a person without the addition of honorific titles such as *san* and the name of a person along with the ending *kun*.

3. *Tamae* ( = please) and *beshi* ( = should) are used extensively as imperative expressions.

4. The term *shikkei* ( = rude (or excuse-me)) is used as a greeting.

5. Apart from this, Sino-Japanese expressions and foreign loanwords are also used extensively.

Here, we should particularly note the use of *-tamae* and the pronouns *boku*, *kimi*, and *wagahai*. The term *-tamae* was used by the samurai of the Edo period, and boku was used by the class of people familiar with Sinology primarily composed of the Edo-era samurai. These are, on the whole, words used by the intellectuals of the samurai class. From these perspectives, it can be seen that <Student Language> was eventually influenced by the language of the samurai class that inherited the Edo period's <Samurai Language>.

### The History of *-tamae* (please)
*Tamau* is a honorific verb that has been used in literature since ancient times.

Originally, it referred to the nobles bestowing something to their inferiors. However, in the Heian period, it was bound with the continuative form of the verb, leading to the development of the auxiliary verb usage, and it was used to express respect to the subject of the action.

*Izure no ohon-toki nika, nyougo koui amata saburafi tamafikeru naka ni ito yamgo-tonaki kifa nifa aranu ga sugurete tokimeki tamafu arikeri.*
(*Genji Monogatari*, "Kiritsubo")
In a certain reign (whose reign it has been?) someone of no very great rank, among all His Majesty's Consorts and Intimates, enjoyed exceptional favor.
(*The Tale of Genji*, Royall Tyler (translation), 2001, Penguin Books, p. 3)

However, as an honorific language, *-tamau* was replaced by *-raru (rareru)*, which emerged in the Heian period, and a form like "*o-kaeri-aru*" (*o* + verbal noun + *aru*) which emerged in the late Middle Ages and was only retained as a part of literary or archaic language usage. Only the imperative form *-tamae* and its negative *-tamau na* were incorporated into the language usage of the men of the Edo samurai class. The following excerpt is an example from the *sharebon* titled *Tatsumi no Sono* (Paradise in the Southeast), published in 1770 (Meiwa 7). Previous context indicates that the *kyaku* (guest) used here refers to a samurai.

Kyaku:
"*Sā, minna, taira-ni, taira-ni* [snip] *Kore kore Yashiki wa yashiki, koko wa koko ja. Taira ni si-tamae.*"
Ok, everyone, make yourselves at home. (…) A mansion is a mansion, this place is this place. Just relax, already.
(*Tatsumi no Sono*, p. 305)

The next example is from *Kikijōzu* (Good Listener), a *hanashi bon* (Shōwa Shū (a collection of funny stories)) edited by Hyakki Komatsu and published around 1773 (An'ei 2). Since the character is described as "kerai o shikaru hito" (one who scolds his servant), he is a samurai.

• *Warui Kuse*
*Kokoro yasui mono ni, yoku kerai o shikaru hito ari. Aru toki kitarite, "Ban niwa mina ga kuru hazu jakara, nanimo naiga, kisama mo kite hanashi tamae." to iu. "Sore wa katajikenai ga, kisama wa hito ga yuku to, yoku kerai o shikaru hito ja ni yotte ikinikui." "Sareba ore mo tashinamu keredo, dou mo shikari-takute naranu. Warui kuse ja. Shitaga, mou ban niwa shikaranu hodo ni, kite kure tamae." to iu yue, "sonnara ikou." to yakusoku shite hanashi ni yuki-keru.*
• bad habit
A person with whom one hang around closely scolds his servants too much. Once, that person came and said, "Since everyone is coming in the evening, I won't be able to treat you to anything, but please come and talk." "I appreciate the offer, but as you are the type of person who scolds the servants too much

## Male Language 73

when people are around, it's hard to go." "In that case, I will hold myself back, but I just can't seem to restrain myself from doing so. It's a bad habit. But I won't scold them tonight, so please come." Upon hearing this, he promised, "In that case I'll go," and went to talk.

(*Kikijōzu*, pp. 397–398)

In this way, -*tamae* was a word used by the men of the samurai class, and it must have been passed on to the Meiji samurai class and incorporated into <Student Language>.

### *Boku* (I) and *Kimi* (You)

Let us now consider the first person pronoun *boku* ( = I). To examine this aspect, we take as a basis Hisao Komatsu's work "Kimi to boku: Edo Tōkyō-go ni okeru tsui-shiyo o chūshin ni" (You and I: focusing pair use in Edo and Tokyo dialect) which comprehensively explains the word *boku* ( = I), especially from the perspective of its paired usage with *kimi* ( = you). According to Komatsu, *boku* was originally a first person pronoun used with a strong awareness of humility by the Confucians, but the actual usage conditions can be followed in *Botan-Dōrō* (The Tale of the Peony Lantern).

1. There is a paired usage of *kimi* and *boku*.

2. The *boku* in *The Tale of the Peony Lantern* has lower status value than the Confucian *boku* and has a milder honorific degree.

3. The paired speaker is a professional male entertainer doctor, not a Confucian, and the word is used in normal conversation.

4. The users of *boku* and *kimi* are not limited to professional male entertainer doctors, but it is widely used by the young *rōnin* (masterless samurai) Shinzaburō.

In addition, in *Kaiwa Hen* (Conversation Volume), a Japanese-language conversation textbook from the end of the Edo Period edited by Ernest Satow (published in 1873 (Meiji 6)), we obtain the following conditions of usage.

1. *Boku* and *kimi* are person pronouns that correspond to each other.

2. They were used on an equal footing among the people of the samurai and educated classes.

From the above, Komatsu says that, the paired use of *kimi* and *boku* can be considered that from before the Meiji era-by the end of the Edo period, it had spread to professional male entertainer doctors, samurais, and those of the educated class. Then, as in the case of -*tamae*, it entered <Student Language> through the samurai class.

Komatsu also traces its development from <Student Language> to <Boy's Language>. Komatsu considers examples of Hidemaro Kiyohara's language from the 1892 (Meiji 25) publication, *Tōsei Shōnen Katagi* (Boys' Habit Nowadays) by Sazanami Ōe (Iwaya). This story describes Hidemaro, a 13-year-old "student of the Gakushūin elementary section" and the third son of the Earl's family who commutes to school by a horse-drawn carriage.

*Ii kara mō naku no wa o-yosi! <u>Boku</u> ga sono udon no dai o dashite yaru kara, sore o motte uchi e o-kaeri!*
That's enough, stop crying. I'll pay for the noodle, so take that and go home.
(Sazanami Iwaya, *Tōsei Shōnen Katagi*, p. 5)

Furthermore, Komatsu takes examples of Nobuyuki's language from Ichiyo Higuchi's *Takekurabe* (Comparing Heights) (1895 (Meiji 28)–1896 (Meiji 29) in Bungaku-kai (Literature Society)). Nobuyuki (or Shinnyo) is the son and heir of the Ryūgeji Temple and since he excels at his studies, he is respected by the other children. The other interlocutor, Chōkichi, is a scaffold constructor's son who is depicted as a quarrelsome, rowdy person. Here, Nobuyuki's *boku* is used in a contrastive manner to Chōkichi's *oira* and *ore*.

Chōkichi:
*"... Oiraa kondo no matsuri niwa dō shite mo ranbō ni shikakete torikaeshi o tsuke-you to omou yo. Dakara Shin san tomodachi-gai ni, sore wa omae ga iya da to iu nomo shireteru keredomo douzo ore no kata o motte,* [snip]*"*
"No matter what happens, I'm going to wreak havoc at the next festival and get my revenge. Shin (=Nobuyuki), I know you don't want to, but if you are my friend, be my ally, (...)"
Nobuyuki:
*"Datte boku wa yowai mono."*
"I'm too weak."
Chōkichi:
*"Yowakutemo ii yo."*
"It's all right if you are weak."
Nobuyuki:
*"Mandō wa furimawase-nai yo."*
"But I can't even swing a lantern."
Chōkichi:
*"Furimawasanakute mo ii yo."*
"You don't have to swing it."
Nobuyuki:
*"Boku ga iru to makeru ga ii kae."*
"If I'm there, you'll lose; are you ok with that?"
Chōkichi:
*"Makete mo ii no sa. Sore wa shikata ga nai to akirameru kara."*
"Losing is fine. We'll just resign ourselves to it."
(*Takekurabe*, pp. 406–407)

In the Meiji 30s, *kimi* and *boku* appeared in textbooks firmly establishing their place as a part of the standard language. *Reihō Yōkō* (Etiquette Guide) (1941 (Showa 16)) by the Ministry of Education stipulated the following about the first person pronoun.

• For the first person pronoun, usually *watashi* is used. When talking to one's elders or superiors, one's last or first name is sometimes used. Toward those of the same age, males may use *boku* but not for one's superiors and elders.
 For the second person, the following is stipulated.

• For the second person, when talking to superiors, an appropriate title must be used depending on the status. For those of the same age, usually *anata* is used, and for males, *kimi* may also be used.

As shown above, our discussion, based on Komatsu's thesis, confirms that the paired use of *boku* and *kimi* along with *-tamae* arose from <Samurai Language>. It was subsequently incorporated into <Student Language> and <Boy's Language>. (One can say that) Hakushu Kitahara's *Amefuri* was a lyric that evidently reflected the typical <Boy's Language> at the time.
 However, *boku*, *kimi*, and *-tamae* subsequently developed into different directions. *Boku*, *kimi*, and *-tamae* still continued to exist in the role language of upper-class males with power and status, such as politicians and professors, which includes <Boss's Language>, the successor of <Student Language>.

*Yamaoka kun, sō iwazu ni tsukiai <u>tamae</u>./Kyūkyoku no menyū zukuri ni kyōmi ga nai to iu kimi no shin'i o, kyō wa dōshite mo kikasete morau yo.*
Yamaoka, come on, don't say no and please join me today./Come what may, today you are going to have to make us hear the truth about why you have no interest in the making of the ultimate menu.

(*Oishinbo* 1, p. 62)

While *-tamae* gradually faded away from <Boy's Language>, the young boys who used *boku* and *kimi* have acquired the image of, for example, a "model student" and "weak." Thus, it can be considered that the transformation of the image of *shōnen* (young boys) in mass media formed the background of this change.

### *Boku* (I) and *Ore* (I)
Currently, the first person pronouns for males in <Standard Language> include *boku*, *ore*, *watashi*, and *watakushi*. *Atashi* and *atakushi* are rather used by females. *Oira*, *asshi*, and *washi* have a high role language degree, and from the definition in this book, they cannot be called <Standard Language>. Among *boku*, *ore*, *watashi*, and *watakushi*, *watashi* and *watakushi* are neutral pronouns used irrespective of gender, and in written language as well as public (formal) speech style. In contrast, *boku* and *ore* are solely used in private (informal) speech style, and they clearly reflect the character of the speaker.

76

The differences in the character of the *boku* speakers and the *ore* speakers had already emerged in pre-war novels. You may recall our early example of the contrast between the characters of Chōkichi and Nobuyuki in *Takekurabe* (example on page 74). Another example is from the *shōnen shōsetsu* (boy's novel) titled *Ā Gyokuhai ni Hana Ukete* (Ah, I am catching petals of cherry blossom on my beautiful cup) (1927 (Showa 2)–1928 (Shōwa 3)) from the *Shōnen Kurabu* (Boy's Club) series, in which the thoughtful and discreet boy Kōichi Yanagi mainly uses *boku*, whereas the rowdy "Seiban" (= savage tribe) Iwao Sakai uses *ore*.

Kōichi:
*"Kono tsugi no nichiyou ni ne, boku no tanjōbi dakara, hiru kara demo ... ban kara demo asobi ni kite kure tamae ne."*
"The next Sunday is my birthday, so please come to play, from afternoon ... or evening onwards ..., anytime."

(*Ā Gyokuhai ni Hana Ukete*, p. 654)

*Seiban wa shibaraku kangaeta ga, yagate ōki na koe de warai dashita. "Omae wa ore ni kenka o yosaseyou to omotterun darō. Sore dake wa ikenai."*
Seiban thought for a moment and finally burst out laughing in a loud voice. "You are thinking of making me not fight, right? That's not to be done."

(ibid., p. 662)

However, the use of *boku* and *ore* is quite relative with Seiban, who also uses *boku* when talking to his father (p. 702). In addition, Kōichi Yanagi uses *ore* in the scene where he expresses his feelings to his friend Senzō Aoki and apologizes to him (p. 775). This type of differentiated usage is based on actual conditions, and it represents the realistic aspect of the work.

The users of *boku* before the war usually used it with <Student Language>, such as *shikkei* and *-tamae*. In other words, young boys using *boku* were *shosei* who were idealistic and dreamt of success in life and were not necessarily weak. Boys heroes in works for boys overwhelmingly used *boku*, irrespective of whether the character appeared in a novel or a *manga*. This trend was, for some time, retained in the world of boy's manga. *Tetsuwan Atomu* (Astro Boy) is a work in which the main character, a young boy (although he is a robot) uses *boku* imbued with this specific image.

Eventually, the aforementioned image of a character brimming with the desire to move up in life began to fade away from boy's manga, and the hero image changed. In other words, the hero emerged as a character with a blazing, raw fighting spirit or one with an air of roughness. Simultaneously, the first person pronoun changed to *ore*. This was probably made decisive by *Kyojin no Hoshi* (Star of the Giants), which was first published in 1966 (Showa 41) and *Ashita no Jō* (Tomorrow's Jō), which was first published in 1968 (Showa 43). Protagonists of both of these series, Hyūma Hoshi and Jō Yabuki, used *ore* for the first person pronoun. This transformation in the image of the hero in boys manga and the shift of first person pronoun reflected an internal cry; that is, an expression of the

*Male Language* 77

suppressed inherent vitality that the children possessed, which had occurred in schools or at home in the real world.

It is unclear what led to this change and from what time it emerged, and I do not know whether there is adequate empirical studies on the subject. Nonetheless, following the *gekiga* (a comic strip with dramatic stories) boom from 1955 to 1965 and the publication of the periodical young adult manga magazine "Rush" in the decade starting in 1965, the manga reading generation suddenly widened, which could be one factor behind the transformation.

Alongside the gradual use of *ore* by the hero, the image associated with *boku* also dramatically changed. More specifically, the pronoun *boku* came to be associated with a tame, spineless character who was protected both at home and in school. For example, in the works of Fujiko F. Fujio, the protagonists of the gag comics targeting boys almost without exception used *boku*, a representative of which is the character of Nobita from *Doraemon* (serialized from 1970 (Showa 45)).

Utilizing the contrast between this aggressive and roguish *ore* and the weak and protégé type of *boku* as well as making a young boy the main character who is made to assume a double personality for some reason, the personality change is effectively portrayed through the differentiated use of *boku* and *ore*. One of the examples, Osamu Tezuka's series *Mitsume ga Tōru* (The Three-Eyed One) (1974 (Showa 49)–1978 (Showa 53)). The same linguistic device is also used in Kazuki Takahashi's *Yu-Gi-Oh!* (It's Time to Duel) and Gōshō Aoyama's *Meitantei Conan* (Detective Konan).

Figure 4-2 *Mitsume ga Tōru* 1
(p. 37/p. 175 ©Tezuka Production)

## 3. Role language as a Kamen (Persona)

The present author once administered a questionnaire survey at a university in Nishinomiya City, Hyogo Prefecture targeting 18 male students regarding their awareness of first person pronouns in daily life. Although no definite conclusion can be drawn as the number of people surveyed was small, the following trends were noted.

• There were comparable numbers of those who responded that they would use *ore* while conversing with family, friends, and persons of the opposite gender that they were familiar with, and those who responded that they would use *boku* (hereafter, we will refer to those who use *ore* as *ore* users and those who use *boku* as *boku* users, respectively).
• However, regarding the use of the pronouns with university professors, there were no *ore* users and most of the respondents chose *boku*, with a few using *watashi*.
• Conversely, in the situation of a job interview, most of the respondents were *watashi* users and exceeded the number of *boku* users. There were also some who used *watakushi*, but naturally there was no one who used *ore* in such a situation.

Furthermore, some students stated that they used *boku* when they were younger but changed it to *ore* around the time when they were in junior high school. In addition, among the female students, the majority had a preference for *ore* usage rather than *boku* usage. When these students were further asked about this point, they stated that the image of *boku* pronoun users was that of feeble, childish characters, whereas the image of *ore* pronoun users was that of masculine characters.

These trends match the author's impressions as well as the impressions of students with whom I interact daily at university. Thus, it can be concluded that role language is not limited to expressions in creative works, but it is also an aspect that is associated with language use in everyday life. In other words, it is related to the manner in which one wants to be perceived by others. Different pronouns are used for different situations, just as one sometimes wears different clothes for different occasions. Precisely, role language can be said to constitute part of a *kamen* (persona. literally, "mask") = personality.

CHAPTER 5

# Where is the Princess?
## Female Language

## 1. Ochō-fujin (Madame Butterfly)

*Ēsu o Nerae!* (Aim for the Ace!), published in *Shūkan Māgaretto* (Weekly Margaret) from 1973 (Showa 48) to 1980 (Showa 55), is the story of Hiromi Oka, a student at Nishi High School, which has a high reputation for tennis. At such a prestigious school, Hiromi has an unobtrusive presence. However, she is discovered by coach Munakata after which she becomes a leading tennis player. In this manga, a particularly conspicuous presence is that of Ochō-fujin. Although she is referred to as *fujin* (literally, wife), she is not married and is just another high school student. Her father is a multi-millionaire and the Director of the Japan Tennis Association; she lives in a castle-like mansion with maids in attendance. Her tennis skills surpass those of the high school level, and she is proud of being an invincible legend. Her pride is also top notch, and she always behaves like a queen. Here, the language of Ochō-fujin is the typical of the so-called <Young Lady from a Good Family Language>. More specifically, there is an extensive use of word forms such as -*te* (*yo*), verb + *wa*, noun + *da* or *desu* + *wa*, and verb ( + *masu*) + *no*. Consider the following excerpt:

Hiromi:
*"Ochō-fujin!"*
"Madame Ochō!"
Ochō:
*"Kyō wa zuibun pōzu ga kuzurete ita yō ne/Ouchi ni kaettara kagami no mae de kufū shinasai./Ketten ga yoku wakatte yo."*
"Today, your form was quite uneven, eh?/When you go back home, practice in

front of the mirror/This way, you can understand your shortcomings."

(Ēsu o Nerae! 1, p. 17)

Club member:
*"Oka san ni wa ... mada senshu wa tsutomarimasen/Otowa san ga tekitō da to ..."*
"Ms. Oka is not yet competent enough to be selected as a player/I think Ms. Otowa is the right one ..."
Ochō:
*"Atakushi mo sansei desu wa/Otowa san wa itsumo senshu de jitsuryoku ga atte."*
"I agree. Ms. Otowa has always been selected as a player and has the competence for it."

(ibid., p. 23)

Ochō:
*"Mattaku, donata mo kan ni sawaru koto bakari nasaru wa ne!!"*
"Good grief! Everyone just keeps getting on my nerves!!"

(Ēsu o Nerae! 2, p. 17)

There is also Ochō-fujin's mother's language in which *koto* is added at the end of the sentence to express feelings of admiration.

Ochō:
*"Okāsama/Dekakete mairimasu/Otōsama ga oshokuji ni sasotte kudasaimashita no."*
"Mother, I am going out/Father has invited me to dinner."
Mother:
*"Mā, ii koto/Itteirashai."*
"How nice! Go on, have a good time."

(Ēsu o Nerae! 4, p.138)

In addition, even if something unpleasant happens and even when she is furious, the language remains absolutely polite with honorific language being used in minute detail.

Ochō:
*"Kōchi ni okotowari shiterasshai./Sono hō ga anata no otame yo."*
"You should go say no to the coach/It's for your own good."

(ibid., p. 24)

Ochō:
*"Mā! Hito o miru me ga oari desu no ne/Takō no senshu ni mo zuibun gorikai ga fukakute irassharu you desu shi!"*
"Wow! You are a fine judge of character, aren't you?/And you seem to have a fairly profound understanding of players from other schools as well."

(Ēsu o Nerae! 2, p. 36)

*Where is the Princess?*　81

Another characteristic of Ochō-fujin is that when she laughs, she always laughs using "ho ho ho" and never "ha ha ha."

Here, the following questions arise:

### ENIGMA 10
Does an *ojōsama* (a young lady from a good family) who speaks like Ochō-fujin actually exist in the current society?

### ENIGMA 11
How is <Young Lady from a Good Family Language> that Ochō-fujin uses similar to or different from the ordinary <Female Language>?

### ENIGMA 12
How did this <Young Lady from a Good Family Language> emerge?

## 2. Gender Differences in Language

### From Grammatical Features

How are gender differences in language currently recognized? First, let us examine grammatical features by focusing on Masuoka and Takubo's *Kiso Nihongo Bunpō* (*Basic Japanese Grammar*, Revised Edition, Part V, Chapter 2, Gender Differences in Language).

The basic characteristics discussed in the chapter are the main expressions primarily used by males and females. The distinctions are quite systematic, but they are not absolute, and usage based on situational and personal differences is also considered to be significant. Furthermore, the following classification is made:

> Generally, female expressions are characterized by avoidance of the conclusive or imperative kind with the manner of speaking such that one's thoughts are not imposed on the other. In contrast to this, male expressions are characterized by the conclusive and imperative kind with most of the expressions being used for making an assertion or for persuasion.
>
> (p. 222)

The gender differences based on the grammatical features listed in the aforementioned book are organized and summarized with slight modifications in Table in the next page.

Table 5-1

| | Masculine feature | Neutral | Feminine feature |
|---|---|---|---|
| Copula *da* | *Kimi wa onna <u>da</u>* (+*yo/ ne/yone*). <br> You are a woman. | | *Anata wa onna* <br> *φ yo(ne/yone)*. <br> You are a woman. |
| *-noka /-noda* | *Kimi mo sono hon katta* <br> <u>*no ka*</u>. <br> Did you also buy the <br> book? <br> *Kore, dare ga* <br> *kaita<u>nda</u>(i)?* <br> Who wrote this? | | *Anata mo sono hon* <br> *katta <u>no</u>?* <br> Did you also buy the <br> book? <br> *Kore, dare ga kaita <u>no</u>?* <br> Who wrote this? |
| Neutral style + *yo* | *Kore, chotto karai <u>yo</u>.* <br> This is hot a little. | | – |
| Imperative/ <br> Prohibitive/ <br> Request form | *Kocchi e <u>koi</u>.* <br> Come here! <br> *Sonna koto suru <u>na</u>.* <br> Don't do that. <br> *Kocchi e kite <u>kure</u>.* <br> (Please) come here. <br> *Kocchi e kite <u>moraitai</u>.* <br> I want you come here. | *Kore yonde.* <br> Read this. | *Kocchi e kite kudasaru?* <br> Would you come here? |
| Interrogative | *Kimi, ashita no pātī* <br> *shusseki suru <u>ka</u>.* <br> Will you attend the <br> party tomorrow? <br> *Kore wa kimi no <u>kai</u>.* <br> Is this yours? <br> *Chotto, soko no hon* <br> *totte kurenai <u>ka</u>.* <br> Would you take me <br> the book? | *Ashita no pātī <u>shusseki</u>* <br> <u>*suru*</u>? <br> Will you attend the <br> party tomorrow? <br><br> *Chotto, soko no hon* <br> *totte <u>kurenai</u>?* <br> Would you take me <br> the book? | (*Chotto, soko no hon* <br> *totte <u>kudasaranai</u>?* <br> Would you take me <br> the book?) |
| Sentence-final <br> particle | *Konna chōshi dewa* <br> *shiken ni ochiru <u>zo</u>.* <br> You will lose the <br> examination at this <br> pace. <br> *Ore wa matteru <u>ze</u>.* <br> I will be waiting. | | *Komatta <u>wa</u>. Henna* <br> *hito ga iru <u>wa</u>.* <br> I'm in trouble. There is <br> a strange person. |
| Interjection | "*Oi.*" "*Kora.*" <br> "Hey!" "Hey!" | | "*Ara.*" "*Mā*" <br> "Oh!" "Alas!" |
| Pronoun | *ore/boku/oira/washi* <br> → I <br> *omae/kimi* <br> → you | *watashi/watakushi* <br> → I <br> *anata/anta/* <br> *otaku(sama)/* <br> *sochira(sama)* <br> → you | *atashi* <br> → I <br> (Women use it more <br> frequently than men.) |

The book also shows that, generally, if polite expressions are used more frequently, then the manner of expression becomes feminine. Consider the following expressions for example:

*Tanaka san mo irasshaimasu.*
Tanaka will also come.

*Sonna koto moushimashita?*
Did I say that?

Note that the sentence-ending particle *wa* is listed as a characteristic of female language, but it is important to consider that *wa* is divided into two types depending on the tone: The rising tone *wa* and the falling tone *wa*. It is only the rising tone *wa* that is considered to be a feature of female language. Females also use the falling tone *wa*, but it is generally used in a masculine manner. Furthermore, the *wa* that appears in the dialects of various regions is the falling tone wa, and its usage is largely gender neutral.

The book also considers as female usage interrogative sentences of the *no ka* and *no da* types from which *ka* and *da* are removed, but the present author deems such forms as neutral. In contrast, the *-no* form, the shortened form of the *no da* (*n da*) in declarative sentences, sounds distinctly feminine.

Masculine expression: *Kore, kinō katte kita-n da.*/I bought this yesterday.
Feminine expression: *Kore, kinō katte kita-no.*/I bought this yesterday.

Also, the book considers it masculine if *yo* is added to the end of the sentence in the neutral style, but the author believes that it sounds relatively neutral. At least, one cannot say that it sounds absolutely masculine.

Furthermore, the self-interrogative expression *kashira* or the *desu mono* in sentences that express reason can be considered to be female expressions. Among speakers of the Tokyo dialect who are somewhat older, males also use kashira. However, the sentence-final particle *sa* is considered to be a male expression.

*Kore, dare no kutsu kashira?* /Whose shoes are these, I wonder?
*Datte, ureshiin desu mono.*/That's because I am happy.
*Kitto jikan dōri ni kuru sa.*/(He/she/it) will surely come on time.

Male- and Female-specific Expressions and Expressions with a Particular Tendency
If the above characteristics are divided into male- and female-specific expressions and expressions with a particular tendency, it will be as follows:

Male-specific expressions: *da*, excluding *da wa* and monologues such as *ara iya da*, imperatives, assertive requests, and interrogative sentences using ordinary style +*ka*(*i*), sentence-ending particles such as *zo* and *ze*, interjections such as *oi* and *kora*, pronouns such as *ore* ( = I), *boku* ( = I), *omae* ( = you), and *kimi* ( = you).

Female-specific expressions: Request expressions such as *-te kudasaru?* and *-te kudasaranai?*, expressions such as *-no*, *-kashira*, and *-desu mono* in declarative sentences, a sentence-ending particle *wa*, interjections such as ara and *mā* (pronoun *atashi* ( = I)).

Expressions with a particular tendency: The more the use of polite expressions, the more the language is feminine.

In *Kiso Nihongo Bunpō* (*Basic Japanese Grammar*), these characteristics are naturally considered to represent the actual conditions of usage in modern Japanese. However, it is also possible to reinterpret them in the context of role language. In fact, the actual conditions are much more diverse, and they cannot be easily or simply generalized. Furthermore, as already mentioned, since we use role language as a persona (= mask), we consciously or unconsciously use role language in our real lives when we want to behave in a masculine or feminine manner.

Now, we can find that the linguistic characteristics of the earlier character Ochō-fujin almost perfectly match the female expressions (as well as the neutral features) seen in this section. However, there are some expressions Ochō-fujin uses but are not included in the female expressions found in this section. They include *-te yo* in "*ketten ga yoku wakatte yo*" (You will thoroughly understand your shortcomings) and *-koto* in exclamatory sentences such as "*mā ii koto.*" (How nice!) In other words, these characteristics are extensions of the ordinary <Female Language>, which are indicators of <Young Lady from a Good Family Language> beyond the (average) <Female Language>.

In this case, historically speaking, from where did the characteristics of modern <Female Language> and of <Young Lady from a Good Family Language> originate? Moreover, what is the current status of <Young Lady from a Good Family Language>?

## 3. Women in *Ukiyoburo* (The Bathhouse of the Floating World)

In Shikitei Sanba's *kokkeibon* (comic novel) titled *Ukiyoburo* (The Bathhouse of the Floating World) (published 1809–1813), there is hardly any difference in the language of males and females of the lower classes in the Edo society. Even if there were any differences, these were only relative differences. Conversely, among the upper-class townspeople, many women acquired the polite female language usage of the samurai-class largely due to the widespread trend of sending daughters (before marriage) to work for samurai families to acquire *gyōgi minarai* (the learning of good manners through apprenticeships with upper-class families). In addition, the language of the samurai-class females has its origins in the *nyōbō kotoba* (secret language) of the ladies of the imperial court. In other words, polite female language propagated through the following process: imperial court → samurai → townspeople. This was called *asobase kotoba* (polite language) and the following are the examples:

Where is the Princess?                                                      85

Yasu:

*"Hai. Ie mō watakushi no danna o ohome mōsu mo ikagade gozaimasu ga, sōbetsu o-kidate no yoi okatadene, omaesan. Anata ga oyashiki ni oide-asobasu jibun wa, oheya-jū de hyōban no o-kekkō-jin de gozaimashita. Watakushi ga ittai sos-okkashii umarede, zonzai-mono de gozaimasu noni, tsui shika, puttsuri tomo osshari-masen. Sore de watakushi mo anmari no arigatasa ni, semete go-konrei made o-tsuki mōsō to zonjimashite, tadaima made tōtō chōnen itasimashita ga, kore kara wa dōzo, o-kosama demo odeki asobasu no o mite, doko e zo katazukimashō to zonjimasu no sa."*

"Yes. I am in no place to praise my mistress, but overall (the young lady) is very well-mannered. When she was at the estate, she was highly spoken of by her peers. I have a careless disposition, with rude qualities; yet, she has never once complained. For that, I am very grateful, and I hope to be of service to her at least until her marriage. As of now, I have been with her for a long time, and now that I see she will have a child, I'm thinking of getting married and leave the service."

(*Ukiyoburo* 2-hen, 2nd Vol., p. 123)

Yasu is a maidservant, and she is not necessarily a character that belongs to the upper class. Since she came to the mansion as a companion to her lady, she has also acquired *asobase kotoba*.

Next, the conventional language of women belonging to the lower class is as follows:

*"Nanno, sharakkuse. O-gushi dano, hettakure no to, sonna asobase kotoba wa mittomune. Hirattaku kami to iina na. Orā kitsui kirē da. Hōkō dakara iu nari ni natte, o-maesama o-jibutsu sama, sayō shikaraba o itte iru keredo, binbō jotē o mocchā irane kotoba da. Semete, yu e demo kita toki wa motimē no kotoba o tsukawane jā, ki ga tsukirā na."*

"What a snob. Saying o-gushi (polite language for "hair of the head") and the like, that sort of asobase-kotoba is unbecoming. Just simply say "kami" (the usual way for saying "hair of the head"). I truly hate that. I know you're speaking in that fancy way because you're mimicking your mistress, but people from common families have no use for such language. If you won't express yourself naturally even at the bathhouse, it's just depressing."

(ibid., p 133)

This is, as expected, the language of a maidservant, and it is interesting that in the utterance, she criticizes the *asobase kotoba* and emphasizes that one's own inherent language should be used. Besides these lower-class townspeople, there were prostitutes in the Edo period who had their own distinctive language. The following is an excerpt from the 1770 (Meiwa 7) publication *Yūshi Hōgen* (The Rake's Dialect) in which *heyamochi* refers to a prostitute. The terms *nansu* and *ozansu* are specifically the language of prostitutes.

Heyamochi (prostitute):
*"Mō okaeri nansu no kae."*
"Going home already?"
Musuko (inexperienced guest):
*"Ai."*
"Yes."
Heyamochi :
*"Mochitto inanse. Mada hayō ozansu."*
"Stay a little while longer. It's still early."
Tōrimono (experienced guest):
*"Moshi watashi oba naze tome nasansen."*
"Hello? Why won't you put me up for the night?"
Heyamochi :
*"Omae oba nushi ga tomenanshō kara, watashi ga tome mōsazu to, yō ozansu."*
"The hostess will put you up; there's no need for me to do so!"

(*Yūshi-Hōgen*, p. 362)

In this way, the prostitutes had a very distinctive way of speaking. However, they still used extremely polite expressions for their clients. It is known that several usages from their language have become widespread to the public.

As shown above, the feminine style of speaking existed in the Edo era, but female-specific expressions found in the modern <Female Language> had not yet appeared.

## 4. Edo Language and Modern <Female Language>

In his article titled "Tōkyō-go ni okeru danjo-sa no keisei: shūjoshi o chūshin to shite" (Formation of gender differences in Tokyo dialect: focusing sentence-final particles), Hisao Komatsu examined and compared language usage by males and females in Sōseki Natsume's *Sanshirō* (published 1909 (Meiji 42)) and Shikitei Sanba's *Ukiyoburo*. A table in the next page (slightly modified) is a summary of the differences in sentence-ending particles.

The following are the aspects that can be recognized from this table and those that should be noted. Expressions used by both males and females in *Ukiyoburo*, particularly forms that are not used by upper-class females, are used by the males in *Sanshirō*, which is acceptable as a matter of course. However, among these forms, some expressions are part of the female usage. First, regarding *da wa* and -*wa*, there is a high possibility that the tones in *Ukiyoburo* and those used by females in *Sanshirō* are differenct. Indeed, it is impossible to directly understand the tone from a literary material, and it is rather inferred from the current Tokyo Shitamachi dialect or traditional performing arts such as *kabuki* and *rakugo*, but the -*da* (*wa*) usage in *Ukiyoburo* is assumed to have been uttered in a falling tone, as seen the following example:

*Where is the Princess?* 87

Table 5-2

| Sentence-final Particle | Tokyo Language* | *Ukiyo-buro* | Comment on usageds in *Ukiyoburo* |
|---|---|---|---|
| -*da* | Male | Male/Female | |
| *dawa* | Female | Male/Female | not used by upper class women |
| *daze* | Male | Male/Female | not used by upper class women |
| *dazo* | Male | Male/Female | not used by upper class women |
| *dana* | Male | Male/Female | not used by upper class women |
| *dane* | Male | Male/Female | |
| *dayo* | Male | Male/Female | |
| *koto* | female | Male/Female | |
| -*sa* | Male | Male/Female | |
| -*ze* | Male | Male/Female | not used by upper class women |
| -*zē* | Male | Male/Female | not used by upper class women |
| -*zo* | Male | Male/Female | |
| -*na* | Male | Male/Female | |
| nominal = *ne* | Female | Male/Female | few examples |
| nominal = *nē* | Female | | not attested |
| -*nano* | Female | | not attested |
| -*no* | Female | Male/Female | |
| *none* | Female | | not attested |
| *noyo* | Female | Male/Female | not used by upper class women |
| -*ya* | Male | Male/Female | various usages |
| nominal = *yo* | Female | Male/Female | |
| -*wa* | Female | Male/Female | |
| *wane* | Female | | not attested |
| *wayo* | Female | | not attested |

*Tokyo Laungage = language in *Sanshirō*

*Ojisan ga sekkaku umete okure <u>dawa</u>.*
Uncle kindly add some cold water to the bath for you.

(Kinbē, *Ukiyoburo*, Zen-pen, Vol. 1, p. 22)

*Kore, ora ga gaki ga, akutare ama ka, unu ga mago ga konjō waru ka, hitosama ga gozonji dawa.*
Now look here, everyone knows whether it's my kid is bad or whether it's your grandkid is a bully.

(Kami-sama, ibid. 2-hen Vol. 2, p. 119)

Furthermore, the usage is quite different since the *da wa* in *Ukiyoburo* is followed by various sentence-ending particles, such as *da wa i, da wa sa, da wa su,* and *da wa na.* However, the *da wa* in modern female language can be followed only by *yo* or *ne.*

Next, regarding nominal + *yo* and *no yo,* the nature of *yo* in Edo language and in modern Tokyo language is quite different. The *yo* in *Ukiyoburo* essentially performs a function equivalent to the declarative auxiliary verb *da* (*de aru*), and it can be directly attached to the nominal. So it does not follow a declarative auxiliary verb. In this regard, it is similar to the sentence-ending particle *sa.* This *yo* always has a falling tone and cannot be used with the rising tone.

*Tōtoi tera wa mon kara to iu keredo, isha sama bakari wa mikake ni yoranu mono yo. uradana ni iru binbō-isha ni kōsha na ōhito ga aru mono sa.*
A great temple looks impressive from the gate, but doctors don't match their appearances. There are talented people even among the poor doctors in the back alleys.

(Kami-sama, ibid. 2-hen, Vol. 2, pp. 130–131)

On the other hand, the nominal+*yo* and the *no yo* in modern Tokyo language result from the omission of the (masculine) *da* from nominal+*da*+ *yo* and *no da*+*yo* forms. In other words, this *yo* cannot function in a manner similar to a declarative auxiliary verb, and in the original usage, it follows *da.* It just looks identical to the *yo* in Edo language when the *da* is omitted in female language. In terms of tone, the nominal+*yo* and *no yo* in modern <Female Language> also has a rising tone (which is more frequent) with some instances of a falling tone. Examples of *yo* such as the following seem to have been pronounced in a rising tone.

*"Hirota sensei wa, yoku, ā-iu koto o ossharu kata nandesu yo" to kiwamete karuku hitorigoto no yō ni itta ato de, kyū ni chōshi o kaete, "Kō iu tokoro ni, kō shite suwatte itara, daijōbu kyūdai yo" to hikakuteki kappatsu ni tsukekuwaeta. Sōshite, kondo wa jibun no hō de omoshiro sō ni waratta."*
"Dr. Hirota is the type of person who says that kind of thing a lot," she said with extreme light tone like a monologue. And then she suddenly changed he tone and added in a comparatively energetic manner, "If you sit in this kind of spot in this sort of way, no worries, you pass." With that, this time, she laughed out of amusement.

(Mineko, *Sanshirō* 5-9, p. 415)

Considering this, the female expressions in *Sanshirō* are not a continuation

*Where is the Princess?*  89

from the Edo language, and we can see that they are actually a new formation even though they appear to have the same form. Among the expressions that are a continuation from the Edo language, the majority are those that have a formation common to both male and female languages and have been incorporated into modern <Male Language>. However, they have gaps in continuity with modern <Female Language>, particularly female-specific expressions.

Now, when, where, and how did the formations specific to modern <Female Language> spread?

## 5. The Emergence of *teyo dawa*

### The Mother and Daughter in *Ukigumo*

Shimei Futabatei's *Ukigumo* (Floating Cloud) (published from 1887 (Meiji 20) to 1890 (Meiji 23)) is the first modern *genbun icchi* novel. In this novel, there are the characters of a mother and daughter, Omasa and Osei, respectively. While the mother's language has inherited characteristics of the Edo language, the daughter's language clearly shows grammatical characteristics of the modern <Female Language>. Let us first examine the language of Omasa.

> *"Ko o motte minakereba, wakaranai kotta keredomo, onna no ko to iu mono wa katazukeru made ga shimpai na mono <u>sa</u>. <u>Soryā</u>, hito sama <u>nyaa</u> anna mon o dō nattemo yosasō ni omowareru darō keredomo, oyabaka towa umaku itta <u>monde</u>, anna mon demo ko dato omoeba, arimo <u>shinē</u> akumyō tsukerarete, hyotto endōku naruto, iyana mono <u>sa</u>. Soreni dare ni shiro, fumitsuke rare<u>reyā</u>, anmari ii kokoromochi mo shinai mono <u>sa</u>, <u>nē</u> bun-san."*

> "These are things you won't understand unless you have a kid, but when it comes to girls, they're nothing but anxiety until you get them married. You know, you wonder if everyone is thinking, it doesn't matter what happens to a kid like that, but as a doting parent, if you always think of them as your child no matter how they are, and a lot of baseless rumors start going around, marriage gets even farther away, it's awful. Isn't that right, Bunzō?"

> (Omasa, *Ukigumo*, p. 150)

The underlined portion shows the characteristics of the Edo language. The fact that a woman uses the sentence-ending particle *sa* indicates that her language is dated. Conversely, let us consider Osei's language.

> *"Desuga ne, kyōiku no nai mono bakari o semeru wake ni mo ikemasen yo nē. Watakushi no hōyū nanzo wa, kyōiku no aru to iu hodo aryā shimasen ga ne soredemo mā futsū no kyōiku wa ukete irundesu yo, soredeite anata, seiyōshugi no wakaru mono wa, nijūgo nin no uchi ni tatta yottari shika nai <u>no</u>, sono yottari mo ne juku ni iru uchi dake de, hoka e dete kara wa ne kuchi hodo nimo naku ryōshin ni assei serarete, minna o-yome ni ittari o-muko o tottari shite shimaimashita <u>no</u>, dakara ima made konna koto o itteru mono wa watakushi bakkari dato omou to, nandaka kokoro bosokutte kokoro bosokutte narimasen, deshitaga ne, konogoro wa*

*anata to iu shin'yū ga dekita kara, anō taihen kijōbu ni narimashita <u>wa</u>.*"
"However, you can't just condemn the uneducated. For example, I wouldn't go so far as to call my friends educated, but they still more or less have had a normal education. But even among them, out of 25 people, only about 4 understand Westernism. And for those 4, it was true only while they were at the private tutoring school; once they get out into the real world, they're all bark and no bite. They totally got persuaded by their parents and got married. So when I realize that I'm the only person who is still saying these kinds of things, I can't help but feeling peerless. However, since I've recently become good friends, so I feel relieved very much."

(Osei, ibid., p. 22)

As the underlined parts indicate, one can see the *-no* at the end of the declarative sentence and the sentence-ending particle *wa*. This *wa* is considered to have been uttered in a rising tone.

Osei is portrayed as an academically oriented young woman: an 18-year-old, she went to the private school in Shiba after graduating from elementary school and started learning English from Bunzō. (However, it gradually becomes clear that her academic passion was shallow and superficial.) The newness of her language (at least for that period) seems to be related to the fact that she goes to school. We will discuss this in more detail later.

### The Criticized *teyo dawa*

Currently, female-specific expressions are often positively evaluated as gentle and elegant language usage. However, from around 1887 (Meiji 20), when these expressions began to appear, until the decade following 1907 (Meiji 40), it was consistently rejected as an undignified, strident, and a rough style of expression in the discourse of leading figures such as scholars, educators, and those in mass media. In addition, it was often described as a language with origins the lower classes of society in *Yamanote*, or a language of low-class geishas, and, which ultimately spread to young women through schools, especially schools for girls. Let us examine the following excerpt from Yoshinori Ishikawa's "Kindai josei-go no gobi: teyo/dawa/noyo" (Endings of modern women's language: *teyo/dawa/noyo*).

As already introduced by Prof. Masahide Yamamoto, a *Genbun Icchi* authority, in his article, its emergence was soon theorized in Kōyō Ozaki's "Hayari Kotoba" (Words in vogue) appeared in *Kijo no Tomo* (The Lady's Friend) (Meiji 21-6). In other words, among the school girls in elementary schools 89 years ago, language with strange sentence endings began to be heard such as "*Ume wa mada sakanakutte yo*" (The plum (flowers) have not blossomed yet), "*Ara mō saite yo*" (Oh, they have already blossomed), and "*Sakura no hana wa mada sakanain da wa*" (The cherry flowers have not blossomed yet). In the past five to six years, this has reached even girls in girls' high school and has permeated even among noblewomen. The origin of this speech is the vulgar language used by "the daughters of the *gokenin* (lower-ranked vassals from the Kamakura

*Where is the Princess?*     91

Period onward up until the Edo Period) living in the Aoyama area when the Edo Shogunate was still in place" and warns that it should therefore not be used. In *Jogaku Zasshi* (The Schoolgirls' Magazine) (July, Meiji 23) two years later, an article titled "Women's Language Usage" (by Hagetsu-shi), language usage such as "*Yokutte yo*" (It's all right), "*Nani nani da wa*" (It's …), and "*Kōen e sanpo ni iku?*" (Coming to the park for a walk?) (where no interrogative particle is placed after *iku* (go), and the interrogative nature of the sentence is indicated solely by raising the tone toward the end, just as in Western languages) that were prevalent among female students are rejected as gruff and unpleasant. In addition, even in 1905 (Meiji 38), which is 15 years later, endings such as "*iya yo*" (I don't like it), "*yokute yo*" (I'm OK) and "*sō da wa*" (Yes it is) were denounced as vulgar by *Kyōiku Jiron* (Educational Commentary) (May, Meiji 38).

(p. 22)

According to the words of Kōyō Ozaki, eight to nine years before 1888 (Meiji 21), that is between 1879 (Meiji 12) and 1880 (Meiji 13), this language spread to elementary schools, which in turn spread to girls' high schools and then to older women. An interesting aspect highlighted in *Jogaku Zasshi* (The Schoolgirls' Magazine) (Hagetsu-shi) was the fact that interrogative sentences in the rising tone without the particle *ka* emerged during that time. In addition, the fact that *da wa* was considered to be "jarring," although it had existed since the Edo period, suggests that it had a different tone than that in the Edo period.

Let us examine the commentary by Yoshifumi Hida in *Tokyo-go Seiritsu-shi no Kenkyū* (Research on the History of Establishment of Tokyo Language).

*… Mukashi wa ushigome hen no basue no go tarishi "Ara yokutte yo" nado ga konnichi nite wa mushiro chūkyū ijō no musume kotoba no yō ni kikaruru mo i-na mono kana, omō ni ko wa yamanote hen no katō shakai yori sono kaiwai no oyashiki e denpa shitaru ga hajime nite, sono oyashiki to iu mono ima no yo no haburi yoki kemmon no rekireki nareba, koko yori yagate shitamachi emo tsutawareru mono naranka.*

… Another odd thing is that phrases like "*Ara yokutte yo*" (Oh, it's all right!), which in the past were heard in the rundown Ushigome area, now appear to be the speech of young women in the middle class and higher. First, the expressions were transmitted from the lower class society uptown to the nearby estates, and as those people were from families who are thought to have good style today, from there, the phrases eventually reached traditional working-class neighborhoods.

(1898 (Meiji 29) *Waseda Bungaku* (Waseda Literature),
April edition, *Zakkai* ("*Reijō Saikun no Kotoba*"
(Young Ladys and Madammes' word)), pp. 204–205)

*Kinnen jogaku no bokkō suru ni shitagai hikakuteki karyū shakai no shijo ga kiwamete tasū ni kaku jogakkō ni nyūgaku suru ni itarishi yori iwayuru otana no musume kodomo ga mochiyuru gengo ga jogakusei kan ni mochiiraruru ni itareru*

*koto sa ni kakaguru rei no gotoshi*
*Nakunacchatta/Ō yāda/Ittete yo/Iku koto yo/Mitete yo/Yokutte yo*
In recent years, girls of comparatively lower classes began entering girls' schools in greater numbers as there was a rapid rise in the number of girls' schools. It is as shown in an example to the left*, the language used by girls working in the so-called "*mizu-shōbai*" (entertainment industry) was consequently adopted by the female students.
It's gone/Oh, I hate it/I will go first/She will go/They saw it/It's all right
(1905 (Meiji 38) March 16, *Yomiuri Shimbun*)
*Because the original text is written vertically, "left" meand "below" in this case

*Atai dano, iya yo dano iu kotoba wa, are wa ganrai geisha-ya no kotoba nanda.*

Figure 5-1 Tōkyō-fu Kōtō Jogakkō
(Tokyo Prefectural Women's High School) Fūzoku Gahō, No.193, September 25, Meiji 32 (1899), Yamamoto, Shōkoku (drawing).

*Where is the Princess?* 93

[snip] *Shikashi sono geisha ni shiro, atai nante iu kotoba wa, dōhai no aida ni tsukatta monode, okyaku no mae e dete wa muron, nēsan ni taishite mo, izen wa kesshite tsukawanakatta. Kanarazu atashi to itta mono dearu. Mata yokutteyo toka iya yo toka iu kotoba wa, ima demo yoku shitajikko ga tsukau ga, izen kara sō de atta. Shikashi kore totemo uchiwa no tsūyōgo de, yoso iki kotoba dewa nakatta monoda.*

(...) Words like '*atai*' ( = I) and '*iya-yo*' ( = no) were originally words used in *geisha* houses. Further, even among the *geisha*, words like '*atai*' were only to be used between equals and never to customers or to the senior *geisha*, as in those cases, '*atashi*' was always used. While '*Yokutte yo*' (It's all right) and '*iya-yo*' have been used by apprentice *geisha* for some time and are still used even today, these were considered insider slangs that were never to be used with outsiders.

(Kyūichi Takeuchi (sculptor) "Tokyo Fujin no Tsūyōgo"
(Tokyo women's vernacular expressions)
*Shumi*, 2-11, 1907 (Meiji 40) November)

This speech style of young women with the *te yo* and *da wa* sentence endings was eventually referred to as the *teyo dawa* language. This language was exactly the modern <Female Language> and <Young Lady from a Good Family Language>. The question of whether the *teyo dawa* language had its origins in the language of those in the lower-class society or geishas is very doubtful since it lacks objective evidence. However, it is almost certain that the spread of this language occurred through schools.

## 6. The Spread of the *teyo dawa* Language

### Girls' Schools as Media

In the Edo period, it was believed that women did not need to be educated. However, in the Meiji era, the admission of girls into elementary schools was approved and over time, even girls' high schools were established. In 1882 (Meiji 15), Fuzoku Kōtō Jogakkō (the Tokyo Women's Higher School) was attached to Tokyō Joshi Shihan Gakkō (the Tokyo Women's Normal School), which marked the beginning of the establishment of *jogakkō* (girls' high school). Subsequently, these high schools were established throughout the country after which a community of young, educated women emerged in Japan.

At that time, families that could send their daughters to girls' high schools had to have a certain income level and social status. Consequently, sending one's daughter to high school became proof of such high status. One can even say that schools such as Kazoku Jogakkō (Women's School for Nobility) (established in 1885 (Meiji 8)) and Joshi Gakushūin (Women's Gakushūin) (established in 1918 (Taisho 7)) were the epitome of such status. In other words, this led to the emergence of the *ojōsama* (a young lady from a good family). Furthermore, influential people of those times such as politicians and businessmen "visited" girls' schools to find brides for their sons (Shōichi Inoue, *Bijin-ron* (An Essay on Beauties)). These "visits" are also mentioned in Kyōka Izumi's *Onna Keizu* (A Woman's Pedigree).

In some cases, a graceful and beautiful girl was selected who married even before graduation. Conversely, those who were not blessed with such beauty and grace were called *sotsugyō-zura* (literally, 'graduation face').

In girls' high schools, regular subjects were naturally taught; besides, information about various cultures and customs was exchanged and transmitted to the general public. While the cultures and customs originating in girls' schools had an intellectual side to them, they were unrealistic and lacked the feel of everyday life. Moreover, they included unique romantic and aesthetic sensibilities that did not exist in Japan up to that point. The visual element that symbolized this type of culture was the *ebicha shikibu* (a girl in the maroon skirt) fashion style of the girl students (See figure 5-1). In addition, the auditory element that symbolized this culture was the *jogakusei kotoba* (female students' language). In *Jogakusei no Keifu: Saishoku Sareru Meiji* (The Genealogy of Girl Students: Colored Meiji), Kazuko Honda evaluates the *teyo dawa* language as "an irresponsible way of talking" that "did not align with the mainstream" and "discreetly obliterated the image of the 'good wife and wise mother' that flourished outside the (school) enclosure" (pp. 132–134).

The modern <Female Language>, simply put, spread as <Female Students' Language>. Although the *teyo dawa* language was known for its negative reputation among intellectuals and journalists, it steadily spread throughout the country's girls' schools. At times, schools themselves function as a powerful medium and in addition to regular subjects, aspects that the teachers did not want to transmit can spread into society. <Female Students' Language> was one such example.

### The *teyo dawa* Language as Seen in Novels

Female students also appeared in novels, which also helped spread female students' language throughout the country. First, let us examine the language of Namiko (a graduate of Kazoku Jogakkō) in *Hototogisu* (The Cuckoo), serialized in the *Kokumin Shimbun* (Citizen's Newspaper) from 1898 (Meiji 31) to 1899 (Meiji 32).

> *"Nami san, kutabire wa shinai ka?"*
> *"Ie, chitto mo kyō wa tsukaremasen <u>no</u>, watakushi konna ni tanoshii koto wa <u>hajimete!</u>"*
> "Nami, aren't you tired?"
> "No, I am not even a little tired today, this is the first time that I am enjoying myself so much!"
>
> (Roka Tokutomi, *Hototogisu* (The Cuckoo), p. 18)

> *Namiko wa sotto Takeo no hiza ni te o nagete toiki tsuki,*
> *"Itsumademo kō shite itō gozaimasu <u>koto!</u>"*
> Namiko gently puts her hand on Takeo's knee and sighs saying,
> "How I want this to last forever!"
>
> (ibid., p. 19)

> *Namiko wa futo omoiidetaru yō ni atama o agetsu.*

*Where is the Princess?*

*"Anata irasshaimasu no, Yamaki ni?"*
*"Yamaki kai, okkasan ga ā ossharu kara ne—ikazuba naru mai."*
*"Ho ho, watakushi mo ikitai wa."*
*"Ikinasai to mo, ikō issho ni."*
*"Ho ho ho, yoshimashō."*
*"Naze?"*
*"Kowai no desu mono."*
"Namiko suddenly raises her head as if she remembered something.
"Will you be going to Yamaki?"
"Yamaki, huh? Mother says so, so I guess I'll have to go."
"Ho ho, I would like to go as well."
"By all means go, let us go together."
"Ho ho ho, I will not do it."
"Why?"
"I'm afraid."

(ibid., p. 69)

Next, let us examine an excerpt from the *Makaze Koikaze* (Winds of Demons and Love) which was serialized in the *Yomiuri Shimbun* (Yomiuri Newspaer) from 1903 on (Meiji 36). The subject matter of this novel covered schoolgirl romance scandals, and the novel became extremely popular at that time.

*"Yoku kite kudasutta wa nē," to kanja wa shimijimi itta. "Watashi, donnani anata ni aitakatta rō ......, Datte, kinō wa mō, konomama shinu tokoro ka to omotte yo."*
*"Bakabakashii, nēsan no you demo nai wa, korenpakashi no kega de shinde dou suru no," to egawo o tsukutte, "Dakedo, kesa shimbun o mita toki wane, watashi jitsu ni bikkuri shite yo ....... Suguni demo kakete koyou to omotta keredomo, kāsama wa, motto attaka ni natte kara de nakya ikenaitte, dō shitemo dashite kurenain desu mono, honto ni kiga kide nakattawa."*
The patient earnestly said, "Thank you for coming!" "I wanted to see you so much. You know, yesterday I thought that was it, I'm going to die like this." "Don't be ridiculous, this isn't like you, sister. You aren't going to die from an injury like this," She said with a smile. "But when I saw the paper this morning, I was really surprised. I thought of running over right away, but mother told me to wait until it got warmer. She wouldn't let me out no matter what. I felt so on edge."

(Hatsuno Hagihara and Yoshie Natsumoto.
Tengai Kosugi, *Makaze Koikaze*, p. 17)

In Soseki Natsume's novels, at least three school girls appear; namely, Yukie from *Wagahai wa Neko de Aru* (I am a Cat) (1905 (Meiji 38)), Yoshiko from *Sanshirō* (1908 (Meiji 41)–1909 (Meiji 42)), and Nui from *Sorekara* (And Then). All three use the vogue words of schoolgirls at that time, such as *yokutte yo* (That's enough/ It's fine), *shiranai wa* (I don't know).

*"Sore ja Yukie san nanzo wa sonokata no yō ni o-keshō o sureba, Kaneda san no bai kurai utsukushiku naru deshō"*

*"Ara iyada. Yokutte yo. Shiranai wa. Dakedo, ano kata wa mattaku tsukuri-sugiru no ne. Nanbo o-kane ga attatte—"*

"If that's the case, then Yukie, if you were to use make-up like her, you could be twice as beautiful as Ms. Kaneda."

"Well, my, that's enough, I don't know about that! But one thing I can say is she really uses too much makeup! No matter how much money she has ..."

(*Wagahai wa Neko dearu* (I am a Cat) 10, p. 442)

*Sanshirō wa kasanai koto ni suru mune o kotaete, aisatsu o shite, tachi-kakeru to, Yoshiko mo mō kaerō to ii-dashita.*

*"Sakki no hanashi o shinakuccha" to ani ga chūi shita.*

*"Yokutte yo" to imouto ga kyozetsu shita.*

*"Yoku wa nai yo."*

*"Yokutte yo. Shiranai yo"*

*Ani wa imouto no kao o mite damatte iru.*

*Imouto wa, mata kou itta.*

*"Datte shikata ga nai ja, arimasenka. Shiri mo shinai hito no tokoro e, iku ka ikanai katte, kiitatte. Suki demo kirai demo nainda kara, nannimo iiyou wa arya shinai wa. Dakara shiranai wa"*

Sanshirō responded that he was not going to lend (money), offered his regards, and began to rise, at which point Yoshiko said she was going home, too.

Brother warned, "We must talk about that issue."

"It's fine," Sister refused.

"It's not fine."

"It's fine. I don't care anymore."

Brother looked at Sister's face in silence.

Sister continued to speak.

"Well there's nothing I can do about it, is there? Asking whether or not I would marry a stranger! It's not about like or dislike, there's just nothing to say. So I don't care anymore."

(*Sanshirō* 9-8, p. 530)

*Nui to iu musume wa, nanika iu to, yokutte yo, shiranai wa to kotaeru. Sou shite hini nanben to naku ribon o kake kaeru. Chikagoro wa baiorin no keiko ni iku. Kaette kuru to, nokogiri no metate no you na koe o dashite osarai o suru. Tadashi hito ga mite iru to kesshite yaranai. Heya o shimekitte, kī-kī iwaseru nodakara, oya wa kanari jōzu da to omotte iru. Daisuke dake ga tokidoki sotto to o akeru no de, yokutte yo, shiranai wa to shikarareru.*

Miss Nui always responds with, "It's good, whatever" when you say something. She does so while tying her ribbon countless times a day. These days, she goes for violin lessons. When she returns, she practices, making sounds like a saw getting set. But she never does it when anyone is looking. She shuts herself up in her room and makes the creaky sounds, so her parents think she is pretty good. Daisuke sometimes gently opens her door, only to be scolded with, "It's

*Where is the Princess?*                                      97

all right, whatever!"

*(Sorekara* 3-1, p. 53)

## 7. The Further Spread of the *teyo dawa* Language

### Beyond Girls' Schools
In *Mon* (The Gate), we come across the following interesting description:

> *"Anata sonna tokoro e neru to kaze hiite yo"* to saikun ga chūi shita. Saikun no
> kotoba wa Tokyo no you na, Tokyo de nai you na, gendai no jogakusei ni kyōtsū na
> isshu no chōshi o motte iru.
> "If you sleep in a place like that, you'll catch a cold," his wife warned. His wife's
> words had a cadence that was Tokyo-esque, yet not Tokyo-esque, with the flavor
> of the speech common to today's female students.
>
> *(Mon* 1-1, p. 348)

Here, one can say that the comment "not Tokyo-esque" highlights the fact
that this language was cut off from the *shitamachi* (downtown) language, which
emerged from the Edo period. Strikingly, this cadence is considered to be a language "common to (the language of) female students."

> *"O-cha nara takusan desu."* to Koroku ga itta.
> *"Iya?"* to Jogakusei ryu-ni nen o oshita Ōyone wa, *"Ja okashi wa"* to itte warai-kaketa.
> Koroku said, "No tea, thank you."
> "No?" said Oyone, verifying in the manner of a female student. "Then how
> about some snacks?" she said, smiling.
>
> (Mon 1-3, p. 353)

"Verifying in the manner of a female student" refers to the way of "raising the end
of a sentence as in a Western language." Furthermore, it is unclear whether the
character of Oyone, the wife of the main character Sōsuke in *Mon* (The Gate),
is a graduate from a girl's school. However, these examples show that even adult
women used female students' language.

The character of Otsuta in Kyoka Izumi's *Onna Keizu* (A Woman's Pedigree)
(1909 (Meiji 42)) is a former geisha of Yanagibashi. In addition, geisha characters
Tsunaji and Koyoshi, former colleagues of Otsuta, also appear. They use the *shitamachi* (downtown) language that includes remnants of the Edo era and a a few
expressions from <Female Students' Language> such as *te yo*. Since geisha cannot
be graduates from girls' schools, this indicates that <Female Students' Language>
has spread beyond girls' schools and has come closer to the domain of <Female
Language> in general.

Tsuta:
*"Kikanai yo, Me no Ji, Takusan nandakara."*
"It's all right, Menoji, you make a big deal out of everything."

Chikara:
*"Mā, omae."*
"Oh, you."
Tsuta:
*"Īe, takusan, daiji na syotai dawa."*
"No, that's enough. They're an important family."
Me:
*"Odorokimasu na."*
"Don't be so surprised."
Tsuta:
*"Watashi, mou shōji o shime te yo."*
"I'll close the door. "

(Kyōka Izumi, Onna Keizu, pp. 357–358)

Tsunaji:
*"Hikkaite yo."* to te o ageta ga, omoidashita youni za o tatte,
"I will scratch you," she said, raising her hand, but stood up from the chair like
she remembered something,
Tsunaji:
*"Dō shitandarō nē, Denwa wa,"* to tsubuyaite deyō to suru.
"What's wrong with this phone, I wonder," she mumbled and tried to leave.

(ibid., p. 462)

Koyoshi:
*"Mā, yoku irashitte nē."*
*to Chikara no hou e aisatsu shite, hohoemi-nagara, koicha ni tsuru-no-ha-komon
no montsuki nimai awase, ai-ke-nezumi no han-eri, shiro-cha-ji ni okina-gōshi no
hakata no maru-obi, kodai moyō sorairo chirimen no nagajuban, tsutsumashiyaka
ni , Sakai ni hikisouta torinashi wa, sashitsukae naku tsumuri ga sagaru ga, wakete
sono yo no shubi dearu kara, Chikara wa teinei ni te o sagete,*
Chikara:
*"Gokigen yō,"* to eshaku suru.
"Well, I'm so glad you came," she said to Chikara, smiling, (clothing description omitted), and modestly accompanied Sakai. This demeanor of hers would
certainly leave a deep impression on anyone. On top of it, since her actions of
that night were so splendid, Chikara politely lowered her hand,
saying,
"Fare thee well." She made slight bow.

(ibid., p. 463)

## Nationwide Spread

<Female Students' Language> originally emerged in Tokyo, but it became wide-
spread through a medium that is girls' schools. In Kunimitsu Kawamura's book
titled *Otome no Inori* (Prayer of Meiden), he introduced letters to the editor
found in the "Shi-yū Kurabu" (Pen Fricends' Club) of *Jogaku Sekai* (The World of

Women's School) (October 1916 (Taisho 5)) in which it was mentioned that "an *Otome's* (virgin) world or a world that did not exist anywhere until now has been created" through the common use of <Female Students' Language> by students of and graduates from girls' schools from various regions nationwide (ibid., p. 48). Let us examine an excerpt from the book.

*Aogirino no ha ga horohoro sabishū chirimasu. Are are are are, mata mushi no koe ga, dokokade, kasukani, utau Rōrerai (Loreley) no oto to tomo ni, watakushi no midareta hāto (heart) o, sosoru you ni hibiite mairimasu. Ā nanto senchimenta (sentimental) deshō. Kakaru yū ... kakaru yo wa, o-natsukashii minasama-gata niwa ikaga o-kurashi nasaimasu <u>no</u>.*

The leaves of the varnishtree scatter so lonesomely. What's this? Somewhere, again the voice of insects' echoes, along with the sound of the Lorelei that softly sings, stirring my restless heart. Ahh, how sentimental, is it not? On evenings like this, on nights like this, how does everyone I miss pass their time?

(Mikawa, Gin no Tsuki, "Shi-yū Kurabu" p. 43)

*Kanashii Shigure-zuki ga otozure-mashita. Onaji kokoro no S sama, impuresshon (impression) fukaki ryō ni sugoshita koro o omoidashi mashou yone. Sabishii kane no ne to tomoni shizukani shizukani kurete itta aki no ichi-nichi ichi-ya o. Utsukushii dentō kara nukedete, hitori ryō no obashima ni yotte shinobinaki shita yoi!! Sono toki watakushi ni yorisoute, amai amai sasayaki o kanashii hāto (heart) ni sosoide kudaimashita kimi, ē soreha onaji kokoro no S sama deshita. Tsuki hosoi koyoi mo watakushi wa ano koro o ...... Soshite hoshi no yō na S san o koute naitemasu <u>no</u>.*

Sad October has come to visit. S, surely, you feel the same; let us remember the time spent at the dorm, which has left such deep impressions. A full day and night in autumn that turned to darkness quietly with the ring of the lonely bell. You, who emerged from the beautiful light and came close to me as I quietly cried alone at the dormitory banister, who filled my sad heart with sweet nothings; yes, that was S, who felt the same. On this night with a slender moon, I (remember) those days ... and I miss and weep for S, who was like a star.

(Shinanoji, Kashiwaba no M-ko, ibid., p. 45)

*O-natsukashiki minasama!! Rōmansu (Romance) na shīzun (season) to narimashita ne. Takan na Aoyagi wa donnani aki ga matareta koto de gozaimashou. Kemuri no miyako nagara, yūbe to nareba, konogoro wa namida o sasou mushi no ne mo itashimasu. Kyō wa ku-gatsu no futsuka, ā, mō ikutsu shitara, oshōgatsu ni naru no deshou ...... Watakushi wa ima yubi otte kazoete mimashita. Eikyū ni otome de itō gozansu kedomo, sō itsumademo shōjo de oshōgatsu o mukaeru koto mo dekimasen <u>wane</u>. Imano shi no yō na hi ga hanayaka na watakushi no sugata to tomo ni kawaranaide ite hoshii!!*

All of you, I miss! The season of romance is upon us. I wonder how long the sentimental willow has waited for fall to come. The city may be filled with smoke, but when the night comes at this time of year, the insects sing their moving songs. Today is September 2nd, ahh, how long until New Year's? I counted it now on my fingers. I wish to always stay a little girl, but I cannot look forward to New Year's as a young lady forever. How I wish my youthful face along with these days might, like poetry, never change!

(Osaka-shi, Aoyagi, ibid., p. 47)

Here, <Female Students' Language> has become a persona of the nationwide "Shi-yū Kurabu" (Pen Friend's Club) of *Jogaku Sekai* (The world of Women's School). Apparently, young schoolgirls and former schoolgirls across the country had acquired <Female Students' Language> and created a virtual community.

Let us consider an example similar to that of the "Shi-yū Kurabu"; namely, the series *Namiko Ririkku Retā* (Namiko Lyric Letters). This was an illustrated letter series aimed at young girls and released by the Benibara Company in 1935 (Showa 10). The letters included poems and letters to the readers.

*Sensei hajimemashite/Takara Midori desu<u>no</u>/Douzo yoroshiku/Hatsu tōkō desu<u>no</u>/ demo korekara doshidoshi otayori itashimasu<u>wa</u>/[snip]/Otomodachi e no otayori taitei Sensei <u>no yo</u>/Datte Jōhin de yasashiin <u>desumono</u>/Sensei mo sonna kata ja nai no <u>kashira</u>/Kono retā (letter) no naka ni sensei no osugata ga haitte iru you ni omoete shikata ga nai <u>no</u>/[snip]/Watashi jogakkō 3nen desu <u>no</u>/Douzo yorochiku ne/Dewa mata sayonara*

Hello, master/I am Midori Takara/Nice to meet you/This is my first post/But I will be sending more and more/[snip]/Most of my correspondence with friends is about you/Your work is so good and gentle/I wonder if you are like that as well/I can't help but see your image in this letter!/[snip]/I am a third-year student at a girls' school/My regards/Talk to you again

(Tokyo, Midori Takara, *Namiko Ririkku Retā*, pp. 83–86)

*Namiko sensei hajimete no otayori de gozaimasu/Gurūpu (group) no minasama douzo yoroshiku onegai itashimasu, honto ni Namiko sensei no o-e nante nante kawaii no deshou/Nakayoshi no binsen de senchi no heitai san ni imon no o-tegami sashiage mashita <u>no</u>/Kitto kitto oyorokobi kudasaru koto to watakushi made ga ureshiku natte shimaimashita./Sensei korekaramo konnano o zehi zehi onegai itashimasu baibai*

Master Namiko, this is my first correspondence/Hello to everyone in the group. I think your drawings are so cute/I sent sympathy cards on friendly stationery to soldiers on the front line/Thinking it will surely make them happy, I got a little happy myself/Master, please, please do this kind of thing (letter sets) more often. Bye bye.

(Sendai, Toshiko, ibid., p. 86)

As an example of <Female Students' Language> in the *Namiko Ririkku Letters* series, let us consider novels for young girls at that time. A typical example is Nobuko Yoshiya's *Sakuragai* (Cherry Shells) (1931 (Showa 6)), serialized in *Shōjo Gahō* (Girls' Pictorial). The following is a conversation among female students at

*Where is the Princess?* 101

the Daiichi Kenritsu Kōtō Jogakkō (The First Prefectural Girls' High School) in City XX near Tokyo.

"*Ejima san, sensei no o diya (dear) deshou, itsumo e no tensai datte o-home ni narun desu mono—Nandeshou, kyō mo mina watakushi tachi o oidashite Ejima san hitori o-nokori nasaitte, zuibun nē.*"
"*Hontō yo, ittai nanno go-yō deshou?*"
"*Kitto, o-futari dake de nakayoku sutōbu (stove) o senryō nasaru o-tsumori yo*"
"*Masaka, —Demo watashi totemo ki ga momeru wa, ato de sotto mado kara nozo-ite mimashou ka*"
"*Mā, sonna shūtai oyoshi asobase yo!*"
"*Demo, Sekido sensei wa seito ni sawagareru wari ni reisei de kōhei mushi ne*"
"*Sou yo, watakushi mou san-do mo kirei na o-hana o sasagete iru noni, chittomo supesharu (special) ni atsukatte kudasaranain desu mono— "*
"Ms. Ejima is the teacher's pet. She is always being complimented on being a painting genius ... it's so terrible! Everybody was shooed out again today, except for her!"
"Really, what does she want with her?"
"Without a doubt, she wants to share a room with a stove, just the two of them."
"Impossible ... but it makes me worry too, afterwards, should I peek in the window?"
"Enough of such ugly behavior!"
"But considering how much of a fuss is made over Ms. Sekido, she is actually very level-headed and impartial."
"I know, I've given her beautiful flowers three times already, but she doesn't treat me as special in the least ..."

(Nobuko Yoshiya, *Sakuragai*, p. 26)

## 8. The Decline of the *teyo dawa* Language

### Changes in <Female Language> after the World War II

In 1945 (Showa 20), Japan was defeated, and subsequently, the country's social structure began to rapidly change. In the same year, the coeducational system was established, which basically removed the barrier between boys and girls in the educational system. Although separate girls' and boys' schools still remain to this day, the category of jogakkō (girls' schools) disappeared. In addition, aristocracy was abolished, and the Gakushūin schools were institutionally no longer different from normal schools. More specifically, the previous system that supported the illusion of the *ojōsama* (young lady from a good family) had collapsed. Indeed, daughters born to families with long and honorable lineages and wealthy families with maids in attendance still exist. However, the social system that once distinguished such people from others no longer exists. Rather, the image of the *ojōsama* only exists in people's conceptions. This raises the following question: In what way is this fact related to <Young Lady from a Good Family Language> ?

We have already discussed how the pre-war female students' language had become quite generalized and how it was increasingly becoming a generic <Female Language>. In fact, even today, -*no* and (*da*) *wa* can be frequently heard as female-specific expressions. However, certain expressions such as -*te yo* and -*koto* are rarely used. Consequently, these -*te yo* and -*koto* type of expressions were gradually absorbed into the conceptual and caricatural <Young Lady from a Good Family Language>. Let us examine how it is the case by focusing on the -*te yo* expression.

If you examine the -*te yo* expression in the CD-ROM version of *Shinchō Bunko no Hyaku Satsu* (Shincho Library 100 Novels), you can see that the -*te yo* expression rapidly disappeared from post-war novels. The following four works include instances of the -*te yo* expression.

• Osamu Dazai, *Ningen Shikkaku* (*No Longer Human*), 1948 (Showa 23):
(*Jibun no e no unpitsu wa, hijou ni osoi hou deshita*)
*Ima wa tada, sakedai ga hoshii bakari ni kaite, soushite, Shizuko ga sha kara kaeru to soreto kōtai ni pui to soto e dete, Kōenji no eki chikaku no yatai ya sutando bā de yasukute tsuyoi sake o nomi, sukoshi yōki ni natte apāto e kaeri,*
"*Mireba miruhodo, hen na kao o shiteiru nē, omae wa. Nonki oshō no kao wa, jitsu wa, omae no negao kara hinto o etanoda*"
"*Anata no negao datte, zuibun ofuke ni narimashite yo. Shijū-otoko mitai*"
 (My painting strokes were extremely slow)
Now, I just paint solely for the purpose of earning some money for drinking, and when Shizuko comes home from the company, I go out in turn, drink some cheap, strong liquor at the liquor stalls and stands near Kōenji station and return to the apartment feeling cheerful,
"The more I see you, the more I feel you've got a funny face. In fact, I got an idea for Nonki Osho's (Easy Going Priest's) face from your sleeping face."
"Your sleeping face has become old too. You look like a 40-year-old man."

(p. 173)

• Takehiko Fukunaga, *Kusa no Hana* (Grass Flowers), 1954 (Showa 29):
—*Sorya atashi datte, kiwamono o kaku hito yori wa erai to omotte yo. Keredone, seikatsu ga aru kara sakuhin ga aruno deshou?*
—*Sore wa sousa.*
—Of course, I think I'm better than writers of novels with temporary topics, but our daily life is the reason why we create works, isn't it.
—Yeah, that is true, no doubt.

(p. 314)

• Junnosuke Yoshiyuki, *Suna no Ue no Shokubutsu-gun* (Plants on Sand), 1964 (Showa 39):
"*Atsuku nan ka nai wa, atatakaku mo nakutte yo.*"
"It is not hot at all, it is not even warm."

(p. 188)

• Hisashi Inoue, *Bun to Fun* (Boon and Phoon), 1970 (Showa 45):

*Where is the Princess?*   103

*Sono interi obasan ga, waraikaketa dake de naku, toshokan o deyō to suru Fun sensei ni mukatte, kou itta no dearu.*

*"Fun sensei, itsumo sensei no go-hon o toshokan ni kifu shite kudasatte arigatou zonjimasu. Konoaida itadaita* Bun *to iu shōsetsu, are wa totemo kekkō de gozanshita. Atakushi, tetsuya de yomashite itadakimashite yo. Atakushidake dewa gozaimasen. Toshokan riyōsha no aida demo hipparidako. Itsumo kashidashichū nande gozaimasu. Mō issatsu, kaiireyōto omoimashitara, hon'ya san demo urikire nandesutte. Sensei,* Bun *wa kessaku de gozansu wa."*

That intellectual lady did not just smile but turned to Phoon Sensei who was about to leave the library and said thus,

"Phoon Sensei, thank you for always contributing books to the library. The novel *Boon* received the other day was really good. I read it overnight. And it is not just me. It is much sought after among the library users as well and it is consistently being lent out. I thought of buying and stocking another copy but it had been sold out at the bookstore as well. Sensei, *Boon* is a masterpiece."

(p. 44)

We must pay attention the fact that his language was used in the jocular conversation by the woman in the first novel *Ningen Shikkaku* (No Longer Human) and in the last humorous novel *Bun to Fun* in which the speaker, an intelligent librarian, is portrayed as a caricature. A decent portrayal of the *-te yo* expression only appears in *Kusa no Hana* (Grass Flowers) and in *Suna no ue no Shokubutsu-gun* (Plants on Sand).

Researchers such as Rinko Shibuya have indicated the decline of female-specific expressions on the whole. This tendency can be accepted as a matter of course in the present time when the gap between males and females has gradually narrowed in regard to educational rights, voting rights, and working conditions, and gender equality is being sought as an ideal. However, is there a reason for the rapid decline of *-te yo* in particular in <Female Language>? The following subsection summarizes the grammar of *-te yo*.

### The Grammar of *-te yo*
In terms of form, the *-te yo* expression can be categorized into the following types:

1. Expressions that convey an issue and attract the attention of the listener.
Examples include "*Yoroshiku(t)te yo*" (It's fine), "*Sensei, irasshite yo*" (Master has come), and "*Koko ni arimashite yo*" (Here it is). In rare cases, *ne* is used instead of *yo*. Furthermore, in the case of an interrogative sentence, *yo* is dropped and the sentence ends with *te*. As in "*Watashi ga mairimasu wa yo. Yokutte?*" (I am going. Okay?), the tone rises at the end of the sentence for both conveying and asking a question.

2. Forms in which the light imperative *-te* is followed by *yo*.
Forms such as "*Hayaku shite yo*" (Hurry up!) and "*Mō, kaette yo*" (Go home already!). Here, the tone falls at *yo*. If *yo* is replaced with *ne*, then it becomes a softer

expression of confirmation. These are feminine expression.

3. When the quotative *-tte* is followed with *yo*, it conveys an utterance of a third person.

Let us examine the following sentence: "*Otōsan, kyō hayaku kaeru-tte yo*" (Father said that he would come home early today). If uttered in a rising tone, then it is considered to be a feminine manner of speaking. If the tone is raised a little at the outset of *yo* and then extended and dropped at the end, then it is considered to be a masculine style of speaking.

4. If the interjectory particle *yo* is attached to the conjunctive particle *te*, it states a presupposition.

Consider the following sentence: "*Kyō wa umi ga shikete te yo, totemo ja nai ga, ryō nyā derarenai yo*" (The sea is rough today, so (we) can't possibly go fishing). If the tone is raised at *yo* and then extended and dropped at the end, then it sounds masculine and "rough."

The *-te yo* in question here is, of course, of the first type. This is used to convey some fact or idea to another person. However, there is no tense distinction. In other words, *-te yo* can be used for both past and present tense, as shown in the following examples:

(a) *Kinō wa, totemo tanoshikutte yo.*/Yesterday, I really enjoyed myself (= was enyoyable).

(b) *Watashi, ima, totemo tanoshikutte yo.*/I am really enjoying myself now (= is enjoyable).

In short, it is a vague and obscure expression where a grammatical item that should ordinarily be distinguished is not distinguished. Perhaps it was understood that, by not clarifying the situation, it better matched the feminine stereotype of "avoiding strong assertion." However, the fact that it is a vaguely worded expression means that it is also an inefficient method of communication. Moreover, in the case of the other *-te yo*, it is an expression in which *te* alone suffices to form a sentence, and the particle *yo* is subsequently attached. This expression can be used with minimum knowledge of grammar, but the first case of *-te yo* on the other hand, is characterized with the fact that the speaker has to know the specific grammatical rule. In this regard, the first *-te yo* is not only semantically vague but also requires sufficient grammatical knowledge; hence, it is an extremely inefficient expression. *-(da) wa*, which is another part of the *teyo dawa* expression, can be used by just adding *wa* to the predicate. Furthermore, expressions, such as "*Suteki yo*" (It's cute) and "*Kino katta no*" (I bought it yesterday), only require the omission of *da*. Hence, they are grammatically simple and could survive much longer compared with *-te yo*.

### Young Girls and <Young Lady from a Good Family Language>

In this way, the withdrawal of the *-te yo* expression from <Female Language> of <Standard Language> has increased its role language degree and was incorporated into <Young Lady from a Good Family Language>. Like the character of Ochō-fujin in the manga *Ēsu o Nerae!* (Aim for the Ace!) discussed earlier, <Young Lady from a Good Family Language> began to appear frequently in the *shōjo* manga (comic books for young girls) and *shōjo shōsetsu* (novels for young girls) as expressions of the young lady character from the 1970s. Consider the following excerpts:

"*Reigi shirazu de kekkō da wa./Isei to shite no dansei nante kyōmi nakute yo.*"
"Mannerless is fine by me./I am not interested in men as a love interest."
(Yukari Ichijō, *Yūkan Kurabu* (Leisure Club) 1, p. 9)

"*Okane nara ginkō de orosu wa yo./Papa ga kusaru hodo sōkin shite kurete te yo.*"
"If I need money, I can withdraw some from the bank./Dad has deposited loads of money."
(Yumiko Suzuki, *Shin Shiratori Reiko de Gozaimasu!* (I am Reiko Shiratori, New Version) 1, p. 169)

"*Nayami goto nara kiite sashiagete yo ....?/Atakushitachi wa mina anata no o-mikata desu mono./Sā! Genki o dashite waratte chōdai.*"
"If you have something to worry about, I can listen to you...?/We are all on your side./Come on! Cheer up and smile!"
(Izumi Kawahara, *Warau Mikaeru* (Laughing Michael) 1, p. 43)

"*Atakushi no namae wa Ayanokōji Reika./Rokumeikan no jidai kara tsuzuku kōkyū shokuhin-ten to shite yūmei na sūpā kōjiya no shachō reijō yo./Fu fu./Nani ka, monku ga atte?/... Sou./Nakereba yoroshī no yo./Ho ho ho ho ho ho ho ho.*"
"My name is Reika Ayanokōji./The daughter of the President of the renowned luxury supermarket chain Kōjiya which has been in existence since the

Figure 5-2 *Yūkan Kurabu* 1, p.62, ©Yukari Ichijō

Figure 5-3 *Warau Mikaeru* 1
(p. 43 ©Izumi Kawahara/Hakusensha (*Hana to Yume Comics*))

Rokumeikan era./Hu hu./Got a problem?/I see … It's all good if you have none./ Ho ho ho ho ho ho ho ho."
(Natsuko Mori, *Ojōsama no Gyakushū* (*Ojōsama* Strikes Back!), p. 8)

The repeated appearance of *ojōsama* in stories with characters of young girls is certainly due to none other than the fact that young girls adore *ojōsama*, a noble and rare species. However, at the same time, these works also indicate that the existence of *ojōsama* is nothing more than an unrealistic fantasy in the modern society. In the manga *Ēsu o Nerae!* (Aim for the Ace!), Ochō-fujin symbolizes a "shadow" that stands in the way of Hiromi Oka, the heroine, who is an ordinary girl, and sometimes symbolizes a great "mentor." Thus, it is not possible for readers to self-identify with Ochō-fujin. Furthermore, in many later works, even if the character is called *ojōsama*, once the so-called mask is "peeled off," she is no more than an ordinary girl. In other words, she is simply a young lady wearing the persona of an *ojōsama*.

On the other hand, if the setting of the story is removed from modern Japan, then the *ojōsama* language comes alive. For example, consider the following excerpts:

"*Jitsu wa kondo …/Ima made no asa no inken to ippan no ekken o toriyameyō to omou no desu ga/Do Gemene kōshaku, dou o-omoi ni nat*te*?*"

"Actually, the next time … I am thinking of stopping giving the morning audience and the general presentation done till now. What do you think, Marquis de Guéméné?"

(Marie Antoinette, Riyoko Ikeda, *Berusaiyu no Bara*
(The Rose of Versailles), p. 294)

Figure 5-4 *Berusaiyu no Bara*
(p.294 ©Riyoko Ikeda Production)

"*Ā, kawaisou ni. Chū bakka, kare o shūri dekite?*"
"Oh, poor thing. Chewbacca, can you repair him?"
(Princess Leia Organa, *Star Wars: Episode V: The Empire Strikes Back*, 1980, Japanese dubbed version)

### <Male Language> and <Female Language> as Role Languages

The distinctive female-specific expressions such as -*te yo* and -*koto* fell from the position of <Standard Language> and have become expressions with high degree of role language. Many other female-specific expressions are also said to be gradually phased out among youths. On the other hand, the use of -(*n*) *da* types of male-specific expressions by females began to appear more frequently. Furthermore, the use of the first person pronoun *boku* and *ore* by junior and senior high school girls is often reported. Overall, it is possible to conclude that modern <Female Language> symbolized by the *teyo dawa* that arose during the Meiji era is in the process of a gradual decline.

If one assumes that the roles of men and women in society have changed and that the gap is narrowing, then it is natural that language gap is also decreasing. This phenomenon cannot be indiscriminately evaluated as "good" or "bad." This is because a thorough examination of why gender differences in language arise and how they function has not been conducted in the first place. In addition, it is customary that gender differences in speech styles are very small in regional dialects.

On the other hand, Chapter 2 introduced the hypothesis of how stereotypes imprinted in childhood will never disappear. If this hypothesis is correct, <Male Language> and <Female Language> as role languages will not be readily forgotten. As long as the knowledge of <Male Language> and <Female Language> is shared among society, writers easily rely on this knowledge. Consequently, the people's knowledge of role language is further strengthened, which leads to another new imprinting of the stereotypes on children.

Furthermore, individual speakers also use <Male Language> and <Female Language> as a part of their persona. The extensive use of female-specific expressions by *okama* (drag queens) and *nyū hāfu* (transsexuals) is an example of the utilization of the role language as a persona. In this way, it is possible to conclude that our knowledge of the role language, more than the actual usage conditions, amplifies the gender differences in language.

CHAPTER 6

# Perception to Aliens

## 1. <*Aruyo* Language>

In Akira Toriyama's manga *Dr. Surampu* (Dr. Slump) (serialized in the magazine *Shōnen Jampu* (Boy's Jump) from 1980 (Showa 55) to 1984 (Showa 59)), there is the Tsun-san family (1982, Volume 20) from China who take off in a spaceship toward the moon. However, they are shot down by Arare-chan and eventually settle in Pengin Mura (Penguin Village). All the family members speak Japanese in a bizarre manner.

Father/Tsuruten:
*"Ko/Konchiwa/Watachitachi/Kondo hikkochite kita Tsun ikka aru/Yorochiku ne."*
"He/hello/We/are the Tsun family, who just moved here/Nice to meet you."
Daughter/Tsururin:
*"Hikkoshi soba aru ne."*
"It's a noodle for the greeting of moving."

(Akira Toriyama, *Dr. Surampu* 5, p. 173)

These Chinese-style accented Japanese expressions were often found in earlier manga. Let us consider examples from Osamu Tezuka's *Mitsume ga Tōru* (The Three-Eyed One) Vol. 5 "Ankoku Gai no Purinsu" (The Prince of the Underworld), first published in 1976 (Showa 51) in *Shūkan Shōnen Magajin* (Weekly Boy's Magazine), and Koremitsu Maetani's *Robotto Santō-hei* (Private Robot) (serialized in *Shōnen Kurabu* (Boy's Club) from 1958 (Showa 33) to 1962 (Showa 37)).

*"Soko no onna koko e koi/purinsu (prince) no aite o suru yoroshii/Omae purinsu no*

Figure 6-1 Dr. *Surampu* 5
(p.173 ©Akira Toriyama)

*o-me ni tomatta <u>aru</u> zo.*"
"You there, girl, come here/Attend to the prince/You have caught the prince's attention."

(Osamu Tezuka, *Mitsume ga Tōru* 10, p. 149)

"*Taichō taihen <u>aruyo</u>/Nihongun ga kita <u>aru</u>.*"
"This is bad, Captain/The Japanese army has come."

(Koremitsu Maetani, *Robotto Santō-hei,* p. 203)

We can find more examples of the same type of language in novels by Yasutaka Tsutsui and Jun'ya Yokota.

Let us refer to this type of Japanese with these special accents as <*Aruyo* Language>, where *aru* is an existential verb and *yo* is a sentence-final particle of affirmation. Below are the features of this language:

1. The expressions *aru* or *aru yo* (affirmative) and *aru ka* (interrogative) are directly attached to the predicate at the end of the sentence. In rare cases, *aru na* may also be attached. As a variation, *arimasu* may also be attached.

2. The expression *yoroshi(i)* is attached to the predicate verb at the end of the sentence to express a command or a request.

3. The particle *o* (sometimes *ga*) is often omitted. For example, "*sake ϕ nomu aru ka*" (Would you like some drink?).

*Perception to Aliens*

Figure 6-2 *Mitsume ga Tōru* 10
(p. 149 ©Tezuka Production)

The grammatical features in the first and second items above do not exist in native Japanese and show characteristics of a pidgin language. A pidgin language refers to a hybrid language created so that two speakers of different languages can communicate with one another. This type of language, similar to the concept of a lingua franca, was frequently used in ports, trade settlements, and plantations. The characteristics of pidgin language include changes in the grammatical features of the original language, followed by a collapse and simplification. In the case of <*Aruyo* Language>, the rich conjugations of the predicate and a plethora of auxiliary groups in Japanese are dramatically simplified and substituted by the affixation of *aru* (*yo*/*ka*).

In manga, speakers of <*Aruyo* Language> are often attributed with certain characteristics visually as well as according to personality:

External Characteristics
• The character has a mustache, most often a thin one.
• The character wears a Chinese hat and clothes.
• The character's hair is styled in a queue.
• Sometimes, the character is extremely overweight.

Personality Characteristics
• The character has a dubious air about him/her (e.g., conducts illegal business).
• The character is calculative and miserly.
• The character is somewhat stupid.
• The character is timid and cowardly.

Figure 6-3 *Robotto Santō-hei*
(p. 203 ©Koremitsu Maetani)

The external characteristics can reflect the older customs of prewar China. For example, the character is portrayed as an overweight Chinese person because in China, corpulence is considered to be a testament of wealth. On the other hand, in regard to personality traits, the characters cannot be said to inspire much respect (however, in newer works, the stereotype of Chinese = Kung-Fu is combined). This seems to reflect the prejudice that the Japanese had against the Chinese in the past. Prejudice, as previously shown, is an emotional manifestation of stereotypes. This prejudice is combined with the incomplete and corrupted Japanese of <*Aruyo* Language> to create the image of a strange Chinese character.

Here, the following questions arise:

**ENIGMA 13**
Did the Chinese actually speak <*Aruyo* Language>? What exactly is the origin of <*Aruyo* Language>?

*Perception to Aliens*

ENIGMA 14

Through what process did <*Aruyo* Language> become associated with the image of a strange Chinese character?

Before answering these questions, let use consider Japanese language spoken by the non-Japanese (or non-human).

## 2. Categorization of the *Ijin* (Alien)

The role languages examined up to this point have included characters that more or less fit within the framework of the modern Japanese society, such as the elderly, males, and females. Let us now examine the *ijin* (alien) , who is considered as not a contemporary Japanese from the beginning, in more detail and consider the type of role languages assigned to them. <*Aruyo* Language> considered earlier is nothing but a language spoken by the *ijin*. Here, we enumerate the diversity of the *ijin*.

Foreigners: Westerners (Whites), Blacks, Chinese, Native Americans (American Indians)

People from previous eras: Samurais, nobles

Non-humans: Gods, ghosts, fairies, aliens, robots

In addition, some characters can be both foreign and from the past, such as "warriors in medieval Europe." How are the languages of these people described? For example, in the case of samurais, there is <Samurai Language>—a language with a historical ground that is considered to be a part of the Japanese language. However, in the case of the others, most of them do not speak the Japanese language nor have we ever heard them speak the Japanese language. Here, the methods utilized are broadly divided into two types: language projection and the adoption of pidgin language.

## 3. Language Projection

### Various Types of Projections

First, let us discuss language projection. For example, in the case of medieval European warriors, <Samurai Language> is often projected. The following example is the speech of Sir Oliver, a 14th-century French feudal lord.

> "Shikashi—*Mā yoi, kokode kojirete wa moto mo ko mo nai. Washi to shite wa, arankagiri no reisetsu to keii o motte, kenja dono no jogen o motomeru nomi ja. Sonata wa kashikoi. Mata, washi wa sonata no eichi o ōi ni hitsuyō to shite oru. —to, koyatsura wa nukashioru.*"

> (Michael Crichton (author), Akinobu Sakai (translation),
> *Taimurain* (Timeline), p. 352)

114

"But come, come, let us not quarrel. With all courtesy and respect, I seek your counsel," Oliver said. "You are wise, and I have much need of wisdom—so these worthies tell me."

(Michael Crichton, *Timeline*, Kindle version, No. 3779)

In reality, Heian-era nobles supposedly spoke in a classical style, such as *"Kyō wa ame nari"* (It is raining today), as seen in *Genji Monogatari* (The Tale of Genji). However, in novels and manga, the manner of speaking is often *"Kyō wa ame de ojaru"* (It is raining today). *Ojaru* is a term that was used among commoners of Kyoto from the end of the Muromachi period to the beginning of the Edo period (around 1600), and this was projected onto the language of the nobles. The origin of <*Ojaru* Language> of the nobles, as a type of role language, is not yet known, but it probably emerged due to the influence of *kabuki*. Finally, regarding ghosts and gods who spoke <Elderly Male Language> or written language, it can also be considered as a type of language projection.

### Black people and <Rural Language>
Another example of language projection that immediately comes to mind is the language of black slaves before their emancipation in America. When black people characters appear, <Rural Language> of the Tōhoku region (northeastern Japan) is often used. It is unclear how such usage emerged, but we can see how it is applied in Gakudō Miura's "Kuroi Ijin" (published in *Shōnen Kurabu* (Boy's Club) in 1929 (Showa 4)). Here, <Rural Language> is spoken by the black man from the village, whereas Būkā (another black people), who is the only person in the village who has finished elementary school, speaks <Standard Language>.

*"Yā kaeri nasatta ka, tsukarete iru tokoro o sumanē ga, sassoku kiite moraimasu bē. Kesa kara uchi no ushi no chichi ga kyū ni denaku natta daga douiu mon deshō kanā?"*

"So, you've returned? Sorry to bother you when you're tired, but I need to ask you now. This morning our cow stopped giving milk all of a sudden, now why do you think that is?"

*"Oi oi deshabaruna. Ora ga saki ni kita de nē ka. Washi no o hitotsu kiite kudasē. Uchi no musume no byōki ga chito ayashii de majinai o hitotsu tanomarete moraitai de na."*

"Hey! Don't push your way in. I was here first. Please listen to me for a moment. Our daughter's illness is sort of strange; please give us a magic spell."

*"Ora no wa sonna kechi nanode nē. Jiken ga ōkii da. Omēsan mo ki ga tsuite iru bē ga ototsui atari kara nishi no sora ga gōgi ni akai de shinpai de nannē. Are wa ittai nanno shirase danbē?"*

"Mine is nothing so small. It's a big problem. Maybe you have noticed too, but since the day before yesterday, the western sky has been very red, and it's worrisome. What kind of omen is that?"

*Atama no hageta ojīsan ya funbetsu zakari no ojisan tachi ga, majime na kao de konna koto o tanomini kitari kiki ni kitari surundesu.*

The bald old men and the middle-aged men come and ask these questions and make these requests with serious looks on their faces.

*"Sonna koto wa boku niwa wakaranai yo. Ushi no koto nara Jūi to sōdan shi tamae. Byōnin wa isha no tokoro e tsurete iku sa. Tentai no mondai wa semmon no gakusha ga aru ja naika. Boku wa shōgakkō no sotsugyōsei da. Sonna koto wa wakaranai yo."*

"I don't know about any of that. For the cow, ask a veterinarian. For the sick girl, take her to a doctor. Surely there are specialists for matters of the sky as well? I'm an elementary school graduate. I know nothing about such things.

(Gakudō Miura, "Kuroi Ijin" (Black Great man), p. 445)

Based on this setting, two aspects are apparent. One is that <Standard Language> is considered to be the language of educated people, whereas <Rural Language> is considered to be the language of the uneducated. The second aspect is that, when we read this story, we first identify ourselves with Būkā. In other words, here as well, <Standard Language> is the hero's language that functions as a "yardstick" for the reader's self-identification. Furthermore, other black people in the story are relegated to supporting and background characters through their use of <Rural Language>.

When white person appears in a story, it is customary to assign <Standard Language> to them. The following excerpt is a conversation between Scarlett O'Hara and Dilcey, her black maid, from the novel *Gone with the Wind* (translation: Yasuo Okubo).

Figure 6-4 "Kuroi Ijin" (Drawing by Hiroshi Mineda)
(Gakudō Miura, "Black Great man", p. 445)

116

"Arigatou, Dirushii. Okāsan ga kaettara, mata sōdan shitemiru wa"
"Arigatou gozēmasu. Ojōsama, dewa, oyasumi nasēmashi."
(Margaret Mitchell(author)/Yasuo Okubo (translation),
*Kaze to tomo ni Sarinu* (Gone with the Wind), p. 80)
"Thank you Dilcey, we'll see about it when Mother comes home."
"Thankee, Ma'm. I gives you a good night," said Dilcey ......
(*Gone with the Wind*, Warner Books, Inc., 1993, p. 66)

Here as well, the following schemas are established:

White people: educated, dominant, object of the reader's self-identification = <Standard Language>

Black people: uneducated, dominated, excluded from the reader's self-identification = <Rural Language>

Indeed, through the repeated portrayals of certain characters, it is possible for such characters to be the object of self-identification even if they speak <Rural Language>. However, it would be impossible to change the reactions of readers during their first reading of the work. In sum, this type of language projection is established by overlapping the Japanese people's perceptions of <Rural Language> with their perceptions of black people.

## 4. The Prototype and Development of *<Aruyo* Language>

### Use of Pidgin Language

Let us now discuss the use of pidgin language. A typical example of pidginized Japanese language is *<Aruyo* Language>. There are often other extremely simplified varieties of Japanese as well as grammatically and phonetically corrupted Japanese that appear as role languages. It can be said that the speakers of these role languages are, in some sense, given personalities of the *ijin* (aliens). For example, American Indians (Native Americans) have been stereotyped as using pidgin language in phrases such as "*Hakujin, uso tsuki, indian uso tsukanai*" (Whites, liars, Indians, no lie). This type of language was established as their role language through the translation of their pidginized English in American cowboy films into Japanese. This manner of speaking contains pidgin characteristics such as omission of particles and simplification of predicate conjugations.

Furthermore, a type of language often seen in recent children's animation is the addition of certain endings at the end of an utterance. For example, fairies called Mōguri (or Moogles) that appear in the video game "Final Fantasy IX" (first sold in 2000 (Heisei 12), SquareSoft) attach the ending kupo, as in "*Nani ka goyō kupo?*" (What is the matter with you?), at the end of a sentence. Let us call such endings that are given to specific characters as "character endings." Utterances, such as "*Sessha ga iku nari*" (I am going) by Korosuke, a with a samurai robot, in Fujiko F. Fujio's *Kiteretsu Daihyakka* (Fantasmo Encyclopedia) ((1974 (Showa 49)

*Perception to Aliens* 117

to 1977 (Showa 52)), serialized in *Kodomo no Hikari* (The Light of Children)), can also be considered to be a type of character ending. Character endings can easily depict characters that are not humans such as aliens, fairies, and robots. Hence, they are frequently used in children's manga.

Character endings are artificially created pidgins that do not exist in the real world. However, on close observation of their inner workings, it is apparent that they match <*Aruyo* Language>. That is, the utterance with a character ending becomes <*Aruyo* Language> once the character ending is replaced by *aru*. In the following section, we will examine the historical circumstances that led to the emergence of <*Aruyo* Language> and how it became associated with the image of strange Chinese characters.

## Yokohama Dialect

In 1879 (Meiji 12), a book titled *Exercises in the Yokohama Dialect* revised by the Bishop of Homoco was published in Yokohama (second edition, Japan Gazette Office, Yokohama (as per Makoto Yanaike's indication)). The title mentions the word "dialect," but it is written in the style of a language study book that presents the forms of pidgin language in the Yokohama settlement at that time. The preface mentions that the Ollendorff system was used, which is a bilingual format applied in the majority of language study books published in Europe during that time (according to a survey by Nina Yoshida). The reviser's name "Bishop of Homoco" is a false name, and his real name is presumed to be F. A. Cope (See Kinsui 2014 *Kore mo Nihongo Aruka? Ijin no Kotoba ga Umareru Toki* (Is this also Japanese?: The Time When Alien's Language), Iwanami Publisher).

In the second edition, a plausible book review newspaper article is cited, but it is made up for the most part. Originally, as one can understand from the quotes mentioned later, the spellings of "Yokohama Dialect" themselves are appropriated spellings of English words that are extremely false sounding. In other words, it is a publication that, on the whole, appears to have been written for the purpose of a parody.

However, if one examines the sentences in the book, they certainly seem to be the prototype of <*Aruyo* Language> of today. Let us consider some examples:

- Is I Ic ill?
  Am buy worry arimas?                                          (p. 20)
- What time is it?
  Nanny Tokey arimasu?
- It is nine
  Cocoanuts arimas                                             (p. 21)
- No, you had better send it up to the Grand Hotel
  Knee jew ban Hotel maro maro your-a-shee                      (p. 29)

At the end of *Exercises in the Yokohama Dialect* of the second edition, there is a chapter on "Nankinized Nippon" (Japanese with a Nanjing accent). According to the preface, this chapter is said to have been attached in response to the demand of Ng Choy, the Hong Kong Attorney General. This can be said to be one variety of pidgin Japanese spoken in the Chinese community. Some additional examples are as follows:

- Twice two are four.
  Fu'tarchi fu'tarchi yohtchi aloo.
- I should like to borrow 500 Yen from you if you have them.
  Anatta go-hakku lio aloo nallaba watark-koo lack'shee high shacko dekkeloo alloo ka. (p. 32)

Furthermore, the following entry is found in Senzō Mori's *Meiji Tokyo Itsubunshi* (Meiji Tokyo History from Unknown Writings) (Toyo Bunko, 1969). It is an excerpt from an 1881 (Meiji 14) article (P. C. from Akihiro Okajima).

*Gaikoku-jin no nihongo (dō-jō)*
"*Shinbashi geigi hyōbanki*" *niwa, "gaikokujin" mo nakamairi shite, "kono ko tai-san beppin <u>arimasu</u>. Odori, shamisen, minamina yoroshii. Watashi, itsudemo doru*

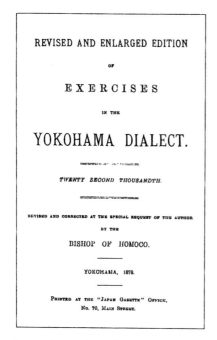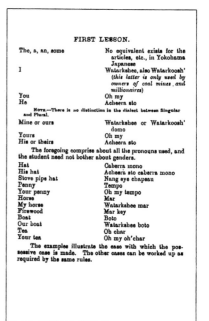

Figure 6-5  Bishop of Homoco (1879) *Exercises in the Yokohama Dialect*, the second edition
(Kaiser, Stephan (ed.) (1995) *The Western Rediscovery of the Japanese Language* 5)

*shinjō arimasu" nado to, katakoto no nihongo o shabette iru.*
In "Yokohama geigi Hyōbanki," "foreigners" are part of the group, saying things like, "This girl is very beautiful. Dance, *shamisen*, everything is wonderful. I will give money anytime," in broken Japanese.

(Senzō Mori, "Foreigner's Japanese," p. 89)

In this example, the speaker seems to be an American. Thus, we can see that the use of <*Aruyo* Language> was not limited to the Chinese (However, it is assumed that the language would naturally have a different intonation when spoken by Westerners or by the Chinese). Also, "*taisan*" is a word meaning 'a log' and 'very' and appeared in the pidgin language at the time.

### The *Arimasu* and *Aru* Types
When we compare the "Yokohama Dialect" and "Nankinized Japanese," the ending used is mostly *arimasu* in the former, but the ending used is *aru* in the latter. For the time being, let us refer to the former and the latter as *arimasu* type of pidgin language and *aru* type of pidgin language, respectively. Forms of both types subsequently appear in the portrayal of the Chinese. The examples from manga cited earlier in the beginning of the chapter are all the *aru* type of pidgin language. The next example is a transcribed document released around the year 1922 (Taisho 11) from "Kantan" (Takarazuka Shōjo Kagekidan (Takarazuka Girls Revue Company)). Here, the *arimasu* type of pidgin language and the expression *nomu yoroshi* (please drink) are used.

(1) (Prologue) *"Kono kageki Mukashi mukashi ōmukasi, o-hanashi arimasu. Tokoro, Shina, Kantan, Mei roshō, seinen arimasu, kono hito shusse shitai arimasu, kyoeishin arimasu, hyakushō kirai arimasu* (Vocal solo) *"Hito no yo no mijikashi ya ware seiun no kokorozashi moyuru tomo yo hakunetsu no, honō to narite tadarakasu, Roshō no chishio wakakushite, rōka tachite utsu mune ya, ta ka sadame ken denpu no ko, ta ka sadame ken suki toru*? (Prologue) *"Seinen Roshō tada shusse shitai arimasu, koshi no kama no te mou iya arimasu, soko ni sennin arimasu, kusuri no sake, anata nomu yoroshi, makura kashimasu, oyasumi nasai, Roshō san, sake you koto taisan arimasu, tsui utouto*
(Synopsis) In Handan of ancient China, there was a young man named Rosei. He was a farmer but hated farming and dreamed of making it big. One day, a sage appeared, made Rosei drink liquor with medicine in it, and lent him a pillow.

("Kantan", p. 67)

In Ryōtarō Shiba's 1970 (Showa 45) essay titled "Hanashi no Kuzukago: Bushi to Kotoba" (Trash box of tales: Samurai and their Language) (*Ōru Yominomo* (All Esseys), September 1970 issue), we have the following part, which is the *arimasu* type of pidgin language.

*"Sayō de gozaru* (It is so)."
That is what warriors say in *kabuki* and the like. Also, this is what they say when

warriors appear in Edo *rakugo*, in an overly serious tone, for example, samurai in "Ganryu-jima," boasting of their martial arts prowess when picking a fight with retired warriors on the same ship say,

"*Sonkō mo ryōtō o tabasande orareru nara, muza to te o tsukanete sessha ni kirare mo itasumai. Sa, shinken no shōbu o sasshai.*" (Should you point your swords at me, you won't be able to cut me with ease. Come now, let's have a real fight) (Enshō, Complete Works). Speaking with "*sessha, sayō, sonkō, shikaraba*" was likely a standard language for warriors of the Edo period. However, not all samurai used this sort of language, for example, just as "<u>*Sore, pokopen arimasu*</u> (that is not useful)" would evoke a stereotypical Chinese person, using the above sort of language in the world of performing arts would make anyone immediately understand, "Aha, that was a samurai." That said, while it seems that real individual samurai didn't speak in this literary fashion on a daily basis, it also doesn't seem to be completely fictional. Teasing out the difference is a complex matter.

(Ryōtarō Shiba, "Hanashi no Kuzukago: Bushi to Kotoba", p. 122)

**Perception of the Chinese**

As stated earlier, the *aru* and *arimasu* types of pidgin language that appeared in the literature around 1880 (around Meiji 10) was also associated with the Chinese, with some evidence of its use by Westerners. Conversely, in the 1922 (Taisho 11) performance of Takarazuka Shōjo Kagekidan (Takarazuka Girls Revue Company), an *arimasu* type of pidgin language was used to actively represent the Chinese. Regarding the changes in this period, it is necessary to explore documents for further evidence, but <*Aruyo* Language> (as a role language) had probably been established by the Taisho period.

Regarding the association of <*Aruyo* Language> with the image of "the strange Chinese," it is important to explore this aspect in more detail. However, it is not difficult to imagine that, in the background, there were probably significant changes in the relations between China and Japan during the Meiji period. From ancient times to the early modern period, China was a nation far superior to Japan in all aspects, including political, cultural, religious, and military, and the Japanese people must have associated the Chinese with a sense of reverence. However, with the defeat of China in the Opium War (1840–1842), the Japanese perception of China had dramatically changed.

In addition, the Sino–Japanese War from 1894 (Meiji 27) to 1895 (Meiji 28) determined the Japanese perception of China in the modern period. The Sino–Japanese War was fought between China (Qing Dynasty) and Japan regarding the control of Korea, and it was the first war that modern Japan experienced. After its victory, Japan became the so-called oppressor country against China, which resulted in Japan's imperialist aggression against Asian countries, such as mainland China, the Korean Peninsula, and Taiwan. Subsequently, the ethnic tensions between Japan and China and between Japan and Korea also increased, leading to the Japanese tendency of perceiving Asia with disdain. For example, in *The Graphic* published April 13, 1895 (Meiji 28), A sketch "the scene of Tokyo street, children who is mocking Chinese men" by Georges Ferdinand Bigot appears.

Perception to Aliens                                                                 121

**From *Norakuro***
Suihō Tagawa's manga series *Norakuro*, from the 1931 (Showa 6) *Norakuro Nitōsotsu* (*Second-class Private Norakuro*) to the 1941 (Showa 16) *Norakuro Tankentai* (*Norakuro Expedition*), was a highly popular series published by the *Shōnen Kurabu* (Boy's Club) magazine. It continued to be written for various magazines after the World War II and was eventually made into a television anime series. The manga begins with a black stray dog named Norakuro, who joins the dog army as a second-class private. Even though he fails repeatedly and makes numerous mistakes, he has no maliciousness and is loved by everyone. In some instances, he achieves success and is noted for his distinguished service. Originally, Norakuro was supposedly conceived as a lovable character that child readers could relate to. However, halfway through the series, he was gradually transformed into an earnest, valiant hero in response to the militaristic atmosphere.

There are two scenes in *Norakuro* where one can see the use of <*Aruyo* Language>. Both reflect the feelings of the Japanese toward this language usage. The first is the use of <*Aruyo* Language> in the 1932 (Showa 7) series *Norakuro Jōtōhei* (*First-class Private Norakuro*) by *dojin* (natives) of the South Pacific. These "pirates" purchase weapons and ammunition from smugglers, but in the end, they are all killed by Norakuro, who accidently witnesses the scene.

Figure 6-6 Georges Bigot "Tōkyō no gaitō no kōkei: Chūgoku kyoryūmin o azakeru nihon no kodomotachi [from his sketches]"

(Among children, there was an increase in the behavior of despising the Qing Chinese) The Graphic, April 13, 1895. (*Bigō Sobyō Korekushon* 3, Meiji no Jiken (Bigot's Sketches Collection 3, Accidents in Meiji Era), p.75. Iwanami Shoten, 1989.

Smuggler:
*"Zenbu de nijūman da"*
"That's 200,000 yen in total."
Pirates:
*"Takai <u>aru</u> / Makeru <u>aru</u>"*
"That's expensive/Make it cheaper."
Smuggler:
*"Makaran yo"*
"Not happening."
Pirates:
*"Teppō bakudan takusan <u>aru na</u>."*
"There are a lot of guns and bombs, huh."
Pirates:
*"Shūchō katte kimashita ze."*
"Chief, I bought everything."
Boss of Pirates:
*"Kayaku ko e shimatte oke."*
"Keep it in a munitions depot."

(Suihō Tagawa, *Norakuro Jōtōhei*, p. 813)

Here, although the pirates use <Standard Language> among themselves, they use <*Aruyo* Language> when speaking to the smugglers. This is very similar to the conditions associated with using the pidgin language. In other words, here, the pidgin language is treated as a provisional language for international trade and is not the native language of the pirates.

Another example is from *Norakuro Buyūdan* (Tale of Heroic Exploits of Norakuro) written in 1938 (Showa 13). Here, the full-scale war between the fierce dog army and the pig army is depicted. Based on the portrayal of the battlefield, one can clearly see that it is an imitation of the Chinese mainland. In other words, the dog army = the Japanese army and the pig army = the Chinese army.

Pig 1:
*"Tatakattemo makeru ni kimatteru."*
"Even if we fight, we're doomed to lose."
Pig 2:
*"Sonna wakaranai taichō wa yattsukeru <u>yoroshi</u>."*
"We can do away with such a clueless captain."
Pig 3:
*"Kora / Taichō no iu koto kikan ka."*
"Hey!/Are you disobeying the captain?"
Pig 4:
*"Kono aida ni nigedase."*
"Let's run away while they are occupied."
Pig 5:
*"Mukō no jinchi ga anzen <u>aru yo</u>."*

"The encampment on that side is safe."

(Suihō Tagawa, *Norakuro Buyūdan*. p. 137)

Here, the fierce dog army is depicted as fighting valiantly as opposed to the pig army, which is depicted as a useless army that is weak and selfish. In addition, the pig army uses <*Aruyo* Language> amongst themselves after which this originally provisional and incomplete pidgin language is established as a characteristic of the weak pig army. Based on the pigs' appearance and lack of abilities as an army and their linguistic characteristic of using the pidgin language, the pig army is depicted as a pathetic army that deserves to lose. These linguistic aspects, in particular, make it difficult for readers to identify with the pig army.

*Norakuro Buyūdan* was written in 1938, one year after the Marco Polo Bridge Incident and the Shanghai Incident. The Sino-Japanese War had become a full-scale war; in Japan, the negative mood against China was increasing. The portrayal of *Norakuro Buyūdan* clearly reflects the Japanese perception of the Chinese based on these social circumstances.

## 5. Beyond Role Language

Finally, regardless of whether the role language was a symbol of the *ijin* (aliens), a type of language projection or a type of pidgin language, it functions as a means of differentiation from the targeted <Standard Language> (speaker = reader's self-identification) and became linked with prejudice ultimately.

Role languages are, in general, easy to understand and instantly convey the image of the user to the recipient. Due to these aspects, they are not only used in children's works or "B-grade works," but they can naturally be incorporated into noteworthy works. Without role languages, works in the Japanese language would not be possible. Therefore, with new conditioning and repeated activation, role languages continue to be reinforced.

Our knowledge of Japanese is, in one way, that of a "virtual Japanese," which is an accumulation of role languages. In general, we live without any doubt regarding this notion. Furthermore, <Standard Language> is positioned at the center of this virtual Japanese. Virtual Japanese is a hierarchical structure based on <Standard Language> and its deviations.

The knowledge of role languages is essential for the Japanese people living in Japan, but it is also important to be aware that knowledge of role languages can hide the diversity and richness of the real Japanese language, thus impoverishing its potential and that also allows prejudice and discrimination to naturally emerge. For example, it is important to know that <*Aruyo* Language> was used to represent the Chinese during a time that was ripe with prejudice. If we see examples of the use of the role languages in the present-day manga, there seems to be no malice or inhibition. However, it is important to think about the feelings of those portrayed who are depicted as those unable to speak anything other than an incomplete Japanese language or pidgin language. Imagine the feelings of watching the depiction of a Japanese individual in American films as short, bespectacled characters that speak a strange, heavily accented "Japanglish."

Therefore, examining the mechanisms of virtual Japanese and sometimes deconstructing it are important to gain a better understanding of the real Japanese language. I believe that this approach is precisely the way to enrich and make the Japanese language a highly productive.

*Appendix*

# Modern Japanese "Role Language" (*Yakuwarigo*): Fictionalised Orality in Japanese Literature and Popular Culture

## 1. Introduction

A newly emerging field in Japanese linguistics examines the connection between spoken language features and the depiction of character types in fiction, popular culture (e.g., *manga* [comic books] and *anime* [animated cartoons]), the Internet, and beyond. Often in Japanese fiction and popular culture, a character's vocabulary and grammar vary greatly according to the person's attributes (gender, age, social status, occupation, region of residence or birthplace, appearance, personality, etc.). Consequently, one can infer the type of role portrayed from the character's vocabulary and grammar. Examples of established character types in popular culture, associated with particular linguistic features, include the elderly male, the young lady of good family, and the Chinese person. Their fictional utterances often make these established character types easily recognisable in Japanese culture, even if actual people fitting these character types are unlikely to produce such utterances in real life. Let us look at a few sample variations of a phrase meaning 'Yes, I know that' in (1). The hypothetical speakers of (1a) to (1c) are an elderly male, a female, and a macho male, respectively.

(1)  a. *Sō-ja*      *washi ga*    *shit-teoru-zo*
        yes-COPULA I      NOM  know-ASPECT-PARTICLE

      b. *Sō-yo*                     *atashi ga* *shit-teiru-wa*
        yes-[ZERO COPULA]-PARTICLE I     NOM     know-ASPECT-PARTICLE

      c. *Sō-da*    *ore ga*    *shit-teru-ze*
        yes-COPULA I    NOM know-ASPECT-PARTICLE

(After Kinsui, 2010: 51)

In these examples,[1] the respective combinations of the copula (i.e., *ja*, [zero copula+] particle *yo*, or *da*), first-person pronoun (i.e. *washi*, *atashi*, or *ore*), aspect form (i.e. *teoru*, *teiru*, or *teru*) and final particle, *shūjoshi* (i.e. *zo*, *wa*, or *ze*) correspond to the character types portrayed (elderly male, female, macho male). These sets of spoken language features (e.g. vocabulary and grammar) and phonetic characteristics (e.g. intonation and accent patterns), associated with particular character types, are called *yakuwarigo* ("role language"), a term coined by Kinsui (2003: 205).

Variations in spoken language, produced according to character type, are not exclusively Japanese; for examples from other languages, see Section 4. In order to help non-Japanese readers understand Japanese role language, we provide similar examples from English below. Comparing role languages in Japanese and English, Yamaguchi (2007) mentions four methods of creating role languages in English: using eye dialect; using stereotyped pidgin varieties; manipulating personal pronouns; and phonological manipulation. Eye dialect uses nonstandard spelling to represent nonstandard pronunciation, including regional and foreign accents. A stereotyped pidgin variety, for instance, dropping articles and *be* verbs, might give an impression of foreign-accented speech. One can also create a role language by replacing the first- and second-person pronouns with the actual names of the speaker and the addressee in the third person, as in '*Dobby has known it for months, sir. Harry Potter must not put himself in peril*,' when Dobby is talking to Harry Potter. Phonological manipulations can represent a baby-talk and/or onomatopoetic effects, e.g. '*I tawt I taw a puddy tat*' instead of '*I thought I saw a pussy cat*' in *Looney Tunes*.

Some role languages may sound quite different from actual speech. However, except for purely imaginary ones (see Section 2.4), most role languages are linguistic stereotypes rooted in non-fictional language usage, whose origins can be traced, as will be shown in Section 3. A good example is elderly male language, where the audience would easily recognise it as such, while being aware that an elderly male would not normally speak 'elderly male' role language, although some features of that role language might be found in real speech. Kinsui has traced the origins of some role languages, including elderly male language, examining historical non-fiction as well as fiction (Kinsui, 2003, 2007b, 2008b). Since Kinsui's initial publication (2003), the study of role language has grown to include an edited volume of papers (Kinsui, 2007a). Role language research now includes studies on 'character-associated endings', *kyara-gobi* (i.e. copulas and particles that connote certain character types), usage on the Internet (e.g. Sadanobu, 2007; Sadanobu and Zhang, 2007). Non-writers' weblogs and electronic bulletin boards are a goldmine, not only for classic role languages, but also for somewhat looser types that are newly and often instantly invented by these bloggers (see Section 2.4).

The present study seeks to introduce non-Japanese readers to the expanding field of research on role language in Japanese. We will give an overview of this emerging research field, drawing on key literature (Kinsui, 2003, 2008b) and related research in literature, popular culture, and Internet resources in Japanese and other languages. Not only does Japanese have a large variety of first-person pronouns and endings (copulas and final particles), it also allows great flexibility in inventing new endings (e.g. Sadanobu, 2007; Sadanobu and Zhang, 2007). All of these features contribute to the continual development of existing role languages and the creation of new ones in Japanese. Through examination of role language and its origins in Japanese, we will show how it is used to characterise minor characters in a story in order to highlight the main characters, which require

*Modern Japanese "Role Language"* (Yakuwarigo)    127

more elaborate portrayal. Some established character types will be analysed and cross-linguistic studies of role language in Japanese and other languages will be reviewed. Similarities and differences across languages will also be noted as well as possible problems role language pose for learners of Japanese. Throughout this paper, we will demonstrate how Japanese – a language with rich data from popular culture and Internet resources, as well as literary works – has much to offer in the development of research on role language, a type of fictionalised orality.

## 2. Some Key Concepts of Role Language

### 2.1 Formation of Role Language

As discussed in Section 3, the origin of role language can often be traced back to actual spoken language, except for purely imaginary varieties. From actual language usage, individuals acquire knowledge about the relationship between a particular variety of the language and its speakers, then categorise and reinforce this knowledge. What is important here is that this kind of knowledge does not remain with a particular individual; rather it disseminates among people and is shared by the community. When such conditions are met, role language becomes established as a linguistic stereotype and an effective communication tool. Role language will then begin circulating in fiction, which now becomes a means for the audience to acquire knowledge about role language. In this way, once established, role language self-perpetuates in fiction, regardless of reality. This process of knowledge propagation through fiction plays an extremely important role in the circulation, dissemination and maintenance of role language (Kinsui, 2008b: 207–208).

By contrast, we surmise that purely imaginary varieties (e.g. role languages of aliens or animals) have been invented at some point, then become current, and maintain themselves in popular culture.

### 2.2 Function of Role Language in Fiction

In order to give the audience immediate access to the storyline unfolding around the main characters, fiction creators make use of stereotypical characters and situations. Characters that are made to speak distinctive role languages (i.e. those not spoken in reality, e.g. elderly male language or stereotypical Chinese language) are not main characters. They are either assigned special roles in the story (e.g. an elderly male language speaker, a mentor, or a trickster) or are simply minor characters that quickly disappear from the scene (Kinsui, 2003: 50). In other words, role language is used to develop the story effectively, by relying on knowledge shared between the creator and the audience.

Role languages are not the only somewhat unnatural or unrealistic expressions found in fiction. Yamaguchi (2007) compares role language with artificial explanatory lines spoken by characters to describe the dramatic setting to the audience, or colourful and verbose gustatory expressions used in Japanese gourmet *manga*. Role language can be considered one type of communication device characteristic of fiction, used to convey the creator's intentions to the audience.

## 2.3 Role Languages versus Sociolects/Actual Speech Styles

How does one distinguish role language from sociolects or speech styles/registers observed in real life, especially as most role language origins can be traced back to actual language use? Role languages and sociolects are similar in that both are language varieties extracted from groups of speakers differing in extralinguistic variables or attributes, such as gender, age, social status, occupation and so forth. By contrast, differences between the two can be explained in terms of research methods, as shown below.

### 2.3.1 Data Sources and Methods of Data Analysis

Role language research primarily examines fictional data sources and describes the speech characteristics of the target character type. Since it originated specifically from interest in language usage in fiction, which is sometimes quite different from actual speech uttered by real people, role language research describes particular character types that are easily recognisable as such (e.g. elderly male language). In addition to fiction in print and other media, data sources now include those that are not fictional in a strict sense, such as Japanese subtitles or the dubbing of interviews with non-Japanese-speaking foreigners and verbal play observed in amateur weblogs (see Section 2.4). By contrast, sociolinguists scientifically observe and collect actual language usage data from informants belonging to groups differing in the social variable under investigation (e.g. gender), and quantify the frequencies of occurrences of the observed variants.

### 2.3.2 Extralinguistic Variables

In addition to the social variables usually examined in sociolinguistics, role language research can also consider such extralinguistic variables as appearance, personality, and even humanity (i.e. whether the character is human or non-human, even though aliens and animals would never speak human language in reality). For instance, in role language research, one can conduct a study on language varieties of good-looking versus physically unattractive characters, as portrayed in fiction. In fact, there are role languages for aliens and animals, neither of which are speakers of Japanese in reality.

## 2.4 Types of Role Language

It is estimated that the number of role language varieties may be as great as that of the types of extralinguistic variables, i.e. an unknown number. Most classic types of role language are those that normally sound very different from utterances produced by real people fitting the character types, including elderly male language and stereotypical Chinese speakers of Japanese. The origins of these types may be traced back to actual language used hundreds of years ago (see Sections 3.1 and 3.2). There are also truly unrealistic types, e.g. the talk of aliens or animals that do not have actual speaker models in reality.

Other types may exhibit a range of expressions from highly unrealistic to near-realistic because these categories can contain numerous subsets; regional dialect speakers and gendered types (see Sections 3.3 and 3.4) form part of this group.

*Modern Japanese "Role Language"* (Yakuwarigo)          129

For instance, Japanese female language can include a range of subtypes from the archaic (e.g. young lady from a good family) to something close to male language (see Section 3.4); somewhere between these two, a more realistic type may be observed, as in the example below:

(2)     *Ara  suteki-da-wa*
        oh     wonderful- COPULA-PARTICLE
        'Oh, that's wonderful!'

An utterance like this may be found in actual speech data as well as in fiction. Translations of non-Japanese speakers' speech in the form of dubbing or subtitling (e.g. interviews with foreign athletes) are another domain where role language is used.

Thus far we have primarily discussed role language in fiction. However, role language research now encompasses 'speech character types', *kyara,* that are created by adopting distinctive *kyara-gobi,* 'character-associated endings' (i.e. copulas and final particles that connote certain character types). In addition to fiction, such speech character types appear in everyday casual written communication data in amateur weblogs and electronic bulletin boards, where users can switch characters for amusement (e.g. Sadanobu, 2006, 2007; Sadanobu and Zhang, 2007). These types are different from the classic types noted above in that they can be instantly invented by non-professionals merely by manipulating the first-person pronouns and endings. These character types may also be nonhuman (e.g. animals and imaginary beings). In the sense that people can switch character types by adopting different sets of first person pronouns and character-associated endings, role language may be considered similar to speech style, as opposed to sociolect.

## 2.5  Role Language Research
Variation in spoken language among or within individuals, so-called styles or registers, have been investigated in traditional Japanese linguistics (e.g. Tanaka, 1999). Since this discipline studies actual language use, its object of study should also be the language actually in use. However, when investigating historical variation, traditional Japanese linguists have also relied on fictional data, such as novels, often uncritically, regardless of whether the data reflected real language in use or simply the expressive intent of the writer. In order to solve this problem, Kinsui (2008b: 206) strongly recommends introducing the concept of role language, which first treats these data in the context of communication between the creator and the audience in a code based on shared knowledge between the two parties, which is the role language of that particular character type.

From this perspective, re-examination of historical data in fiction, such as passages containing role language, can reveal that possible role language usage, distorted by the author's intention, may have been alleged to be historical fact in previous research. An example can be drawn from Takayama (2007) as cited in Kinsui (2008b: 211–212), where a passage containing utterances by learned men from *Genji Monogatari* by Murasaki Shikibu is reanalysed using a role language

130                                  *Appendix*

framework. From the viewpoint of Japanese language history, it has been pointed out that the learned men's utterances are full of Japanese renderings of Chinese words, reflecting the actual speech styles of intellectuals of that period. However, Takayama casts doubt on this traditional view, which tries to overly conform to historical fact. Instead, he suggests that the exaggerated use of Japanese renderings of Chinese words is a role language of this character type, used by the author to fit the stereotype of learned men. In this way, role language research can challenge traditional interpretations of fictional utterances and encourage researchers to reexamine alleged facts in the study of language history.

## 3. Analyses of Established Role Languages in Japanese Fiction

Let us analyse some established role languages in Japanese fiction. The first two subsections deal with classic examples of role language, namely elderly male language and the *aruyo* language of a Chinese-speaker; both have lexical markers and it is unlikely that people actually fitting these categories (i.e. an elderly Japanese male or a Chinese-speaker) speak these role languages. Section 3.3 discusses regional speaker types, which have most commonly been documented in other languages as well (see Sections 3.3 and 4). Lastly, gendered types, namely female and male role languages, will be discussed as examples of reinteracting with actual language usage and influenced by language ideology.

### 3.1   Elderly Male Language[2]

In Japanese *manga*, a bald or grey-haired elderly man, often with facial hair, or an elderly man with a cane, will almost always speak using a set of characteristic lexical items: the verb of existence *oru* (instead of *iru*); copula *ja*; negative *n*; and the first-person pronoun *washi*. Interestingly, it has been reported that there is no such lexical equivalent that connotes that the speaker is an elderly man in English (Yamaguchi, 2007) or Korean (Jung, 2007), although these languages also have stereotypes of elderly speech in terms of pragmatics or phonetics (e.g. choice of topics, turn-taking, phonetic characteristics). Let us look at an example of the English original and the Japanese translation of *The Hobbit* by J.R.R. Tolkien.

(3) a. "Of course!" said Gandalf. "…You are a very fine person, Mr. Baggins, and I am very fond of you …"

(Tolkien, 1982: 305)

   b. *"Mochiron-**ja**" to gandarufu ga īmashita. "… Anta wa, makotoni sutekina hito*
      of course-COPULA
   *nan-**ja** yo. Baginzu-dono. **Washi** wa, kokoro kara anta ga suki-**ja**…."*
   INFLECTION-COPULA       1st PERSON MALE            fond-COPULA

(Tolkien/Seta, 2000: 267)

Example (3) clearly shows two characteristics that make elderly male language a classic role language. Whereas Gandalf, an elderly male wizard, speaks Standard

English in the original version, the Japanese translation makes abundant use of elderly male language features, such as the copula *ja* and the first-person pronoun *washi*. If we were to remove these features and make him speak standard Japanese, it would ruin the atmosphere of the work completely. Therefore, the first important characteristic of Japanese elderly male language as role language is that it has typical lexical markers as well as pragmatic and phonetic characteristics.

In addition, in reality, speakers who use a variety of speech similar to elderly male role language are only found in western Japan (e.g. Okayama, Hiroshima), although fictional elderly male characters in Tokyo and elsewhere are likely to speak this variety. Table 1 compares elderly male language, Western Japanese and standard Japanese/Eastern Japanese.[3]

Table 1 Comparison of elderly male role language, Western Japanese and standard Japanese/Eastern Japanese

|  | Elderly male Language | Western Japanese | Standard Japanese/ Eastern Japanese |
|---|---|---|---|
| Affirmation | *kyō wa ame ja**<br>It is rainy today. | *kyō wa ame ja / ya*<br>It is rainy today. | *kyō wa ame da*<br>It is rainy today. |
| Negation | *shiran / shiranu†*<br>I do not know. | *shiran / shirahen*<br>I do not know. | *shiranai‡*<br>I do not know. |
| Existence of animate beings | *oru*<br>be | *oru*<br>be | *iru*<br>be |
| Progressive/Stative | *shitteoru /shittoru*<br>I know. | *shitteoru /shittoru*<br>I know. | *shitteiru /shitteru*<br>I know. |

*Elderly male characters may use *da* quite often and *ja* only occasionally, just to give a flavour of this character type. †*Shiranu*, as an alternative to *shiran*, is a classic Japanese form using a classic negative auxiliary *nu*. ‡In addition, *shiranē* is included in the Eastern Japanese dialect.

(After Kinsui, 2008b: 216–217)

Examination of this table reveals that, apart from some minor differences, elderly male language is similar to Western Japanese. In other words, the characteristics of elderly male language are regional, not age-related. Of course, it is highly unlikely that people (especially those outside Western Japan) would suddenly start speaking differently (i.e. a variety similar to Western Japanese) when they reach a certain age. Nevertheless, these unrealistic cases occur quite often in the world of comics; furthermore, Japanese readers find it quite natural. Because of these characteristics – the lexicon and the unreality of this variety – we can say that elderly male language is a classic example of role language.

The origins of elderly male role language were investigated by Kinsui (2008b: 218–228) through an extensive historical review of Japanese fiction and traced back to late 18th century in Edo (Tokyo), the capital of the Tokugawa shogunate. While the younger generation was more likely to speak the eastern dialect of Edo, the older educated generation tended to speak the more conservative, normative western dialect of Kyoto. Older learned males, such as scholars and medical

132                                    *Appendix*

doctors, would often use the more traditional dialect of the imperial capital and appear old-fashioned to younger speakers of the emerging and changing Edo dialect. This contrast between the rising younger Edo generation and the conservative older authorities was emphasised and stereotyped by writers of that period and incorporated into popular plays and novels. This resulted in the transformation of western dialectal characteristics into a fictional attribute of elderly male language.

### 3.2  Chinese Person Type: *Aruyo* Language

Another example of a role language with relatively solid characteristics that has developed independently from real spoken language is *aruyo* language, which is often associated with Chinese people (Kinsui, 2003: Ch. 6, 2007b, 2008a, 2008b). The following is an example:

(4)     *Yasui aru-yo,*              *hayaku kau yoroshi*
        cheap exist-PARTICLE     soon  buy good
        'It's cheap. You had better buy it now.'

Grammatical characteristics of *aruyo* language include: 1) use of *aru* immediately following the base form of a verb or adjective, or negative *nai*, or the stem of an adjective verb (*yasui aru* above); 2) use of *yoroshi(i)* after the base form of a verb (*kau yoroshi* above) as a request or command form.

The origin of *aruyo* language can be traced back to a pidgin Japanese that emerged in the Yokohama area at the end of the Edo period and beginning of the Meiji period. Yokohama was one of the ports opened under pressure from the West and settlements for foreign residents developed there. It is documented that pidgin Japanese was used in these port areas, especially in Yokohama, where Westerners and Chinese needed to communicate with Japanese nationals. While these expressions are actually observed in documents recording the language used in those days, they also started being used in novels and dramas. That *aruyo* language is based on pidgin Japanese makes it hard for readers to identify with characters speaking this role language (Kinsui, 2003: 200–201), which denotes it to use by minor character types.

Although international affairs in East Asia underwent drastic changes, *aruyo* language expressions have continued to be associated with Chinese characters in some films, *manga* and *anime* during the post-war period. The character types speaking *aruyo* role language were confined to suspicious or comical adult males. The use of this language evokes a sense of discrimination by Japanese toward Koreans, Chinese and Taiwanese, who lived under Japan's pre-war occupation. From the late 1970s to the 1980s, the character types speaking *aruyo* language in fiction (especially in *manga* and *anime*) shifted to young women dressed in traditional Chinese costumes (e.g. Shampoo in *Ranma 1/2* and Tsururin Tsun in *Dr. Slump*). However, this shift of speaker types for *aruyo* language should be regarded as a cultural preference, rather than a reflection of reality (Kinsui, 2008a, 2008b).

## Modern Japanese "Role Language" (Yakuwarigo) 133

### 3.3 Regional Dialect Speaker Types

Regional dialect speaker types are thought to be the most commonly found role language type in other languages (e.g. Hosokawa, 2010; Jung, 2005). Drawing on Kinsui (2003: Ch. 3), this subsection summarises accounts of regional dialects and standard Japanese as role languages in fiction.

The main character in Japanese fiction generally speaks standard Japanese, while minor characters are assigned regional dialect role languages. Growing up immersed in Japanese culture as native Japanese speakers, the audience can empathise with the standard-Japanese-speaking character (main character), irrespective of their own native dialects, while perceiving dialect-speaking characters as marginal. Kinsui (2003: Ch. 3) explains how standard Japanese became the language with which the audience identifies.

After the Edo period, the Meiji Government needed <Standard Language> to modernise the country. The dialect spoken in the Tokyo area was adopted as standard Japanese for several reasons, including: 1) it was the language of Tokyo, the centre of politics and business for centuries; 2) much of Japanese literature and the performing arts were written and performed in this dialect; 3) many intellectuals spoke this variety. As a result of adopting Tokyo dialect as the standard, Japanese speakers are now all educated in standard Japanese. Therefore, they can identify with standard Japanese speakers regardless of their own dialects. Newly developed mass media (i.e. print, visual, and audio media) played a significant role in establishing, disseminating, and reinforcing standard Japanese among speakers throughout the country.

On the other hand, various role languages in nonstandard Japanese were also produced and circulated via the mass media. Such dialects spoken by regional characters are often not consistent and are made up of a number of regional dialects (Kinsui, 2003: 54–58). As a playwright, Kinoshita (1982: 273) mentioned that he assembled rustic words from various regional dialects into a dialect for supporting roles (*fuhen hōgen* 'universal dialect'), as opposed to his main character's language, which is standard Japanese. This same phenomenon (i.e. making up a dialect based on multiple regional sources) has also been found in Korean (Jung, 2005) and German (Hosokawa, 2010). Cooley has also discussed the case of African American literary dialect, where a Caribbean variety 'constituted a prototype for other early African-American representations regardless of provenance' (1997: 53)

However, there is also an established role language of a regional dialect in Japanese, that of the Osaka or Kansai speaker (Kinsui, 2003: 81–101). He traces the origin and transformation of the images of this dialect speaker type from classic literature through modern mass media.

Ironically, perhaps, the role language of dialect speakers becomes most prominent in Japanese translations of foreign literature (Gaubatz, 2007; Inoue, 2003). Kinsui (2003: 184–187) remarks on the association between African American characters and Japanese translations using northeastern Japanese regional dialects. Gaubatz (2007) hypothesises that Nishida (1977) translated dialects in *The Adventures of Huckleberry Finn* into Japanese role language rather than any actual

134                                    *Appendix*

regional dialect. To confirm his hypothesis, Gaubatz elicited Japanese speakers' impressions of excerpts from Nishida's translation. The survey results revealed that Huck's language gave Japanese respondents an impression of a role language of somewhat rural origin, although they felt closer to Huck than to other characters, including Jim (speaking a stronger dialect in the Japanese rendering). Gaubatz states that, because role language is a tool in 'virtual reality', role languages are more effective in the translation of fiction than existing dialects, which are closely connected to the culture, geography and society where they are spoken.

Inoue (2003: 325–327) analyses a translation of *Gone with the Wind* from English into Japanese and highlights differences in translations of dialogue of Caucasian main characters versus those of African American supporting characters. While the dialogue of the Caucasian characters was translated into male and female role languages (see the next subsection for characteristics of these role languages), those of African American characters used 'ungrammatical forms, or some unspecified 'regional dialect,' at best'. In other words, we can say that these African American characters were deprived of gendered language in the Japanese rendering (setting aside the issue of whether gendered renderings are good or bad).[4]

To summarise these two subsections on speakers of foreign and regional accents, we would like to introduce an American study that has investigated linguistic stereotypes depicted by contrived accents in American animated films (Lippi-Green 1997: Ch. 5). Lippi-Green deals with accents as spoken in animated films. She conducted a large-scale survey of Disney feature films involving an investigation of a total of 371 characters. Among the relationships observed between the language varieties and attributes of the characters, the relationship between mainstream US or British accents and positive roles is comparable to that observed in Japanese role language studies, that is, main characters speak <Standard Language>.

### 3.4 Gendered Types: <Female Language> and <Male Language>

A significant body of research has considered gendered varieties of Japanese language to analyse how Japanese men and women speak differently (e.g. Ide and McGloin, 1990). However, the gendered role languages discussed here should be distinguished from the actual language used by men and women. At the same time, these gendered role languages are also transformed, being influenced by real social changes. Kinsui (2003: Ch. 4) states that male language developed from Edo (current Tokyo) language during the Edo period and was strongly influenced by *shosei kotoba* (male student language) during the Meiji period (see also Nakamura, 2005).

Modern female language was strongly influenced by *teyo dawa* language (schoolgirl language) used by female students during the Meiji period (Nakamura, 2004, 2007a). The following lines spoken by a female cat, Mikeko (Tortoiseshell) from *Wagahai wa Neko dearu* (1905) by Sōseki Natsume, illustrate examples of *teyo dawa* language:

(5)      *"Ara iyada, minna burasageru-**noyo**."*
                               hang-PARTICLE

*"Ara goshujin datte, myō nanone. Oshishō-san **dawa**. ..."*
mistress-HONORIFIC PARTICLE

*"Anata taihen iro ga warukut-**teyo**. ..."*
bad- PARTICLE

English Translation
"Really? Everyone hangs them [bells]."
"Oh, my master? That sounds strange. Mine is a mistress [of the two-stringed harp]. ..."
"Your colour looks very bad. ..."

(Natsume, 1961: 19)

Characteristics of *teyo dawa* language include: 1) *te(yo)* ending (as in the third line above); 2) final particle *wa* following the base form of a verb; 3) *wa* following a copula *da* or *desu* (second line); and 4) final particle(s) *no(yo)* following the verb (+ *masu*) (first line).

According to Nakamura (2004, 2007a), female students first used varieties of language that included male student language during the Meiji period. However, the use of male student language by female students started being criticised and was discouraged by the contemporary media. Then, in opposition to the roles assigned to females (i.e. *ryōsai-kenbo*, 'good wife and wise mother'), which were promoted in the single-sex education system newly introduced at the time, female students started *teyo dawa* language, which also came in for criticism by the media, who maintained that women should only use polite language. However, despite such criticisms and because writers started using this variety for female student characters in novels written in the *genbun icchi*⁵ ('speech and writing unified') style, *teyo dawa* language quickly spread among female students who read novels.⁶

Nakamura's view is that knowledge and evaluation of schoolgirl language were constructed by the media and fiction writers, and did not emerge naturally from female students' actual language use. What is also important is her statement that the speaker's knowledge of gendered language, constructed by media and fiction (i.e. language ideology), influences and constrains the speaker's actual language in the interaction between gendered language and actual language usage. Here, female student language is different from elderly male language: while knowledge of elderly male language can be used for language play when adopting the character type, it is unlikely to be associated with any specific language ideology.

Today, while such apparently feminine language has been disappearing in reality, it continues to exist as a language for imaginary young ladies of good family (*ojōsama*) in popular culture. The varieties of role language styles used by female characters in current popular culture can range from traditional female language to something like male language, depending on the genres, character attributes (especially age), creators, etc. Translations of foreign works are among the most conservative varieties, where female characters still tend to use exclusively female endings as in *teyo dawa* language. By contrast, male language can be used for female characters in some comics featuring girls of high school age. While this type of phenomenon may be viewed as a loosening of norms in contemporary society, we may also consider it an example of a new identity created by shifting existing language resources (see Nakamura, 2007b: 16).

## 4. Crosslinguistic Studies of Role Languages

Initial crosslinguistic studies conducted by Kinsui's research project members have been published in Japanese (Jung, 2005, 2007; Sadanobu, 2007; Sadanobu and Zhang, 2007; Yamaguchi, 2007), among which those published in Kinsui (ed.) (2007a) are accompanied by English summaries at the end of the collection. These initial studies inspired other linguists, resulting in embryonic crosslinguistic studies presented at the symposium held in March 2009 on *Yakuwari/Kyarakutā/Gengo* ('Roles/Characters/Languages) (Hosokawa, 2010; Kaneda, 2010).

As a Korean teacher of Japanese, Jung's motivation for studying role language in both languages was to apply her research findings to improve the translation quality of printed and visual media between the two languages (Jung, 2005, 2007). Sharing grammatical characteristics with Japanese, such as word order (SOV), and being an agglutinative language with final particles (see also Sadanobu, 2007), Korean has also developed a rich range of role languages. According to Jung's (2005) experimental results, despite existing role language varieties, it is possible that Korean speakers are less aware of the existence of role languages. Also, the character types portrayed by role language do not necessarily match between Korean and Japanese since role languages in the two languages apparently have different areas of expertise: whereas Japanese has finer gender distinctions, Korean distinguishes generational differences better. These languages' differences can result in loss of the original portrayal differences in the translation renderings, especially from Japanese into Korean. It should be noted that Korean also has a 'universal dialect', consisting of a combination of features from various regional dialects (see Section 3.3). As a follow-up study, in addition to having a third participant group of Japanese learners of Korean for the same experiment as in Jung (2005), Jung (2007) collected impressions of Korean regional dialects from native speakers and compared these with Japanese speakers' impressions of Japanese regional dialects from the 1980s (Inoue, 1980, 1983). Although the results of the impression comparisons are somewhat mixed, the kinds of knowledge obtained from this research are deemed useful for improving translation quality by matching the impressions of dialects used between the two languages.

Drawing on online communication data, Sadanobu and his colleagues have compared character-associated endings in Japanese with those in Korean (Sadanobu, 2007) and Chinese (Sadanobu and Zhang, 2007). Under *kyara-gobi* ('character-associated endings'), two subtypes are identified in Japanese, namely *kyara-kopyura*, 'character-associated copula' and *kyara-joshi*, 'character-associated particle'. A *kyara-kopyura* is a copula-like ending resembling an actual copula morphologically and phonologically, whereas a *kyara-joshi* does not resemble any copula, and occurs only sentence-finally. After identifying these two types in Chinese, Sadanobu and Zhang (2007) found a third type, *kyara-shūjoshi* 'character-associated final particle', which can occur where normal sentence-final particles can occur (i.e. phrase-finally), both in Japanese and Chinese. The first two types are also found in Korean (Sadanobu, 2007). Sadanobu (2007: 45–46) surmises that, in addition to enjoying the verbal play itself, language users may adopt such speech character types that display cuteness or comicality in order to smooth over the immediately following (face-threatening) communication (e.g. avoiding arguments, making requests, asking for forgiveness). Su (2009) also discusses the functions of verbal play in online communications. Switching character types became apparent in the 1980s, when characters were detached from individual fictional works and began circulating as autonomous objects in younger speakers' language (Kinsui, 2008b). It may also be connected with the propagation of typed language, such as mobile telephone text messages (Tanaka, 2007).

Illustrating four ways of creating English role languages, Yamaguchi (2007) states that English has disadvantages in producing new role languages freely compared with Japanese. As introduced in Section 1, English has the following four means of creating role languages: using eye dialect; using stereotyped pidgin varieties; manipulating personal pronouns; and phonological manipulation. Eye dialect in English can be compared to regional dialects in Japanese fiction; however, English eye dialect inevitably gives readers an impression of the speaker's lack of education due to nonstandard spelling, limiting the character type using that role language. Using pidgin English, for instance, dropping a set of lexical items including articles, *be* verbs, and the subject of the sentence, results in less diversity and productivity of role language in English. Replacing the first- and second-person pronouns with the actual names of the speaker and addressee is an awkward way of composing sentences with limited productivity. Lastly, phonological manipulation is also limited, as in the example mentioned in Section 1: Tweety Pie's line simply relies on baby talk and onomatopoetic expressions (*tweet, twitter*) sharing similar phonological patterns. Despite these limitations, English still utilises role language for effect – by making a character speak role language, the creator signals that this is a minor character that will not be described to detail.

Hosokawa (2010) examined how Japanese role language in comics is translated into German. According to him, as translations of Japanese *manga* have become popular, a new method of comic translation has been developed, utilising *Kunstdialekt* (artificial dialect) to invent an alternative when a regional dialect in the original language has no counterpart in German. An example is shown where, by making a character speak a mixture of northern and southern dialects (i.e. 'universal dialect'), the translator can create an image of a rural/uneducated character. Hosokawa also mentions that there have been borrowings of Japanese terms of address (e.g. *dono* 'Mr/Ms/Esq.') and sentence-final expressions (e.g. *sōrō*, an archaic copula), directly by transliteration, in order to retain the original image of the samurai character.

Based on important grammatical characteristics that signal role languages in Japanese, Korean and Chinese, Kaneda (2010) attempts to determine universal grammatical characteristics contributing to the creation and development of role languages. He examined French and English translations of Japanese popular media, with regard to these three factors: phonological manipulation, use of specific lexical items (e.g. unmarked lexical forms such as infinitive, or omission of articles) and variation in personal pronouns. He also investigated sentence-final discourse markers (e.g. tag questions, English *you know*, *huh*, French *n'est-ce pas*, *hein*) and terms of address/swear words that occur sentence-finally. Of these, terms of address or swear words occurring sentence-finally were deemed effective as role language, connoting specific character types. He also notes that transliterations of Japanese character-associated endings in English translations suggest the emergence of a new grammatical category devoid of grammatical or semantic function, which exclusively signals speaker attributes.

To conclude this section, we would like to mention a few studies that attempt to apply findings from crosslinguistic role language research to language education and to further develop this research field. As role language is a form of linguistic stereotyping, which could lead to bias and discrimination, introducing it into education should be done with caution. At the same time, because role language plays such an important role in Japanese across varieties of media, appropriate knowledge of role language should be useful and beneficial to Japanese learners. Given that the number of students of Japanese as a foreign language that are motivated by interests in Japanese popular culture has been on the rise recently, it is necessary to teach the difference between role language and actual language usage. Onzuka's (2008) paper was written from this point of view, asserting that textbooks biased towards 'natural Japanese' (i.e. Japanese as used in real-life situations, having less clear-cut differences between genders) could actually be more difficult for students. Advocating the introduction of role language instruction into Japanese language education, she maintains that it is necessary to develop textbooks incorporating 'virtual reality' (i.e. role language) suitable for the target levels and purposes. Jung (2010) describes an effort to include role language in education more consciously. Based on her contrastive research on Japanese and Korean role languages, mentioned above (Jung, 2005, 2007), she devoted three class hours to incorporating role language translation of parts of novels in her Japanese-Korean translation seminar for advanced Korean learners of Japanese.

## 5. Conclusions

This review introduces non-Japanese readers to the world of role language research in Japanese, drawing on key literature (Kinsui, 2003, 2008b). After presenting key concepts, we discussed analyses of some established role languages, followed by summaries of existing crosslinguistic studies. As has been shown, Japanese provides great flexibility in inventing new role languages, thanks to a wide selection of first-person pronouns and endings (copulas and particles), and as a result, it has developed many varieties of role language types for fictionalised orality. Therefore, we think research on Japanese role languages can contribute to the study of fictionalised orality. For a particular language to develop role languages, the following two conditions appear important: typological tendencies (Kaneda, 2010) and penetration of popular culture (e.g. translations of Japanese *manga* and *anime*) and electronic media. The first point has been explored experimentally in Kaneda

(2010). Among other things, we also consider the variation in personal pronouns (especially first- and second-person pronouns), accompanied by an absence of subject-predicate agreement, and variation in sentence-final expressions, including terms of address and swear words, to be important contributing factors. The penetration of popular culture and electronic media has also been pointed out in Sadanobu (2007).

In role language research, we first treat discourse data from fiction as a portrayal of character by the creator and as clues to investigating the stereotypical knowledge of a certain character type shared between the creator and the audience. Among such shared knowledge, there may be some that encompasses language ideologies constraining actual language use (i.e. female role language). It has also been shown that there are varieties of role languages that, after their creation, based on actual language usage, underwent exaggeration and transformation and are still in use, irrespective of their basis in linguistic reality (e.g.. elderly man language, *aruyo* language). In addition, we have looked at a group of studies investigating everyday language use that plays with role languages by switching character types (e.g. Sadanobu, 2007).

Role language is still a new, emerging area of research filled with problems to be solved from historical, crosslinguistic and educational perspectives. Nevertheless, it is an interesting field of multidisciplinary inquiry in the humanities and social sciences,[7] providing strong incentives to develop this research topic further in order to elucidate the nature of fictionalised orality, which may be confounded with reality in conventional analyses.

Mihoko Teshigawara (Komazawa University, Japan)
Satoshi Kinsui (Osaka University, Japan)
"Modern Japanese 'Role Language'(Yakuwarigo):
fictionalised orality in Japanese literature and popular culture,"
*Sociolinguistic Studies* 5-1: 37–58, Sheffield: ©Equinox Publishing Ltd. 2011

## NOTES

[1] Throughout this paper, transliterated Japanese words may be divided into morphemes by using hyphens to indicate morpheme boundaries, when relevant to the discussion, while maintaining word boundaries elsewhere in the text.

[2] For an extensive analysis, see Kinsui (2008b: Section 7.4).

[3] Standard Japanese and Eastern Japanese are presented in the same column because standard Japanese was based on the Uptown Tokyo dialect and therefore inherits features of Eastern Japanese.

[4] This interplay of race, language variety and sexuality in the Japanese renderings may be comparable to that between accent and sexual attractiveness and availability of the character pointed out in Lippi-Green (1997: 97, 102–103), where she states that for characters to be sexually attractive and available, they must not have strong accents.

[5] For more details in English, see Inoue (2002), Nakamura (2004, 2005) and references

140    *Appendix*

cited therein.

[6] See Nakamura (2004, 2007a) for descriptions of how *teyo dawa* language was demeaned after it spread in popularity.

[7] Although not discussed here, there are also researchers in a role language research group, led by Kinsui, studying phonetic aspects of role languages in Japanese *anime* (Teshigawara, 2007, 2009), and *manga* characters' faces and bodies from the viewpoint of stereotyping, that is, visual aspects of role 'languages' in *manga* (Yoshimura 2007, 2008).

## ACKNOWLEDGEMENTS

We would like to express our gratitude to the editors and anonymous journal reviewers for their time, effort, and detailed comments, which were extremely helpful, and to J. C. Williams, our reader in Japan. We gratefully acknowledge the support of KAKENHI Nos. 19320060 and 19700173 of the MEXT, Japan.

## REFERENCES

Cooley, M. (1997) An early representation of African-American English. In C. Bernstein, T. Nunnally and R. Sabino (eds) *Language Variety in the South Revisited* 51–58. Tuscaloosa and London: University of Alabama Press.

Gaubatz, T. M. (2007) Shōsetsu ni okeru beigo hōgen no nihongoyaku ni tsuite [Translating dialect in Mark Twain's *The Adventures of Huckleberry Finn*]. In S. Kinsui (ed.) (2007a) 125–158.

Hosokawa, H. (2010) Komikku hon'yaku o tsūjita yakuwarigo no sōzō [Creation of role language through translation of comics]. In *Proceedings of the Symposium 'Yakuwari/ Kyarakutā/Gengo'* [Roles/Characters/Languages], March 28–29, 2009, Kobe University, Japan. 55–67.

Ide, S. and McGloin, N. H. (1990) *Aspects of Japanese women's language*. Tokyo: Kurosio.

Inoue, F. (1980) Hōgen no imēji [Image of dialect]. *Gengo Seikatsu* [Language Life] 341: 48–56.

Inoue, F. (1983) Hōgen imēji no tahenryō kaiseki ni yoru hōgen kukaku [Distinguishing dialects by dialectal images using multivariate analysis]. In Hirayama Teruo Hakase Koki Kinen Kai (ed.) *Gendai Hōgengaku no Kadai* [Issues in Modern Dialectology] Vol. 1, 71–98. Tokyo: Meiji Shoin.

Inoue, M. (2002) Gender, language and modernity: toward an effective history of Japanese women's language. *American Ethnologist* 29 (2): 392–422.

Inoue, M. (2003) Speech without a speaking body: "Japanese women's language" in translation. *Language & Communication* 23: 315–330.

Jung, H. (2005) Nihongo to kankokugo no yakuwarigo no taishō: Taiyaku sakuhin kara miru hon'yaku jō no mondai o chūshin ni [Contrastive study of role language in Japanese and Korean: focusing on translation issues as exhibited in bilingual texts of literary works]. *Shakai Gengo Kagaku* [The Japanese Journal of Language in Society] 8 (1): 82–92.

Jung, H. (2007) Nikkan taishō yakuwarigo kenkyū: Sono kanōsei o saguru [Possibility of the contrastive study of role language in Japanese and Korean]. In S. Kinsui (ed.) (2007a) 71–93.

Jung, H. (2010) Yakuwarigo o shudai toshita Nikkan hon'yaku jugyō no jissen: Kadai suikōgata no hon'yaku katsudō o tōshite no kizuki to sukiru kōjō [Conducting a seminar on Japanese–Korean translation with role language as its theme: raising awareness and improving skills through task-performance type translation activities]. In *Proceedings of the Symposium 'Yakuwari/Kyarakutā/Gengo'* [Roles/Characters/Languages], March 28–29, 2009, Kobe University, Japan. 101–112.

Kaneda, J. (2010) Yakuwarigo kara mita bunmatsushi taishō [A contrastive study of sentence-final discourse markers from the view of role language]. In *Proceedings of the Symposium 'Yakuwari/Kyarakutā/Gengo'* [Roles/Characters/Languages], March 28–29, 2009, Kobe University, Japan. 37–47.

Kinoshita, J. (1982) *Gikyoku no Nihongo* [Japanese Language in Dramas]. Tokyo: Chuo Koronsha.

Kinsui, S. (2003) *Vācharu Nihongo: Yakuwarigo no Nazo* [Virtual Japanese: Enigmas of Role Language]. Tokyo: Iwanami shoten.

Kinsui, S. (ed.) (2007a) *Yakuwarigo Kenkyū no Chihei* [New Horizons of Role Language Research]. Tokyo: Kurosio.

Kinsui, S. (2007b) Yakuwarigo toshite no pijin nihongo no rekishi sobyō [Historical sketch in the pidgin Japanese as a role language]. In S. Kinsui (ed.) (2007a) 193–210.

Kinsui, S. (2008a) Nihon manga ni okeru ijin kotoba [Foreigners' speech in Japanese *manga*]. In K. Ito (ed.) *Manga no Naka no "Tasha"* ["Other" in *Manga*] 14–60. Kyoto: Rinsen Shoten.

Kinsui, S. (2008b) Yakuwarigo to nihongoshi [Role language and Japanese language history]. In S. Kinsui, Y. Inui and K. Shibuya (eds.) *Nihongoshi no Intafēsu* [Interfaces in Japanese Language History] 205–236. Tokyo: Iwanami shoten.

Kinsui (2010) On "role language" in contemporary Japanese: An investigation of stereotypical styles in Japanese language. In *Proceedings of the Symposium 'Yakuwari/Kyarakutā/Gengo'* [Roles/Characters/Languages], March 28–29, 2009, Kobe University, Japan. 51–54.

Lippi-Green, R. (1997) *English with an Accent: Language, Ideology, and Discrimination in the United States*. London: Routledge.

Nakamura, M. (2004) Discursive construction of the ideology of "women's language": "Schoolgirl language" in the Meiji period (1868–1912). *Nature-People-Society* 36: 43–80.

Nakamura, M. (2005) Construction of "men's national language" in Japan (1868–1926). *Nature-People-Society* 38: 91–125.

Nakamura, M. (2007a) *"Onna Kotoba" wa Tsukurareru* [Women's Language Is Constructed]. Tokyo: Hitsuji Shobo.

Nakamura, M. (2007b) *"Sei" to Nihongo: Kotoba ga Tsukuru Onna to Otoko* [Gender and Japanese Language: Women and Men as Language Constructs]. Tokyo: NHK Books.

Natsume, S. (1961) Wagahai wa neko dearu [I am a cat]. In *Nihon Gendai Bungaku Zenshū 23 Natsume Sōseki Shū*. Vol. 1, 5–201. Tokyo: Kodansha.

Mark T. (1835), Nishida, M. (trans.) (1977) *Hakkuruberī-Fin no Bōken*. (Adventures of Huckleberry Finn) Tokyo: Iwanami shoten.

Onzuka, C. (2008) Kyōkasho ni arawareru yakuwarigo no yakuwari: kyōkasho ni okeru bācharu riaritī no susume [The role of role language as observed in textbooks: a suggestion for the introduction of virtual reality into textbooks]. *Nihongo Kyōiku Kenkyū* [Research on Japanese Language Education] 14: 37–48. Kankoku Nihongo Kyōiku Gakkai [Japanese Education Association of Korea].

Sadanobu, T. (2006) Kotoba to hatsuwa kyarakuta [Speech and speech characters]. *Bungaku* [Literature] 7 (6): 117–129.

Sadanobu, T. (2007) Kyara joshi ga arawareru kankyō [The occurrence environment of "character-particles" in Japanese and Korean]. In S. Kinsui (ed.) (2007a) 27–48.

Sadanobu, T. and Zhang, L. (2007) Nihongo, chūgokugo ni okeru kyara gobi no kansatsu [Observation of character-associated endings in Japanese and Chinese]. In F. Peng (ed.) *Nitchū Taishō Gengogaku Kenkyū Ronbunshū: Chūgokugo kara Mita Nihongo no Tokuchō, Nihongo kara Mita Chūgokugo no Tokuchō* [Collection of Research Papers on the Contrastive Study of Japanese and Chinese: Characteristics of Japanese Language from a Chinese Language Perspective, Characteristics of Chinese Language from a Japanese Language Perspective] 99–119. Osaka: Izumi Shoin.

Su, H. (2009) Reconstructing Taiwanese and Taiwan guoyu on the Taiwan-based Internet. *Journal of Asian Pacific Communication* 19 (2): 313–335.

Takayama, M. (2007) Kundoku-go to hakase-go [Japanese renderings of classical Chinese words and role language of the elderly learned male type]. Paper presented at Kyūshū University Graduate School of Letters Seminar 'Gengo to bungei: Wakan koten no sekai [Language and Literature: The World of Japanese and Chinese Classics]', July 28, 2007, Fukuoka, Japan.

Tanaka, A. (1999) *Nihongo no Isō to Isō-sa* [Japanese Registers and Register Variation]. Tokyo: Meiji Shoin.

Tanaka, Y. (2007) "Hōgen kosupure" ni miru "hōgen omochaka" no jidai [Age of regional dialect play as encountered in 'cosplay' using dialects]. *Bungaku* [Literature] 8 (6): 123–133.

Teshigawara (2007) Seishitsu kara mita koe no sutereotaipu: Yakuwarigo no onseiteki sokumen kara mita ichi kōsatsu [Voice qualities of vocal stereotypes of good guys and bad guys: A phonetic study in the role language framework]. In S. Kinsui (ed.) (2007a) 49–69.

Teshigawara (2009) Vocal expressions of emotions and personalities in Japanese *anime*. In K. Izdebski (ed.) *Emotions of the Human Voice,* Vol. III: *Culture and Perception* 275–287. San Diego: Plural Publishing.

Tolkien, J. R. R. (1982) *The Hobbit*, Revised Edition. New York: Ballantine Books.

Tolkien, J. R. R. (2000) T. Seta (trans.) *Hobitto no Bōken* [The Hobbit's Adventure] Vol. 2. Tokyo: Iwanami Shoten.

Yamaguchi, H. (2007) Yakuwarigo no kobetsusei to fuhensei: Nichi-Ei no taishō o tōshite [Universals and specifics of role language in popular fiction: a contrastive analysis between Japanese and English]. In S. Kinsui (ed.) (2007a) 9–25.

Yoshimura, K. (2007) Kindai nihon manga no shintai [Bodies in modern Japanese manga]. In S. Kinsui (ed.) (2007a) 109–121.

Yoshimura, K. (2008) Rekishi hyōshō toshite no shikakuteki "nihonjin" zō [Visual images of the Japanese people as historical icons]. In K. Ito. (ed.) *Manga no Naka no "Tasha"* ['Other' in *Manga*] 62–95. Kyoto: Rinsen Shoten.

143

# Sources of Texts

**CHAPTER 1**

"Tetsuwan Atomu 1"… Tezuka, Osamu, *Tetsuwan Atomu* (Astro Boy) 1, Tezuka Osamu Manga Zenshū 221, Kodansha, 1979.

"Meitantei Konan 1" … Aoyama, Gōshō, *Meitantei Konan* 1, Shogakukan, 1994.

"Poketto Monsutā 1" … Anakubo Kōsaku, *Poketto Monsutā* (Pocket Monster) 1, Shogakukan, 1996.

"Tamanegi Hakase Ichi gō Tariran" … Yadama, Shirō, *Tamanegi Hakase Ichi gō Tariran,* Iwasaki Shoten, 1999.

"YAWARA! 1" … Urasawa, Naoki, *YAWARA!* 1, Shogakukan, 1987.

"Hitsuji Otoko no Kurisumasu" … Murakami, Haruki and Sasaki, Maki, *Hitsuji Otoko no Kurisumasu* (Christmas of the Sheep Man), Kodansha Bunko, 1989.

"Kasei Hakase" … Tezuka, Osamu, *Kasei Hakase* (Doctor Mars), Tezuka Osamu Manga Zenshū 339, Kodansha, 1994.

"Shin Takarajima" … Tezuka, Osamu, *Shin Takarajima* (New Treasure Island) (Revised Edition), Tezuka Osamu Manga Zenshū 281, Kodansha, 1984.

"Yūrei Otoko" … Ban, Toshio and Tezuka Production, *Tezuka Osamu Monogatari/ Osamushi Tōjō,* Asahi Shimbun-sha, 1992.

"Robotto Hakase" … Unno, Jūza, *Unno Jūza Shū,* Shōnen Shōsetsu Taikei, Vol. 9, San-ichi Publishing, 1987.

"Uchū Joshū Dai Ichi Gō" … Unno, Jūza, *Uchū Joshū Dai Ichi Gō,* Aozora Bunko (original sourse: Jūhachiji no Ongaku-yoku, Hayakawa Shobo, 1976).

"Kokkei Daigaku" … *Gendai,* Vol. 36, No. 4, Kodansha, 2002. Original sourse: *Shōnen Kurabu* (Boy's Club) Shōwa ku nen ni gatsugō, Kodansha, pp. 194–195.

"Sarutobi Sasuke" … Jinbutsu Ōraisha (ed.) *Tatsukawa Bunko Kessaku Sen,* Jinbutsu Ōraisha, 1967.

"Kaidan Botan Dōrō" … San'yūtei Enchō, *Kaidan Botan Dōrō,* Iwanami Bunko, 2002.

"Yabu Isei no Fuyōjō" … Kokuritsu Kokugo Kenkyūjo (National Institute for Japanese Language and Linguistics) (ed.) *Gyūnabe Zōtan Aguranabe Yōgo Sakuin,* Shuei Shuppan, 1975.

"Ukiyo-buro" … Jimbo, Kazuya (recension and annotation), *Ukiyo-buro, Kejō Suigen Maku no Soto, Daisen Sekai Gakuya Saguri,* Shin Nihon Koten Bungaku Taikei 86, Iwanami Shoten, 1989.

"Tokaidō Yotsuya Kaidan" … Tsuruya, Nanboku/Kawatake, Shigetoshi (recension and revision), *Tokaidō Yotsuya Kaidan,* Iwanami Bunko, 1956.

**CHAPTER 2**

"Sutā Uōzu/Teikoku no Gyakushū" … G. Lucas (Director)/Hirata, Katsushige (Translation for Japanese Edition), *Sutā Uōzu/Teikoku no Gyakushū* (Tokubetsu-hen) (Star Wars/The Empire Strikes Back (Special Edition)), 20th Century Fox Entertainment Japan Co. Ltd., 1997.

"Harī Pottā to Kenja no Ishi" … J. K. Rowling/Matsuoka, Yūko (translation), *Harī*

144

*Pottā to Kenja no Ishi* (Harry Potter and the Philosopher's Stone), Seizansha, 1999.

## CHAPTER 3

"Yūzuru" … Morimoto, Kaoru, Kinoshita, Junji, Takana, Chikao and Iizawa, Tadasu, *Morimoto Kaoru/Kinoshita Junji/Tanaka Chikao/Iizawa Tadasu Shū,* Gendainihon Bungaku Taikei 83, Chikuma Shobo, 1970.

"Yume no Heishi" … Abe, Kōbō, *Abe Kōbō Zenshū* 7, Shinchosha, 1998.

"Sesetsu Shingoza" … Sharebon Taisei Henshū Iinkai (ed.), *Sharebon Taisei,* 7, Chuokoron-sha, 1980.

"Ukiyo-buro" … Jimbo, Kazuya (recension and annotation), *Ukiyo-buro, Kejō Suigen Maku no Soto, Daisen Sekai Gakuya Saguri,* Shin Nihon Koten Bungaku Taikei 86, Iwanami Shoten, 1989.

"Daisen Sekai Gakuya Saguri" … Jimbo, Kazuya (recension and annotation), *Ukiyo-buro, Kejō Suigen Maku no Soto, Daisen Sekai Gakuya Saguri,* Shin Nihon Koten Bungaku Taikei 86, Iwanami Shoten, 1989.

"Katō Hōgen Hakomakura" … Sharebon Taisei Henshū Iinkai (ed.), *Sharebon Taisei* 27, Chuokoron-sha, 1987.

"Hyōjungo ni tsukite" … Sanada, Shinji, *Hyōjungo wa Ikani Seiritsu Shitaka: Kindai Nihongo no Hatten no Rekishi,* Sotakusha, 1991.

"Pāman 1" … Fujiko F. Fujio, *Pāman* 1, Shogakukan Korokoro Bunko, 1997.

"Tōkaidōchū Hiza-kurige" … Aso, Isoji (recension and annotation), *Tōkaidōchū Hiza-kurige,* Nihon Koten Bungaku Taikei 62, Iwanami Shoten, 1958.

"Ukiyo-doko"…Nakanishi, Zenzō (recension and annotation), *Ukiyo-doko,* Nihon Koten Zensho, Asahi Shimbun-sha, 1961.

"Sōkei-sen" … Kojima Teiji, *Manzai Sesō-shi,* Mainichi Shimbun-sha, 1961.

"Tōkei" … Kon, Tōkō, *Tōkei,* Kadokawa Shōsetsu Shinsho, 1957.

"Ero-goto-shi-tachi" … Nosaka, Akiyuki, *Ero-goto-shi-tachi,* Shincho Bunko.

"Meitantei Konan 10" … Aoyama, Gōshō, *Meitantei Konan* 10, Shogakukan, 1996.

## CHAPTER 4

"Taiyō to Mokujū" … Kitahara, Hakushū, *Hakushū Zenshū* 28, Iwanami Shoten, 1987.

"Kaijin Nijū-mensō" … *Shōnen Kurabu Meisaku-sen* 2, Kodansha, 1966.

"Tetsuwan Atomu 1"… Tezuka, Osamu, *Tetsuwan Atomu* (Astro Boy) 1, Tezuka Osamu Manga Zenshū 221, Kodansha, 1979.

"Tōsei Shosei Katagi" … Inagaki Tatsurō (ed.) *Tsubouchi Shōyō Shū,* Meiji Bungaku Zenshū 16, Chikuma Shobo, 1969.

"Bungaku Jihyō" … Takayama, Chogyū, Bungaku Jihyō, Dokuritsu Gyōsei Hōjin Kokuritsu Kokugo Kenkyūjo (ed.) *Taiyō Kōpasu* (Taiyō Corpus) Ver. 5, Dokuritsu Gyōsei Hōjin Kokuritsu Kokugo Kenkyūjo, 2002 (Original source: Taiyō No. 13, Hakubunkan, 1901).

"Wagahaiwa Neko de aru" … Natsume, Kinnosuke, *Sōseki Zenshū,* 1, Iwanami Shoten, 1993 (English Translation Version: Soseki Natsume, Aiko Ito and

Sources of Texts 145

Graeme Wilson (translation), *I Am a Cat,* Charles E. Tuttle Company, Inc. Rutland, Vermont, and Tokyo, Japan, 1972. p. 143.).

"Genji Monogatari" ... Yamagishi, Toppei (recension and annotation), *Genji Monogatari* (The Tale of Genji) 1, Nihon Koten Bungaku Taikei 14, Iwanami Shoten, 1958.

"Tatsumi no Sono" ... Mizuno, Minoru (recension and annotation), *Kibyōshi Sharebon Shū,* Nihon Koten Bungaku Taikei 59, Iwanami Shoten, 1958.

"Kiki-jōzu" ... Odaka, Toshirō (recension and annotation), *Edo Shōwa Shū,* Nihon Koten Bungaku Taikei 100, Iwanami Shoten, 1966.

"Tōsei Shōnen Katagi" ... Fukuda, Kiyoto (ed.) *Meiji Shōnen Bungaku Taikei* 95, Chikuma Shobo, 1970.

"Takekurabe" ... Higuchi, Ichiyō/Shiota Ryōhei, Wada, Yoshirō, and Higuchi Etsu (eds.), *Higuchi Ichiyō Zenshū* 1, Chikuma Shobo, 1974.

"Oishinbo 1" ... Kariya, Tetsu (original story)/Hanasaki, Akira (comic), *Oishinbo* 1, Shogakukan Bunko, 2000.

"Aa Gyokuhaini Hana Ukete" ... Katō, Ken'ichi (ed.), *Shōnen Kurabu Meisaku Sen* 1, Kodansha, 1966.

"Kyojin no Hoshi 1" ... Kajiwara, Ikki (original story)/Kawasaki, Noboru (comic), *Kyojin no Hoshi* 1, Kodansha Manga Bunko, 1995.

"Ashita no Jō 1" ... Takamori, Asao (original story)/Chiba, Tetsuya (comic), *Ashita no Jō* 1, Kodansha Manga Bunko, 2000.

"Mitsume ga Tooru 1" ... Tezuka, Osamu, *Mitsume ga Tooru* 1, Tezuka Osamu Manga Zenshū 110, Kodansha, 1980.

## CHAPTER 5

"Ēsu o Nerae! 1" ... Yamamoto, Sumika, *Ēsu o Nerae!* 1, Chūkō Bunko Komikku Ban, 1994.

"Ēsu o Nerae! 2" ... Yamamoto, Sumika, *Ēsu o Nerae!* 2, Chūkō Bunko Komikku Ban, 1994.

"Ēsu o Nerae! 4" ... Yamamoto, Sumika, *Ēsu o Nerae!* 4, Chūkō Bunko Komikku Ban, 1994.

"Ukiyo-buro" ... Jimbo, Kazuya (recension and annotation), *Ukiyo-buro, Kejō Suigen Maku no Soto, Daisen Sekai Gakuya Saguri,* Shin Nihon Koten Bungaku Taikei 86, Iwanami Shoten, 1989.

"Yūshi Hōgen" ... Sharebon Taisei Henshū Iinkai (ed.), *Sharebon Taisei* 4, Chuokoron-sha, 1979.

"Sanshirō" ... Natsume, Kinnosuke, *Sōseki Zenshū* 5, Iwanami Shoten, 1994.

"Ukigumo" ... Futabatei, Shimei, *Futabatei Shimei Zenshū* 1, Chikuma Shobo, 1984.

"Hototogisu" ... Tokutomi, Roka, *Hototogisu,* Iwanami Bunko, 1938.

"Ma-kaze Koi-kaze" ... Kosugi, Tengai, *Ma-kaze Koi-kaze Zen-pen,* Iwanami Bunko, 1951.

"Wagahai wa Neko de aru" ... Natsume, Kinnosuke, *Sōseki Zenshū,* 1, Iwanami Shoten, 1993 (English Translation Version: Soseki Natsume, Aiko Ito and Graeme Wilson (translation), *I Am a Cat,* Charles E. Tuttle Company, Inc.

Rutland, Vermont, and Tokyo, Japan, 1972. p. 143.).

"Sorekara" ... Natsume, Kinnosuke, *Sōseki Zenshū* 6, Iwanami Shoten, 1994.

"Mon" ... Natsume, Kinnosuke, *Sōseki Zenshū* 6, Iwanami Shoten, 1994.

"Onna Keizu" ... Izumi, Kyōtarō, *Kyōka Zenshū* 10, Iwanami Shoten, 1940.

"Shiyū Kurabu" ... Kawamura, Kunimitsu, *Otome no Inori: Kindai Josei Imēji no Tanjō,* Kinokuniya Shoten, 1993 (Original Source: Jogaku Sekai, 1916 nen 10 gatsugō).

"Namiko Ririkku Retā" ... Karasawa, Shun'ichi, *Karasawa Dō Hen-sho Mokuroku,* Gakuyō Shobō, 2000.

"Sakura-gai" ... Yoshiya, Nobuko, *Sakura-gai,* Jitsugyo-no-Nippon-Sha, 1935.

"Ningen Shikkaku" ... CD-ROM Ban, *Shincho Bunko no Hyaku-satsu,* Shinchosha, 1995.

"Kusa no Hana" ... CD-ROM Ban, *Shincho Bunko no Hyaku-satsu,* Shinchosha, 1995.

"Suna no Ue no Shokubutsu-gun" ... CD-ROM Ban, *Shincho Bunko no Hyaku-satsu,* Shinchosha, 1995.

"Bun to Hun" ... CD-ROM Ban, *Shincho Bunko no Hyaku-satsu,* Shinchosha, 1995.

"Yūkan Kurabu 1" ... Ichijō, Yukari, *Yūkan Kurabu* 1, Shuei-sha, 1982.

"Shin-Shiratori Reiko de Gozaimasu! 1" ... Suzuki, Yumiko, *Shin-Shiratori Reiko de Gozaimasu!* 1, Kodansha, 1992.

"Warau Mikaeru 1" ... Kawahara, Izumi, *Warau Mikaeru* 1, Hakusen-sha, 1992.

"O-jōsama no Gyakushū!" ... Mori, Natsuko, *O-jōsama no Gyakushū!,* Gakushu-kenkyusha, 1991.

"Berusaiyu no Bara 1" ... Ikeda, Riyoko, *Berusaiyu no Bara* 1, Shueisha Bunko, 1994.

## CHAPTER 6

"Dr. Surampu 5" ... Toriyama, Akira, *Dr. Surampu* (Dr. Slump) 5, Shueisha Bunko, 1996.

"Mitsumega Tooru 10" ... Tezuka, Osamu, *Mitsumega Tooru* 10, Tezuka Osamu Manga Zenshū 110, Kodansha, 1980.

"Robotto Santō-hei" ... Kitajima, Noboru (ed.), *Shōwa Manga-shi,* Bessatsu Ichiokunin no Shōwa-shi, Mainichi shimbun-sha, 1977.

"Taimu Rain" ... Michael Crichton/Sakai, Akinobu (translation), *Taimu Rain* (Time Line), Jō, Hayakawa Shobō, 2000.

"Kuroi Ijin" ... Katō, Ken'ichi (ed.) *Shōnen Kurabu Meisaku Sen* 1, Kodansha, 1966.

"Kaze to tomoni Sarinu" ... Margaret Mitchell/Ōkubo, Yasuo (translation), *Kaze to tomoni Sarinu* (Gone with the wind) I, Mikasa-ban Gendai Sekai Bungaku Zenshū, Bessatsu I, 1953.

"Gaikoku-jin no Nihongo" ... Mori, *Senzō, Meiji Tōkyō Itsubun-shi,* Jō-kan, Toyo Bunko, Heibon-sha, 1969.

"Kantan" ... *Nipponohon Onpu Monku Zenshū,* Revised and Enlarged Version, 6th Edition (Kurata, Yoshihiro and Okada, Norio (Supervision), Taishō-ki SP Ban

Rekōdo Geinō/Kashi/Kotoba Zen-kiroku 9, Ozora-sha, 1997).

"Hanashi no Kuzukago: Bushi to Kotoba" ... Shiba, Ryōtarō, *Yowa to shite,* Bunshun Bunko, 1979.

"Norakuro Jōtō-hei" ... Katō, Ken'ichi (ed.) *Shōnen Kurabu Meisaku Sen* 1, Kodansha, 1966.

"Norakuro Buyūdan" ... Tagawa, Suihō, Norakuro Buyūdan, Kodansha, 1969 (reprint).

# References

Akita, Minoru (1984) *Ōsaka Shōwa-shi* (History of Humorous Stories in Osaka), Henshū Kōbō Noa.

Amino, Yoshihiko (1998) *Higashi to Nishino Kataru Nihon no Rekishi* (History of East and West Japan), Kodansha Gakujutsu Bunko.

Asakura, Kyōji, Mizoguchi, Atsushi, Yamanouchi, Yukio and others (2000) *Jitsuroku Yakuza to iu Ikikata* (Document: Yakuza Life), Takarajima Bunko.

Ban, Toshio and Tezuka Production (1992) *Tezuka Osamu Omonogatari: Osamushi Tōjō* (A Story of Osamu Tezuka: Here comes Osamushi) Asahi Shimbun-sha (included Asahi Bunko, 1994).

Brewer, Marilynn. B. (1988) "A dual process model of impression formation," T. K. Srull and R. S. Wyer, Jr. (eds.) *Advances in Social Cognition*, Vol. 1, pp. 1–36, Academic Press, New York.

Campbell, Joseph (1956) The Hero with a Thousand Faces, Meridian Books, New York.

Devine, Patricia. G. (1989) "Stereotypes and prejudice: Their automatic and controlled components," *Journal of Personality and Social Psychology*, 56, pp. 5–18.

Doihara, Sakurō (1995) *Kansai no Terebi Dorama-shi* (A History of TV drama in Kansai), Kamigata Geinō Shuppan Sentā.

Endō, Orie (ed.) (2001) *Onna to Kotoba: Onna wa Kawatta ka Nihongo wa Kawatta ka* (Women and Language: Did women change? Did Japanese Language Change?), Akashi Shoten.

Furuta, Tōsaku (1986) "*Tōkaidō Yotsuya Kaidan* ni oite kamigata-fū, tōgoku-fū no ii-kata o shite iru hito tachi" (Poeple who speak in a kamigata-like or togoku-like manner in *Tōkaidō Yotsuya Kaidan*), *Matsumura Akira Kyōju Koki Kinen Kokugo Kenkyū Ronshū*, pp. 449–493, Meiji Shoin.

Furuta, Tōsaku (1987) "*Tōkaidō Yotsuya Kaidan* ni oite kamigata-fū no kotoba-zukai o suru hito tachi" (Poeple who speak in a kamigata-like manner in *Tōkaidō Yotsuya Kaidan*), *Kindaigo Kenkyū*, 7, pp. 437–458, Meiji Shoin.

Furuta, Tōsaku (1993) "*Tōkaidō Yotsuya Kaidan* ni oite tōgoku-fū no kotoba-zukai o suru hito tachi" (Poeple who speak in a togoku-like manner in *Tōkaidō Yotsuya Kaidan*), *Kindaigo Kenkyū*, 9, pp. 231–256, Meiji Shoin.

Hudson, R. A. (1980) *Sociolinguistics*, Cambridge University Press, Cambridge.

Hida, Yoshifumi (1992) *Tōkyō-go Seiritsu-shi no Kenkyū* (Research on the History of Establishment of Tokyo Language), Tokyo-do Shuppan.

Honda, Kazuko (1990) *Jogakusei no Keifu: Saishoku Sareru Meiji* (Genealogy of Girl Students: Colored Meiji) , Seido-sha.

Ide, Sachiko (ed.) (1997) Josei-go no Sekai (The World of Women's Language), Nihongo-gaku Sōsho, Meiji Shoin.

Inoue, Shōichi (1991) *Bijin-ron* (An Essay on Beauties), Libro Port.

Ishikawa, Yoshinori (1972) "Kindai josei-go no gobi: teyo/dawa/noyo" (Endings of modern women's language: *teyo/dawa/noyo*), *Kaishaku*, 18-9: 22–27, Kyōiku Shuppan Sentā.

Kaiser, Stefan (ed.) (1995) *The Western Rediscovery of the Japanese Language*, Vol. 5, Curzon Press Ltd., Richmond.

Kaiser, Stefan (1998) "Yokohama Dialect: nihongo bēsu no pijin" (Yokohama Dialect: a Japanese-based pidgin), Tokyo Daigaku Kokugo Kenkyū-shitsu Sōsetsu Hyaku-shūnen-kinen-kai (ed.) *Tokyo Daigaku Kokugo Kenkyū-shitsu Sōsetsu Hyaku-shūnen-kinen Kokugo Kenkyū Ronshū*, pp. 83–106, Kyuko Shoin.

Kaishaku to Kanshō Henshū-bu (ed.) (1992) *Kokubungaku Kaishaku to Kanshō/ Tokushū: Kotoba to Josei* (Japanese Literature, Its Reading and Appreciation/ Featured Theme: Language and Women), Vol. 56, No. 7, Shibundo.

Kamei, Hideo (2000) *Meiji Bungaku-shi* (History of Literature in Meiji Era), Iwanami Shoten.

Kamise, Yumiko (2002) *Sutereotaipu no Shakai-shinri-gaku: Henken no Kaishō ni Mukete* (Social Psychology of Stereotype: towards the Solve of Prejudice), Serekushon Shakai-shinri-gaku 21, Saiensu-sha.

Karasawa, Shun'ichi (2000) *Karasawa Hensho-dō Mokuroku* (Book List of Karasawa Hensho-dō), Gakuyō Shobō.

Karatani, Kōjin (1980) *Nihon Kindai Bungaku no Kigen* (Origins of Modern Japanese Literature), Kodansha.

Kawamura, Kunimitsu (1993) *Otome no Inori: Kindai Josei Imēji no Tanjō* (Prayer of Meiden: the Birth of Modern Women's Image)

Kikusawa, Sueo (1933) *Kokugo Isō-ron* (Essays on the Japanese Register), Kokugo Kagaku Kōza, Meiji Shoin.

Kikusawa, Sueo (1936) *Shin-Kō Kokugo-gaku Josetsu* (New Introduction of the Study of Japanese Language), Bungaku-sha.

Kinoshita, Junji (1982) *Gikyoku no Nihongo* (Japanese Language in Drama), Nihongo no Sekai, 12, Chuo-Koron-sha.

Kinsui, Satoshi (1996) "Oru no kinō no rekishiteki kōsatsu" (Historical research of the function of *oru*), Yamaguchi Akiho kyōju Kanreki Kinen-kai (ed.) *Yamaguchi Akiho kyōju Kanreki Kinen Kokugogaku Ronshū*, pp. 109–132, Meiji Shoin.

Kinsui, Satoshi (2000) "Yakuwarigo tankyū no teian" (A proposal of the research of role language) Satō, Kiyoji (ed.) Kokugo-shi no Shin-shiten, *Kokugo Ronkyū*, 8, pp. 331–351, Meiji Shoin.

Kinsui, Satoshi (2001) 'Shiryō shōkai' Meiji Taishō jidai SP rekōdo monku-shū ni tsuite" ('Bibliography' On the text collections of SP record in Meiji and Taishō era), Osaka Daigaku Kokugo Kokubun Gakkai (ed.) *Gobun*, No. 75/76: 80–88.

Kinsui, Satoshi (2002) "Kindaigo to sutereotaipu" (Modern Japanese and stereotype), Tokyo Daigaku Kokugo Kokubun Gakkai (ed.) *Kokugo to Kokubungaku* 79-11: 85–95.

Kinsui, Satoshi (2014) *Kore mo Nihongo Aruka? Ijin no Kotoba ga Umareru Toki* (Is This Also Japanese? The Time When Arien's Language Emerged), Iwanami Shoten.

Kojima, Teiji (1978) *Manzai Sesō-shi* (A history of Manzai and Social Conditions), Mainichi Shimbun-sha.

Komatsu, Hisao (1974) "*Ichidoku Santan Tōsei Shosei Katagi* no edo-go-teki tokushoku" (Edo-language-like features of *Ichidoku Santan Tōsei Shosei Katagi*), *Saitama Daigaku Kiyō,* No. 9, pp 17–28, Saitama Daigaku Kyōyō Gakubu.

Komatsu, Hisao (1985) *Edo-jidai no Kokugo: Edo-go* (Language in Edo era: Edo Language), Tokyo-do Shuppan.

Komatsu, Hisao (1988) "Tōkyō-go ni okeru danjo-sa no keisei: shūjoshi o chūshin to shite" (Formation of gender differences in Tokyo dialect: focusing sentence-final particles), Tokyo Daigaku Kokugo Kokubun Gakkai (ed.) *Kokugo to Kokubungaku* 79-11: 85–95.

Komatsu, Hisao (1998) "Kimi to boku: Edo Tōkyō-go ni okeru tsui-shiyō o chūshin ni" (You and I: focusing pair use in Edo and Tokyo dialect), Tokyo Daigaku Kokugo Kenkyū-shitsu Sōsetsu Hyaku-shūnen-kinen-kai (ed.) *Tokyo Daigaku Kokugo Kenkyū-shitsu Sōsetsu Hyaku-shūnen-kinen Kokugo Kenkyū Ronshū,* pp. 667–685, Kyuko Shoin.

Komiya, Toyotaka (1980) *Meiji Bunka-shi 10: Shumi Goraku* (Cultural History of Meiji Era 10: Hobby and Recreation), Hara Shobo.

Kuroda, Isamu (1999) "'Jibun' katari-dashita kansai dorama" (Kansai dramas have begun speaking about themselves) *Asahi Shimbun,* September 3, evening edition.

Kushima, Tsutomu (editor in chief) (1999) "Anime tokusatsu nenpyō (Shōwa-shi)" (Chronology of animation and "tokusatsu" in Shōwa), *Nichiyō Kenkyū-ka,* No. 14, pp. 87–98, Fusosha.

Kyokudō Konanryō (2000) *Engei-sokki-bon Kiso Kenkyū* <Sei/Zoku> (Fundamental Research on Stenographic Books of Entertainment <Part 1/2>), Taru Shuppan.

Labov, William (1972) *Sociolinguistic Patterns,* University of Pennsylvania Press, Philadelphia.

Lippmann, Walter (1922) *Public Opinion.* Lippmann/Kakegawa, Tomiko (translation) *Seron,* Jō/Ge, Iwanami Bunko.

Mainichi Shimbun-sha (ed.) (1977) *Shōwa Manga-shi* (History of Manga in Showa), Bessatsu Ichioku-nin no Shōwa-shi, Mainichi Shimbun-sha.

Masuoka, Takashi and Takubo, Yukinori (1922) *Kiso Nihongo Bunpō* (Basic Japanese Grammar) (revised version), Kurosio Publishers.

Minami, Hiroshi, Okada, Norio and Takeyama, Akiko (eds.) (1988) *Yūgi/Goraku* (playing/Recreation), Kindai Shomin Seikatsu-shi, 8, San-Ichi Shobo.

Mizuhara, Akito (1994) *Edo-go/Tōkyō-go/Hyōjun-go* (Edo Language/Tokyo Language/Standard Japanese), Kodansha Gendai Shinsho.

Nakamura, Michio (1948) *Tōkyō-go no Seikaku* (Character of Tokyo Language), Kawata Shobo.

Ozaki, Yoshimitsu (1997) "Josei sen'yō no bunmatsu-keishiki no ima" (Contemporary sentence-final forms of Japanese for the exclusive use of women only), Gendai Nihongo Kenkyūkai (ed.) *Josei no Kotoba: Shokuba-hen* (Language of Women: Office Version), pp. 33–58, Hituzi Syobo.

Sanada, Shinji (1991) *Hyōjungo wa Ikani Seiritsu Shita ka: Kindai Nihongo no Hatten no Rekishi* (How was Standard Japanese Established?: A History of Development of Modern Japanese), Sotakusha.

Sanada, Shinji (2000) *Datsu Hyōjungo no Jidai* (The days of Post-Standard Japanese) Shogakukan Bunko.

Sanada, Shinji (2001) *Hōgen wa Zetsumetsu Suru no ka: Jibun no Kotoba o Ushinatta Nihonjin* (Will Dialects become Extinct?: Japanese People Have lost Their Own Language) PHP Shinsho.

Seto, Tatsuya and Yamamoto, Atsushi (1999) *Manga Hakase Tokuhon* (Reader of Doctors in Manga), Takarajima-sha (included Takarajima Bunko, 2000).

Shiba, Tsukasa and Aoyama, Sakae (1998) *Yakuza Eiga to Sono Jidai* (Yakuza Movies and their Times) Chikuma Shinsho.

Shiba, Ryōtarō (1970) "Hanashi no Kuzukago: Bushi to Kotoba" (Trash box of tales: Samurai and their language) *Ōru Yomimono*, Shōwa 45 Nen 9 Gatsu-go (included in *Yowa to shite*, Bunshun Bunko, pp. 122–130, 1979).

Shibuya, Rinko (2002) "Sex exclusive difference as the norm: Japanese women's language," (manuscript), 9th UCLA Graduate Student Symposium for Japanese Studies.

Shimizu, Isao (2000) "20 seiki hajime no shōsetsu ni okeru josei no kotoba: Tōkyō chūryū no josei no kotoba to hyōjungo" (Women's language in novels at the beginning of 20th century: the language of middle class women in Tokyo and the standard Japanese), *Kokubungaku Kaishaku to Kanshō*, Vol. 56, No. 7, pp. 38–44, Shibundo.

Shimizu, Yoshinori (2000) *Nihongo Hisshō Kōza* (The Funny Course of Japanese Language) Kodansha.

Shimokawa, Kōshi (2002a) *Kindai Kodomo-shi Nenpyō: Meiji Taishō Hen* (Modern Chronology of Children: Meiji and Taishō Volume), Kawade Shobo Shinsha.

Shimokawa, Kōshi (2002b) *Kindai Kodomo-shi Nenpyō: Shōwa Heisei Hen* (Modern Chronology of Children: Shōwa and Heisei Volume), Kawade Shobo Shinsha.

Shimotsuki, Takanaka (1998) *Tanjō! 'Tezuka Osamu'* (The Birth of Osamu Tezuka!), Asahi Sonorama.

Takebe, Yoshinobu (2000) *Zenbu Ōsaka no Eiga ya nen* (These Are All Osaka Movies) Heibonsha.

Takeuchi, Hiroshi (1991) *Risshi/Kugaku/Shusse* (Setting Aim/Self-supporting Student Life/Success), Kodansha Gendai Shinsho.

Tanaka, Akio (1983) *Tōkyō-go: Sono Seiritsu to Tenkai* (Tokyo Language: Its Establishment and Development), Meiji Shoin.

Tanaka, Akio (1999) *Nihongo no Isō to Isō-sa* (Registers and Differences between Registers), Meiji Shoin.

Tanaka, Satsuki (2002) "'Ojōsama kotoba' no seiritsu: 'Romeo to Jurietto' no hon'yaku o shiza to shite" (Establishment of young lady's language: From the viewpoint of translations of 'Romeo and Juliet'), a graduation Thesis of School of Letters, Osaka University.

Toriyama, Hiromu (1986) *Nihon Terebi Dorama-shi* (A History of TV drama in Japan), Eijin-sha.

Trudgill, Peter (1974) *Sociolinguistics; An Introduction*, Penguin Books Ltd., Harmondsworth. Trudgill/Tsuchiya, Shigeru (translation) *Gengo to Shakai*,

Iwanami Shinsho, 1975.

Tsugawa, Noriko (1994) "Hon'yaku ni miru hōgen imēji no katsuyō gihō" (Images of dialects and techniques of application in translation), *Tōkyō Joshi Daigaku Gengo Bunka Kenkyū*, No. 3, pp. 90–101.

Tsuzome, Naoya (1993) "Nama no hōgen/Kyakushoku sareta hōgen" (Raw dialects/dramatized dialects), *Gengo*, 22-9: 68–75.

Vogler, Christopher (1998) *The Writer's Journey,* second edition, Michael Wiese Productions, Studiocity.

Washi, Rumi (1996) "Gendai nihongo seisa ni tsuite no ichi-kōsatsu: onna kotoba to shite no shūjoshi 'wa' o megutte" (An consideration on gender differences in contemporary Japanese: focusing the sentence-final particle *wa* as a women's language), *Nihongo/Nihon-bunka Kenkyū*, No. 6, pp. 43–56, Osaka Gaikokugo Daigaku Nihongo Kōza.

Yasuda, Toshirō (1999) *<Kokugo> to <Hōgen> no Aida: Gengo Kōchiku no Seijigaku* (A Gap between <National Language> and <Dialects>: Politics of Language Construction), Jinbun Shoin.

Yoda, Megumi (2003) "Seiyō rashisa o ninau yakuwarigo: 'Oo, Romio!' no bunkei kara" (A role language that bears western-like atmosphere: from the search of the sentence pattern 'Oh, Romeo!'), *Gobun*, No. 79, pp. 53–65, Osaka Daigaku Kokugo Kokubun Gakkai.

Yomota, Inuhiko (2000) *Nihon Eiga-shi 100-nen* (100 years of Movie History in Japan), Shueisha Shinsho.